"The Gospel has been hijacked! In *Christians Against Christianity*, Dr. Obery Hendricks affirms the population of people who have given their talents, skills, and abilities to religion and church only to find themselves marginalized, disenfranchised, and vilified. He clearly states that it is time to liberate Jesus and emancipate the heart of the Gospel that is trapped by pseudo-Christianity behaving badly! I recommend this book as a road map to freedom both for the prisoners and the practitioners of Bad Religion. Buy several copies and set captives free!"

—REV. DR. YVETTE FLUNDER, presiding bishop, The Fellowship of Affirming Ministries, and author of *Where the Edge Gathers*

"Obery M. Hendricks Jr. is one of the most brilliant and consequential biblical scholars of the twenty-first century. *Christians Against Christianity* extends the intellectual arc of his classic *The Politics of Jesus*, as Hendricks illuminates the moral hypocrisy and spiritual corruption of right-wing evangelicals who are more white than Christian. Touching on all the hot-button issues—from abortion to gun control, from immigration policy to commercialized religion, from gay rights to xenophobia—Hendricks reads the scriptures through a prophetic lens. He writes with the poetry of a novelist, the learning of a world-class scholar, and the artistry of a thunderous preacher sharing a burning jeremiad. This book is pure fire!"

—MICHAEL ERIC DYSON, author of *Long Time Coming*

"Dr. Obery Hendricks's latest book, *Christians Against Christianity*, is a powerful, prophetic denunciation of the brand of right-wing, overwhelmingly white evangelicalism that has done such grievous damage to the body politic and the body of Christ in the United States, as well as to the witness of the Christian church in the United States around the world. In reflecting on the damage of the last four years in particular, Hendricks describes the dangerous heresy and idolatry of Trumpism that has even further distanced far too many right-wing evangelicals literally from the true teachings of Jesus Christ. The witness of the Trumpian evangelicals is truly anti-Christ. Only by following Jesus's two greatest commandments—to love God and to love our neighbors as ourselves—along with his teachings in Matthew 25 that the test of discipleship is how we treat the 'least of these,' can these right-wing evangelicals find their way back to Jesus. I strongly recommend this book."

—JIM WALLIS, founder of *Sojourners* and
New York Times best-selling author of *Christ in Crisis*

"We are at a time of turmoil, a crossroads that will determine what Christianity will mean and how it will be practiced in the twenty-first century. Any Christian who cares about the central message of the Gospels must read Dr. Obery Hendricks's urgent and important work."

—REV. AL SHARPTON, president, National Action
Network, and host of *Politics Nation*, MSNBC

"Obery Hendricks Jr. reminds us that two crucial measures of our faith are loving God and neighbor and that whatever we do for the 'least of these' we do for Jesus. Now more than ever we must live out 'the life-affirming, justice-insistent message that Jesus proclaimed' for our nation's children. Like Jesus, who put the child among the disciples, as we reclaim the transformative power of Christian faith, we must move children from the margin to the center of our nation's priorities."

—MARIAN WRIGHT EDELMAN, president emerita,
The Children's Defense Fund, and author of
The Measure of Our Success

"Dr. Obery Hendricks is one of the country's most insightful voices on faith in the public square and racial justice and equity. This book is a critical contribution to our political and religious debate and deserves to be read and understood by policy and political leaders and people of faith alike."

—JOSHUA DUBOIS, CEO of Values Partnerships,
CNN contributor, and former director, White House
Office of Faith-Based and Neighborhood Partnerships

"*Christians Against Christianity* is a brilliantly and powerfully written prophetic indictment of right-wing evangelicals who misuse the Bible while abusing those they otherize to further their political agenda. Obery Hendricks does a masterful job of shining a spotlight of gospel truth on their hypocrisy, masked as piety, while extending a redemptive invitation to experience and be emancipated by the liberating love of the sable-skinned Savior who majored in ministry to those on the margins. This is the gospel truth!"

—DR. FREDERICK D. HAYNES III,
co-chair of the Samuel DeWitt Proctor Conference

"A masterful and grounded challenge to right-wing evangelical theology and politics—but one not for theologians alone. Powerfully written, forcefully argued, and morally anchored, *Christians Against Christianity* offers hope and thoughtful insight to all progressives and fair-minded readers."

—GAR ALPEROVITZ, author of *What Then Must We Do?*
Straight Talk About the Next American Revolution

"It's a sign of our unsettling times when a figure like Obery Hendricks Jr.—respected biblical scholar, former seminary president, and elder in the church—calls on his fellow Christians to rise up against what much of contemporary Christianity has become. *Christians Against Christianity* is a searing indictment of white evangelicals' allegiance to white supremacy and political power and a clarion call to all Christians to go back to the Bible to reclaim a faith rooted in love and responsibility for others rather than domination and self-interest. This is a must-read book for this crucial moment in our nation's history."

—ROBERT P. JONES, CEO and founder of PRRI,
author of *White Too Long: The Legacy of
White Supremacy in American Christianity*

CHRISTIANS
AGAINST
CHRISTIANITY

CHRISTIANS

HOW RIGHT-WING EVANGELICALS

AGAINST

ARE DESTROYING OUR NATION

CHRISTIANITY

AND OUR FAITH

OBERY M. HENDRICKS JR.

BEACON PRESS, BOSTON

BEACON PRESS
Boston, Massachusetts
www.beacon.org

Beacon Press books
are published under the auspices of
the Unitarian Universalist Association of Congregations.

24 23 22 21   8 7 6 5 4 3 2 1

This book is printed on acid-free paper that meets the uncoated paper
ANSI/NISO specifications for permanence as revised in 1992.

Text design and composition by Kim Arney

Library of Congress Cataloging-in-Publication Data

Name: Hendricks, Obery M. (Obery Mack), author.
Title: Christians against Christianity : how right-wing Evangelicals are
destroying our nation and our faith / Obery M. Hendricks, Jr.
Description: Boston : Beacon Press, [2021] | Includes bibliographical
references and index.
Identifiers: LCCN 2021003292 (print) | LCCN 2021003293 (ebook) |
ISBN 9780807057407 (hardcover) | ISBN 9780807057414 (ebook)
Subjects: LCSH: Church controversies—United States—History—21st
century. Evangelicalism—United States. | Christian conservatism—United
States. | Christianity and politics—United States—History—21st
century. | Christians—Political activity—United States.
Classification: LCC BR526 .H378 2021 (print) | LCC BR526 (ebook) |
DDC 261.80973—dc23
LC record available at https://lccn.loc.gov/2021003292
LC ebook record available at https://lccn.loc.gov/2021003293

To my beloveds, the bearers of my greatest hopes:

My daughters, Tahirah and Serena,

My granddaughters, Mariam and Diata,

and

My great-granddaughter, Nimah

May your world be more kind,
and may you always strive to make it so

He said to them, "Isaiah prophesied rightly about
    you hypocrites, as it is written,
'This people honors me with their lips,
but their hearts are far from me;
in vain do they worship me,
teaching human precepts as doctrines.'
You abandon the commandment of God and hold
    to human tradition."

—MARK 7:6–8

I was in hopes that the enlightened and liberal policy,
which has marked the present age, would at least
have reconciled Christians of every denomination
so far that we should never again see the religious
disputes carried to such a pitch as to endanger the
peace of society.

—PRESIDENT GEORGE WASHINGTON
(letter to Edward Newenham, October 20, 1792)

CONTENTS

INTRODUCTION

A TRAVESTY. THAT'S HOW I would characterize Christianity in America today. A travesty, a brutal sham, a tragic charade, a cynical deceit. Why? Because the loudest voices in American Christianity today—those of right-wing evangelicals—shamelessly spew a putrid stew of religious ignorance and political venom that is poisoning our society, making a mockery of the Gospel of Jesus Christ. Their rhetoric in the name of their Lord and Savior is mean-spirited, divisive, appallingly devoid of love for their neighbors and outright demonizes those who do not accept their narrow views—even fellow Christians. Perhaps most shocking is their enthusiastic, almost cultish support for the cruel, hateful policies and pronouncements of President Donald Trump, whose words and deeds more often than not have been the very antithesis of Christian faith.

I do not make these claims lightly. And I can't be dismissed as a contentious outsider; I offer these observations as an ardent insider of the faith. I am a proudly ordained elder in the African Methodist Episcopal Church, a former president of its flagship theological seminary, and a dedicated biblical scholar trained at the highest levels of academia. But most significantly, I speak from a lineage of faithful Christians who know the Gospel of Jesus Christ that right-wing evangelicals seem to have left behind: the Gospel that tells us to love our neighbors, to respond to the cries of the poor and the vulnerable, to accept the immigrant stranger, to seek fairness and justice for all. Some might call me a "progressive"

Christian, although I reject that and all other labels. I simply believe in the life-affirming, justice-insistent message that Jesus proclaimed and died for. I have little interest in the doctrinal bells and theological whistles that drive so much of Christendom today.

You see, I am the product of two deeply religious families in rural Virginia, the place of my birth. From both I have been gifted with a legacy of deeply devoted church pastors, trustees, deacons and deaconesses, Sunday school teachers, lifelong ushers, and gifted church musicians.

My maternal grandparents loom particularly large in that blessed legacy. The loving, openhearted generosity of my grandmother, Laura Banks, easily rivaled that of the Good Samaritan. She was a funny, kind soul, easy to laugh, whose love for her many grandchildren, it seemed to us at least, was second only to her love for her omnipresent God. Grandma began every day in the early morning dark, sometimes humming, sometimes singing, "Take My Hand, Precious Lord" (she pronounced it "Pryshush") as she prepared enough bacon, ham, salmon cakes, scrambled eggs, and buttered hoecakes to feed the first three pews of her beloved St. Louis Baptist Church, which she attended in life and in which she was funeralized in death.

Perhaps most impressive in spiritual temperament among my forebears was my beloved maternal grandfather, Joseph Baker Banks, a well-respected mahogany-hued man of medium height, powerful build, proverbial quiet strength, loving demeanor, and unmistakable dignity. Although orphaned at the age of twelve, and being raised, in a fashion, until his teens by his mother's white employer, he grew into a man well respected by his community, a paragon of his black Presbyterian church and a deeply devoted Christian gentleman in every sense of the word. He regularly led in solemn prayer my grandmother and their nine children, all of whom grew into good-hearted, upstanding citizens and faithful Christians, among them a pastor, two deacons, a pastor's wife, and assorted lay officers.

Then there were my loving and devoted parents. My father, Obery Sr., was a trustee at Calvary Baptist, which had become our church home after he'd led my mother and me (my sister, Linda, did not grace the world until a couple of years later) on the oft-trod road from the Jim Crow South to the somewhat less hostile racial environs of Newark, New Jersey, to settle in a three-room apartment at the end of an alley off a street that no longer exists. Then, as his fortunes rose, on to East Orange, a nice contiguous sister city once voted the "Cleanest City in the Nation," but which by then was on the fast track from a bedroom community of elegant shops and theaters to a struggling city that became known as the willing host to a gaggle of fast-food restaurants and a bare-knuckled police force. A man fiercely proud of providing for his children and his stay-at-home wife, my father had bricklayer's hands so rough that you could strike a match on them, yet his heart was nearly as tender as a saint's.

My beautiful red-haired mother, Willie Beatrice, called Billie by family and friends, was a talented self-taught painter and sculptor and as religious as her siblings. For years she made an art of sitting on church committees, both official and not, with very important-sounding names attached to less important missions, which were usually convened by older folks with little else to do. In her later years, my mother shifted into a higher spiritual gear that earned her the honorific of "mother of the church" of which she was very proud until her dying breath. Although she was hard on me, her wayward son, to save me from falling into the eternal fires of hell and the earthly hell of prison, she was kind, witty, gracious, and uniformly described in death with the high compliment, "she was such a lady."

For our part, my younger sister Linda and I regularly, and under considerable duress, performed the pew-sitting duty required by our church-possessed parents, which led us to wonder whether we had truly emerged from the womb in hospital delivery rooms, as we'd been told, or had instead entered the world in the Calvary

Baptist Sunday school room in the presence of the loving, imperious church mother Mrs. Gibson and the other unexcited children she fussed at—and fussed over—weekly. There, for Sundays on end, we learned lessons that reside within us yet. It was there that we learned about the love of Jesus. It was there we were taught that other than the Son of Man, it is the loving unselfishness of the Good Samaritan that we should embrace and emulate.

Our wonderful church family gifted us children with magnificent blessings that only became apparent as we ventured into the world. It was there, in the godly stronghold of Calvary Baptist Church, that we were treated as treasures from God. It was there that the church men, in their sober suits, and the church ladies, with their modest raiment and church hats perched like crowns, modeled for us the lessons of decorum, sobriety, and unflappable dignity that still run as deeply as marrow. These loving Christians worked hard to ensure that we felt our God-given worth in a society that did not fully value children like us. No slouching, they admonished; stand tall and proud and "act like somebody." Mumbling was unacceptable; we had to speak up and look the other firmly in the eye. With stories from the Bible, they alerted us to the deleterious seductions of the world, insisting that girls embody the carriage of dignified young ladies, and boys, the bearing of dignified young men. They celebrated our accomplishments, no matter how modest, with pride, encouragement, appreciative words, and dimes and quarters slipped with a wink into our eager little hands.

From our parents and our church family my sister and I learned that Christian living is synonymous with compassion (we were taught to pool our pennies to help families in need who, truth be told, were not much less well off than we), synonymous with respect for proper authority (which held in its purview virtually every grown-up who was not vicious or creepy), and synonymous with honesty (I can still hear my mother admonish, "If you will lie, you will steal"). We mourned with those who mourned and were taught to look beyond external differences to behold the humanity of all in God's household by welcoming strangers, no matter how ragtag, beaten by demon rum, or halting their English. Most of all, we were taught to love and to never hate—not even the murderous faux Christians of the Ku Klux Klan, the embodiment of all things evil for every black person of sound mind.

By word and deed we were taught that there is no true love without the willingness to sacrifice for others, which was coupled with a stern insistence that all our dealings be fair and just. My sister and I never witnessed our parents taking unfair advantage or turning their backs to anyone who reached out in genuine need. In short, what I witnessed at home and at church was unstinting decency by people who would willfully hurt no one and would pray for anyone; large-hearted folks who did their daily best to plant gardens of grace they nurtured with the nectar of goodwill, if not outright love.

This is the faith to which I am heir. It is a faith that takes seriously the ethical demands of the Gospel to love our neighbors as ourselves and to seek the salvation and well-being of the whole people, like the New Testament figure Simeon, who being "righteous and devout," with "the Holy Spirit rested upon him," prayed for the *common good*, the "consolation," or deliverance of his whole people from their travails at the hands of their Roman oppressors (Luke 2:25).

But today the contours of this faith, this venerable faith, are barely recognizable, particularly in the public square. Too many of the faithful, especially right-wing "evangelical" Christians, seem to have forgotten that loving our neighbors is as crucial to authentic faith as loving God, when in actuality, loving our neighbors is the only real evidence of love for God. It is as if right-wing evangelicals have embraced "a different gospel" (paraphrasing the apostle Paul's words in 2 Corinthians 11:4), a harsh, self-serving ideology of domination like the one Jesus died standing against, a heretical ideology that refracts and distorts the love and truth of his teachings through a lens of xenophobia, political rancor, and narrow self-interests.

I have endeavored at the outset to share the faith tradition of my youth to give context to my horror at what Christianity has become at the hands of the modern right-wing evangelical movement and to explain my reason for writing this book: to defend the truth and majesty of the Gospel, if you will, from right-wing evangelicals' crude caricature of it, a caricature so ugly and crude that it has unleashed in the public square new levels of incivility, bullying, cruelty, race-baiting and xenophobia, and birthed a cottage industry of conspiracy theories and grotesque demonizations aimed at anyone who dares to point out the rot at the root of their politics.

The faith of my forebears is offended. I am offended. I believe the Gospel itself is offended by the political wrongs in this nation that are regularly perpetrated in its name. For those who truly believe in the Gospel of Jesus Christ, in its call for a world of justice, love, and inclusion for all, it is time to set the record straight. That is what I have strived to do here.

A note on my use of the Bible. I am a biblical scholar by profession, training, and dedication. Therefore, I base my observations, assertions, and critiques not on religious dogma or the silliness of the prosperity antigospel or even the inspired ruminations of systematic theology, but rather upon the pronouncements of the biblical writings themselves in their historical and cultural contexts. Any study of the Bible that does not engage the writings in their respective historical and cultural contexts is at best incomplete, if not fatally misleading. As one of my professors at Princeton Theological Seminary once said, any reading of the biblical *text* that does not consider its *context* is a *pretext*. My favorite seminary professor, the late J. Christiaan Beker, a New Testament scholar, taught us that the Bible is "a word on target," which means every one of its writings is written to a particular group of people to address a particular issue or circumstance in a particular time and place. I trust that the importance of this observation will become evident in the course of this book. In addition, I refer to the totality of Jesus's teachings as the New Testament relates them for us as capitalized, i.e., the *Gospel*. When referring to any of the four books that narrate his life and ministry, I use the lowercase, i.e., *gospel*.

I do not claim that my readings and interpretations of the biblical text are the only reasonable ones. But because those I offer are informed by years of faithful critical scholarship and supported by ample documentation, I ask that challenges or rejections of my readings be similarly informed. "I disagree" or "I don't believe that" without a plausible alternative reading does not do honor to the solemn task of biblical interpretation. All biblical citations are from the New Revised Standard Version (NRSV), which I find to be among the most accurate and authoritative, unless otherwise noted. Where necessary I will augment the NRSV with direct literal translations from the Hebrew and Greek texts, as indicated.

Because the various writings in the Bible were written over numerous centuries in different cultural, social, and political settings in life, even when they are handled with discretion and integrity the values they espouse can appear to be in conflict. Obvious examples include the cry of the psalmist for his enemies' infants to be fatally dashed against rocks (Psalm 137:9) and Paul's angry wish that certain disciples of Jesus "would castrate themselves" for insisting that all Christian males must be circumcised (Galatians 5:12). Passages such as these are in opposition to the central love ethic of Jesus as expressed in the Gospel of John: "I give you a new commandment, that you love one another. Just as I have loved you, you also should love one another" (John 13:34). Thus, it is not enough to simply declare oneself a "Bible believer." Because our values guide our conduct in the world, it is necessary for each of us to be clear about the biblical values upon which our faith is based.[1] I believe that to keep faith with my readers it is appropriate that I also declare the hierarchy of biblical values that informs and guides my judgments in this book.

The biblical passages upon which my hierarchy of values rests are two. The first is Jesus's response to the scribe's inquiry:

> Teacher, which commandment in the law is the greatest? He said to him, "You shall love the Lord your God with all your heart, and with all your soul, and with all your mind." This is the greatest and first commandment. And a second is like it: "You shall love your neighbor as yourself." (Matthew 22:36–39)

Because I will be engaging primarily the politics of right-wing evangelicals rather than just their professions of faith, it is the second of these commandments, "love your neighbor as yourself," that I will stress throughout.

The second passage in my hierarchy of Gospel values is what Jesus presents in parable form as God's primary mode of judgment of the way people live their lives in the world. Called the parable of the sheep and goats, I quote it here in its entirety:

> When the Son of Man comes in his glory, and all the angels with him, then he will sit on the throne of his glory. All the nations will be gathered before him, and he will separate people one from another as a shepherd separates the sheep from the goats, and he will put the sheep at his right hand and the goats at the left. Then the king will say to those at his right hand, "Come, you that are blessed by my Father, inherit the kingdom prepared for you from the foundation of the world; for I was hungry and you gave me food, I was thirsty and you gave me something to drink, I was a stranger and you welcomed me, I was naked and you gave me clothing, I was sick and you took care of me, I was in prison and you visited me." Then the righteous will answer him, "Lord, when was it that we saw you hungry and gave you food, or thirsty and gave you something to drink? And when was it that we saw you a stranger and welcomed you, or naked and gave you clothing? And when was it that we saw you sick or in

prison and visited you?" And the king will answer them, "Truly
I tell you, just as you did it to one of the least of these who are
members of my family, you did it to me." Then he will say to
those at his left hand, "You that are accursed, depart from me
into the eternal fire prepared for the devil and his angels; for I
was hungry and you gave me no food, I was thirsty and you gave
me nothing to drink, I was a stranger and you did not welcome
me, naked and you did not give me clothing, sick and in prison
and you did not visit me." Then they also will answer, "Lord,
when was it that we saw you hungry or thirsty or a stranger or
naked or sick or in prison, and did not take care of you?" Then
he will answer them, "Truly I tell you, just as you did not do it to
one of the least of these, you did not do it to me." And these will
go away into eternal punishment, but the righteous into eternal
life. (Matthew 25:31–46)

It is my fervent belief that to be fully true to the faith, Christians must strive to focus and refract every public policy and every
deed in the public square through the prism of the values these
passages impart. The subtext of both these seminal Gospel pronouncements is that believers have responsibility for the health
and well-being not only of our personal circles of friends and loved
ones but also for the good of all, particularly those in need. The
martyred Salvadoran priest Oscar Romero insisted, "We cannot
segregate God's word from the historical reality in which it is proclaimed. It would not then be God's word. . . . It would be a pious
book, a Bible that is just a book in our library. It becomes God's
word because it vivifies, enlightens, contrasts, repudiates, praises
what is going on today in this society."[2] Therefore, I will refer to
both these passages throughout this book, for I believe that they
comprise the core of the Gospel witness: love and responsibility
each for the other, embraced and enacted as a social norm. Unfortunately, the actions and public pronouncements of right-wing
evangelicals today suggest that the crucial messages these passages

contain do not carry the same weight for them. That is why their rhetoric is so loveless and divisive.

It is time for the truth to be told about the harm their deformed presentation of the Gospel is doing to our nation and to our faith. God declared through the prophet Hosea, "My people are destroyed for lack of knowledge" (4:6). Jesus said, "You will know the truth, and the truth will make you free" (John 8:32). Both sayings imply the same, that there is no time like the present to set the record straight.

That is what I have endeavored to do with this book: to set the record straight.

CHRISTIANS
AGAINST
CHRISTIANITY

CHAPTER 1

WE HAVE NO KING BUT CAESAR

Genuflecting at Strange Altars

IT IS TRUE that throughout history much suffering, oppression, exploitation, and unspeakable horrors have been committed in the name of Jesus Christ. But it is also true that no justification or sanction for such abominations can be found in the words or actions of Jesus in the four gospels. When it is kept in mind that Jesus, his disciples, and most of his biblical followers were Jews, and that virtually every word he speaks in the gospels is spoken to Jews, it becomes evident that not even the few sayings of Jesus that are routinely used to justify anti-Semitism actually contain that ugly meaning. Indeed, anyone who has read the New Testament knows that the core message of Jesus is love. He couldn't have made it any plainer when he declared to his disciples and gathered followers: "I give you a new commandment, that you love one another. Just as I have loved you, you also should love one another" (John 13:34). That is why it is such a curious thing, perhaps blasphemy even, that today so many Christians seem to define themselves not by those they love, but by those for whom they have *no* love: Muslims, gays, immigrants, women who seek to exercise full sovereignty over their own bodies, and those who seek succor and asylum in our land from deadening poverty and the threat of deadly violence in their own. These Christians cry bitter tears for the unjust execution of Jesus two thousand years ago, but have few tears for the injustice visited daily upon those among us for whom Jesus expressed great love: the desperately poor, the sick and vulnerable, the refugees struggling to find a better life for the babies at their breasts. Nonetheless, I must admit that, even having long been aware of this twisted strand of Christianity in our society, I still was shocked to learn that millions of Christians, particularly the vast majority of right-wing evangelicals—some 81 percent—who so zealously preach moral rectitude and personal piety, could actually champion a man like Donald Trump. Like the character Stamp Paid in Toni Morrison's classic novel *Beloved* after he witnessed malevolence he could not comprehend, I, too, asked the heavens: "What kind of people are these?"

Trump's daily, indeed, hourly flurries of ugly insults, violent, hateful rhetoric, outrageous lies, destructive divisiveness, and malicious name-calling reflect a fatal lack of respect for the most basic Christian civility. Yet in May 2019, the Pew Research Center reported that support for Trump by evangelicals remained extremely high, with seven out of ten (69 percent) approving of him.[1] How can this be? The answer should be obvious to anyone who has paid attention to current events: it is the result of successful shilling for Trump by a cadre of influential evangelical leaders who seem to have decided that the teachings of Jesus can be ignored when those teachings get in the way of their quest to dominate American society.

But what does it mean to be an evangelical Christian? *Evangelical* comes from the Greek *euangelion,* meaning "good news" or "gospel." In historical accounts the term has been used to describe widespread Christian religious revivals in America in the eighteenth and nineteenth centuries. Respectively referred to by historians as the First and Second Great Awakenings, these religious eruptions emphasized Bible-based sermons and conversion experiences that were often accompanied by religious ecstasy and reveries. Then as now, rather than denominational formalities, evangelical faith focuses on the "good news" of salvation brought by Jesus Christ, emphasizing experience of God as the ground of knowledge. Those with evangelical sensibilities do not comprise a single denomination as such. They are found in many Protestant denominations and, to a lesser extent, in Catholicism as well. Rather than a denominational identity, what all evangelicals have in common is a belief in four basic tenets: (1) that the Bible is the ultimate authority for life (which they profess to accept literally although, as we shall see, they tend to ignore or tendentiously construe passages that do not suit their purposes); (2) that Jesus died to atone for the sins of the world; (3) that a conversion experience, or being "born again," is necessary for heavenly salvation; and (4) that believers should engage in evangelistic outreach.

In the late twentieth century the term *evangelical* as a religious description also took on a political dimension. As scholars Hannah Butler and Kristin Du Mez explain, "It seems reasonable to assume that when Americans self-identify as evangelicals today, many are identifying with the movement as it has taken shape in recent decades—a conservative politicized movement—and not with a static conception rooted in centuries-old history."[2] That seems reasonable to me as well. In this book I will focus on the trajectory of what we might call modern right-wing evangelicalism, a phenomenon that emerged in roughly the mid-twentieth century, as an essentially political movement anchored in evangelical beliefs, albeit loosely at times. What distinguishes right-wing evangelicalism from more mainstream evangelicalism is that right-wing evangelicalism contains an unabashed and inextricable substratum of Christian nationalism. "Christian nationalism is the engine that drives white American evangelical politics. It is the ideology . . . that the United States is intended by God to be a Christian nation."[3] "This movement is a form of nationalism," explains Katherine Stewart, "because it purports to derive its legitimacy from its claim to represent a specific identity unique to and representative of the American nation."[4] Christian nationalism not only purveys the myth that America was founded as a Christian nation but also that it should be governed according to the biblical precepts that Christian nationalists themselves identify as germane. They routinely ignore all evidence to the contrary, no matter how compelling, including the testimony of founding fathers like Thomas Jefferson and John Adams that America was *not* founded as a Christian nation.[5] Thus, Christian nationalism is best understood as a political ideology that holds that America's government is not legitimate, nor can it be, until its laws and policies are thoroughly consistent with the Christian nationalists' narrow, sometimes idiosyncratic, and at times convoluted readings of the biblical text. Thus, while the tenets of evangelicalism essentially comprise right-wing evangelicals' religious beliefs, Christian nationalism is the political ideology that guides and motivates the pursuit of their social and political interests in the world. The spectacle we see in the public square today is right-wing evangelicals' Christian nationalist convictions taking precedence over their religious beliefs. This is fully reflected in right-wing evangelicals' voter turnout for Donald Trump. A major 2018 study observes that the "single factor that most accurately predicted whether one would vote for Trump [in 2016] was the belief that America is and should be a Christian nation."[6] Indeed, despite his well-earned reputation for racism and moral indecency, those who most enthusiastically supported his candidacy are numbered among the most ardent evangelical believers. A poll by the Barna organization, a respected Christian pollster, indicates that "higher levels of church attendance correlates with stronger levels of Trump support."[7]

While white and black evangelicals share similar basic beliefs, relatively few black evangelicals are found in Christian nationalist ranks. Why? "Sociologically, the principal difference between white and black evangelicals is that we believe that oppression exists," says African American evangelical activist Lisa Sharon Harper, citing a nationwide study of Christians from 2000 called *Divided by Faith*.[8] In addition, Christian nationalism contains a distinct underpinning of white supremacy that most black people want no part of. In the Christian nationalists' myth of our nation's beginnings, blacks have no purchase in the nation's founding except subservience to the white overclass. In this myth blacks are either completely absent or present only as enslaved nonpersons with no personal agency. Thus for blacks to embrace right-wing evangelicalism, they must embrace repugnant white supremacist assumptions as well. As the scholar Robert P. Jones demonstrates in his book *White Too Long,* right-wing evangelicalism is inextricably shot through with white supremacist sensibilities.[9] As a result, the ranks of black right-wing evangelicals remain exceedingly thin. Therefore, when speaking of right-wing evangelicals, it is overwhelmingly white evangelicals to which I refer.

Those evangelicals who led the fight for Trump's candidacy number among the most prominent right-wing evangelical preachers and thinkers. The religious scholar John Fea calls them Trump's "court evangelicals," because they are reminiscent of "the members of Kings' courts during the Middle Ages and the Renaissance, who sought influence and worldly approval by flattering the monarch rather than prophetically speaking truth to power."[10] Predictably, most are white. These include Franklin Graham, the son of the renowned evangelist, Billy Graham; Jerry Falwell Jr., Pat Robertson, Robert Jeffress, Ralph Reed, Paula White, James Dobson, the famously jet-setting Kenneth Copeland, and several black clergy, including Harry Jackson and Darrell Scott (who called Trump "the greatest pro-black president in my lifetime"[11]). Each has done their part to mislead their flocks to believe that a man who has perhaps debased Christianity in America more than anyone before him is instead a man of decency and a committed follower of Jesus Christ.

Even recognizing the deceit and cynicism in Trump's court evangelicals' glossing over his true character and essentially nonexistent Christian witness, many people are still left to wonder why these evangelicals picked Trump as their standard-bearer. After all, there were candidates with more traditionally held Christian bona fides who actually evinced respect for the canons of Christian civility, such as Ted Cruz, Ben Carson, and Mike Huckabee. The answer to this question is apparently as ironic as it is cynical: they chose Donald Trump because in all of his five decades of public life he has shown absolutely no evidence of a moral core. His blank-page malleability, easy susceptibility to flattery, and a moral compass so skewed as to be virtually nonexistent made him the perfect candidate to help them realize their primary stated political goal of appointing Supreme Court justices willing to gut *Roe v. Wade* and support "religious freedom," which in their view apparently applies only to them. Franklin Graham put it succinctly: "What's at stake," he averred, "is the future of the Supreme Court."[12] No mention of decency, honesty, integrity, or the leavening influence of love as factors they should consider. Yet, as important as control of the Supreme Court is to right-wing evangelicals, that is not their ultimate concern.

What is seldom voiced outside their circles is that the eventual goal of right-wing evangelical leaders is to force every aspect of American life to genuflect at the altar of their narrow brand of Christianity. In actuality, then, they are not only right-wing evangelical Christian nationalists, they are also Christian supremacists, who justify their goal of world domination by interpreting Genesis 1:28 ("have dominion over . . . every living thing that moves upon the earth") and Matthew 28:19 ("go and make disciples of all nations") as divine mandates to take control of all political institutions and offices in America, if not the world. The problem with their use of the Bible to justify their goal of domination is that neither of the verses they cite has the dominionist meaning they ascribe to it. Genesis 1:28, written long before the Christian era, assigns dominion over the created world to humanity in general, not to Christians. And in Matthew 28:19 the Greek term from which "disciple" is translated, *mathetes,* means "student," "pupil," "apprentice," "one who engages in learning through instruction from another."[13] In other words, Matthew 28:19 instructs believers to bring the meaning of the Gospel to the world, not to bring the world under Christian domination, and certainly not under the domination of a *particular* group of Christians. Yet that is their claim and their goal. In a November 2016 post on the Billy Graham Association website, Franklin Graham maintained that there is a divine call for a "Christian revolution in America" that will place control of this nation firmly in the hands of right-wing evangelical Christians. On his *700 Club* television show, Pat Robertson declared outright that "God's plan for His people . . . is to take dominion. What is dominion? Well, dominion is Lordship. He wants His people to reign and rule with Him."[14]

Trump's evangelicals saw in him a willing booster of this theology of dominion, which, in their reading of the Bible, mandates destroying abortion rights, rolling back the newly granted federal protections of the constitutional rights of gay Americans, and recognizing Jerusalem as the capital of Israel, which many of them believe to be a prophesied precursor for the Second Coming of Christ.[15] Trump's choice of former Indiana governor Mike Pence as his running mate, which immediately made the cloying Pence the most powerful evangelical politician in America, further bolstered their hopes for attaining political supremacy.

A revealing example of the Christian supremacist strategy in action is the weekly White House Bible study, led by right-wing evangelist Ralph Drollinger.[16] Drollinger, who is president and founder of the evangelical Capital Ministries and a former professional basketball player, denounces women holders of political office who have young children as "sinners" and Catholicism as "one of the primary false religions in the world."[17] Sponsored by no fewer than ten senior Cabinet officials, the White House Bible study had a prominent place in the Trump administration. In addition, Drollinger led study groups for both houses of Congress. In Bible study sessions, Drollinger advised those he considered the righteous people in government—those who subscribe to his Christian supremacist ideology—to actively engage in religious discrimination by hiring only other righteous people, by which he meant similarly thinking persons. Extremist teachings like Drollinger's have major implications for governance. The domestic policy implications of his declarations that social welfare programs "have no basis in scripture" are obvious. With regard to foreign policy, he explicitly urged members of the president's Cabinet to use their positions of power and influence to forcefully enact Jesus's directive in Matthew 28 to "make disciples of all nations." In his letter to Christians in Rome, Paul admonished them to obey the governing authorities out of concern that they would incur the empire's wrath by words or actions that could be construed sedition (Romans 13:1–6). In sermons, Drollinger appropriated Paul's sentiments and applied them to the Trump administration, declaring that "the institution of the state" is "an avenger of wrath" with the God-given responsibility "to moralize a fallen world through the use of force."[18] Given Trump's arrogant bellicosity and triumphalist "America First" ethos, coupled with the sordid history of American military excursions masquerading as missionary efforts,[19] it is hard not to conclude that for Drollinger and his allies, making "disciples of all nations" construed evangelicalism's call to proselytize as a mandate to make all countries submit to the Trump administration's toxic ideological admixture of American nationalism and Christian supremacy, underpinned by America's brutal legacy of white supremacy.

But there is another factor that made Trump such an attractive candidate to the evangelical elites. As Robert P. Jones observes, "As a candidate in 2008, Obama offered a theologically sophisticated account of how his faith connected with his life and work as an elected official."[20] Yet Trump actively questioned both his faith and his citizenship. As the result of his years of enflaming racist resentment with his Obama "birther" lie, candidate Trump entered the election with a ready-made constituency of whites who had constantly fed on his racist dog-whistle screeds. Although he has crowed, with typical bravado, "I am the least racist person you will ever meet," Trump has a history of racism with public implications. It goes back at least to 1973, when he and his company,

Trump Management, were sued by the Department of Justice for housing discrimination against African American renters. (We will explore the depths of his racism in a bit.)

Thumbing their noses at the moral rigor expected of their Gospel calling, evangelical leaders chose to ignore the venomous, un-Christian rhetoric of Trump and his campaign and instead enthusiastically embraced his ugly message. In a monumental betrayal of both the faith and the faithful, these false prophets and court evangelicals exhorted believers to vote for a man who arrogantly eschews even the most basic tenets of Christian decency. With great fanfare and pomposity in both the pulpit and the press, they happily assumed the role of Trump's sycophants and court jesters.[21] Jerry Falwell Jr. fawningly crowned Trump America's "dream president."[22] Crowed evangelist Franklin Graham, "He defends the Christian faith more than any President in my lifetime."[23] Evangelical leaders have gone so far as to declare that voting for Trump was every Christian's Gospel duty.

Thankfully, not all evangelical leaders have defiled the integrity of their faith by backing Trump. During the 2016 presidential campaign, Russell Moore, president of the Ethics and Religious Liberty Commission of the Southern Baptist Convention, scathingly criticized evangelical leaders who continued to trumpet support for Trump after the release of the *Access Hollywood* tape, on which Trump boasted of sexually molesting unsuspecting women. "What a disgrace," Moore tweeted on October 7, 2016. "What a scandal to the gospel of Jesus Christ and to the integrity of our witness." In a *Washington Post* op-ed in 2016, Al Mohler, president of the Southern Baptist Theological Seminary and a leading conservative evangelical, called Trump's candidacy an "immediate and excruciating crisis," adding, "I am among those who see evangelical support for Trump as a horrifying embarrassment—a price for possible political gain that is simply unthinkable and too high a price to pay."[24] (In a head-scratching about-face in April 2020, Mohler announced that he would vote for Trump's reelection.)

In a July 2015 open letter to candidate Trump, Rev. William Barber, president of the social justice organization Repairers of the Breach, wrote,

> Your campaign . . . does not represent . . . the call of justice, or the ethics of Biblical evangelicalism. Instead, your campaign presents an extremist philosophy of hate, greed, racism, classism, and xenophobia. . . . Despite your support from people like Franklin Graham and Jerry Falwell, Jr.—people who claim to be evangelists—neither your views nor theirs are authentic evangelicalism.[25]

During Trump's campaign for reelection, Mark Galli, editor in chief of *Christianity Today,* the evangelical periodical cofounded by Billy Graham, in a December 2019 editorial went so far as to call for Trump to be removed from office. With Trump at the nation's helm, he warned, America is "playing with a stacked deck of gross immorality and ethical incompetence."[26]

Unfortunately, those voices of Christian integrity and reason have been drowned out in evangelical circles by patently false depictions of Trump as a pious practitioner of Christian faith. Christian publisher Don Nori claimed that Trump "believes Jesus is His Savior, reads his Bible, and prays every day,"[27] as if prayer, Bible study, and confessions of belief are substitutes for decency. Megachurch prosperity preacher and Trump "spiritual advisor" Paula White proclaims she is "one hundred percent" certain that Trump has been "born again," although she offers no evidence to support her assertion and Trump himself seemingly has never made such a claim.

But no matter how effusively evangelical leaders characterize President Trump as a man of faith, reality painted a radically different picture. Their assertions could not hide the fact that Donald Trump has evinced little interest in even the most fundamental tenets of Christianity. By word and by deed he has shown that biblical values and even basic rituals and confessions of Christian faith hold little meaning for him.

For Christians, repentance is fundamental to their faith and a crucial precondition for divine salvation. But in early 2016, when Trump was asked if he had ever repented for his sins, the supposedly born-again candidate replied, "I don't think so. I think if I do something wrong, I think, I just try and make it right. I don't bring God into the picture. I don't."[28] In other words, he answers to himself alone. In a perverse demonstration of evangelical leaders' convoluted claims, David Brody, news anchor at CBN (the Christian Broadcasting Network founded by Pat Robertson), contended that by not having confessed his sins to the Lord, Trump is somehow an even more admirable Christian.[29]

Trump's take on Easter, the most solemn holy day in the Christian calendar, reflects a similar ignorance of Christianity, if not complete indifference. Incredibly, his description of the significance of Easter makes no mention of God, crucifixion, resurrection, or Jesus himself:

> Well, it really means something very special. I'm going to church in an hour from now and it's going to be—it's a beautiful church. I'm in Florida. And it's just a very special time for me. And it really represents family and get-together and—and something, you know, if you're a—a Christian, it's just a very important day.[30]

His response to the crucial faith question "Who do you say Jesus is?" could have easily passed as the description of the head of a military platoon or a cartoon superhero. "Jesus to me," he said in June 2016, "is somebody I can think about for security and confidence. Somebody I can revere in terms of bravery and in terms of courage and, because I consider the Christian religion so important, somebody I can totally rely on in my own mind."[31] No mention of salvation. No mention of an atoning death. No mention of Jesus as his Lord and Savior. When asked in a May 2020 interview by his former press secretary Sean Spicer if, during his presidency, he'd grown as a *believer,* incredibly Trump answered as a *benefactor* of the faith: "I think maybe I have, from the standpoint that I see so much that I can do. I've done so much for religion."[32] In October 2020, his son Eric took his father's claim a step further, declaring without a hint of irony that he had "literally saved Christianity."[33]

Yet Trump's court evangelicals continue to tout him as God's anointed, whose rise was divinely prophesied. Some proclaimed him a modern "Cyrus messiah"[34] who would bring America "back to God."[35] In a 2019 op-ed, Miriam Adelson, wife of billionaire Republican donor and casino mogul Sheldon Adelson, asked, "Would it be too much to pray for a day when the Bible gets a 'Book of Trump,' much like it has a 'Book of Esther' celebrating the deliverance of the Jews from ancient Persia?"[36] Jim Bakker, the evangelical preacher who spent six years in prison for fraud and who is now a hawker of outrageous conspiracy theories and dubious survivalist products, on his daily cable television show prophesied that if Trump were to lose his reelection bid, "leaders of the church and leaders of the gospel and conservative political leaders" will die, supposedly at the hands of Trump's political opponents, although many—perhaps a plurality, if not a majority—of Trump's political opponents are Christians themselves.[37]

Others went to even more absurd lengths to paint Trump as holy. Florida evangelist Mary Colbert pronounced a curse upon everyone who opposes him: "If you come against the chosen one of God"—that is, Trump—"you are bringing upon you and your children and your children's children curses like you have never seen."[38] At a summit of right-wing evangelicals, Paula White prayed for God's condemnation upon anyone who criticized Trump: "Any tongue that rises against him will be condemned according to the word of God."[39] Incredibly, Jerry Falwell Jr. compared Trump to both Martin Luther King Jr. *and* Jesus Christ, claiming that, like them, Trump is persecuted for "radical" and "politically incorrect" ideas.[40] Robert Jeffress, a particularly enthusiastic court evangelical sycophant of Trump, offered a public prayer in which he referred to the pathologically self-obsessed, malignant narcissist as selfless: "Today we thank you for Donald Trump, who is willing to selflessly offer himself for service to this nation."[41]

Yet despite the image that right-wing evangelicals project, evangelicalism has not always been led by xenophobes, right-wing reactionaries disdainful of the poor, and those who are more readily willing to compromise their morality than to sacrifice even a sliver of their personal political and economic interests. Evangelicals as a group were once dedicated to championing the poor, the vulnerable, and the socially marginalized rather than demonizing those that did not look or believe as they. In fact, fifty years or so after its mid-eighteenth-century beginnings, evangelicalism had become one of the most progressive social forces in America.

The abolitionist Frederick Douglass, in "What to a Slave Is the Fourth of July?," his famous July 5, 1852, oration at Corinthian Hall in Rochester, New York, indicted the Christian church of his day: "These ministers . . . strip the love of God of its beauty, and leave the throng of religion a huge, horrible, repulsive form. It is a religion for oppressors, tyrants, man-stealers, and thugs. It is not that 'pure and undefiled religion' which is from above." Douglass's remarks were appropriately bitter and condemnatory for his time, but generally he was not referring to evangelical Christians for, in fact, most abolitionists of his day were evangelicals. One example is Elijah H. Pilcher, a white Methodist preacher in Ohio who in 1852 published an abolitionist polemic, "The Unconstitutionality of Slavery and the Fugitive Slave Law."[42] Another is S. H. Waldo, a white Ohio minister who extolled communitarian, egalitarian economic and political justice in an 1849 address to the Society of Inquiry at Oberlin College. "Civil Government," he wrote, "where Christianity has its appropriate influence, is framed for the promotion of the universal good of the state [i.e., the common good], and not for the benefit of a few."[43] Charles Grandison Finney (1792–1874), a Rochester, New York, lawyer turned evangelical preacher who was perhaps the most influential evangelical of the nineteenth century, offered this challenge to enslavers: "Would a man that loved God with all his heart, perfectly, hold his neighbor as a slave?"[44]

None of this means that the evangelical ranks were immune to racism. To be sure, racism has permeated the fabric of America from its founding. As Jared Yates Sexton observes, "Exiting the British Empire meant a new sovereignty, but it wouldn't mean an entirely new society, as past hierarchies predicated on race and wealth remained firmly in place, and the country that would be birthed from the Revolutionary War entrenched those hierarchies in its laws and foundations."[45] Racism is even embedded in the United States Constitution and myriad Supreme Court rulings.[46] However, several major evangelical leaders, like Basil Manly Sr., William Capers, and James Henley Thornwell, three of Southern Presbyterianism's most influential scholars, vigorously defended the enslavement of black people.[47] They and other enslavers employed cherry-picked verses from the Bible devoid of historical nuance as their primary tools of pro-slavery argumentation. Favorites included Ephesians 6:5–9 ("Slaves, obey your earthly masters with fear and trembling, in singleness of heart, as you obey Christ")[48]—sentiments that, by the way, are not consistent with any saying of Jesus's—and the so-called curse of Ham in Genesis 9:18–27 ("Cursed be Canaan; lowest of slaves shall he be to his brothers").[49]

There were other white evangelicals of the period who, while acknowledging the sinfulness and inhumanity of slavery and working hard to abolish it, still believed that black people were morally and intellectually inferior. As a result, their stands against the maltreatment of blacks were often patronizing and at times given to convoluted thinking. The eighteenth-century evangelist and preacher George Whitefield is a major figure in American religious history, dubbed the "founder-hero" of American evangelicalism by historian Sydney Ahlstrom for his outsized role in promoting evangelical religion in America.[50] He was also a slave owner, an advocate of slavery, and a prime example of the convoluted racial calculus of the time. On the one hand, he excoriated abusive enslavers as "monsters of barbarity." Yet in an open letter to planters in the colonies, he simultaneously urged kinder treatment for enslaved blacks while also advising that cruelty could have the positive consequence of increasing "the sense of their natural misery," which would cause them to have a heightened receptivity to the Gospel.[51] Even Charles Finney forbade the election of blacks as trustees in his church and segregated the races in the pews, although he might have done so out of fear of offending his congregation. Some evangelical leaders were not above openly perpetuating white supremacy, even with violence, yet they were still able to remain members in good standing in both their churches and the KKK. Consider Los Angeles pastor Robert Pierce "Fighting Bob" Shuler (1880–1965). Through the first decade of the twentieth century he sat on the board of the evangelical Bible Institute of Los Angeles (now Biola University) at the same time he was organizing Klan rallies at his church.

Despite the racism so deeply embedded in American society, a number of evangelical periodicals rose above it to become major voices for justice. An 1828 article in the *Christian Reformer* declared, "Let us not forget that we are disciples of a reformer, the most thorough reformer, the most zealous reformer, the most courageous reformer that mankind ever saw. . . . Every man is bound, by his responsibility to God, to promote the best interests of his fellow creatures."[52] A writer in the *Piscataqua Evangelical Magazine* declared that a benevolent person "will not say to a brother or sister destitute of food, depart in peace, be thou warmed and filled, and, at the same time, give not those things that are needful for the body."[53] Charles Finney also vigorously insisted on the social responsibility of Christians, especially to care for the poor and vulnerable. "God's rule," he declared, "requires universal benevolence. . . . God loves both piety and humanity" (i.e., treating others humanely).[54]

Evangelical benevolent advocacy, mostly in the form of sermons and writings in journals and periodicals, touched on a number of issues, including support for prison reforms, financial relief for the poor, and the rights of women. Evangelicals were also major advocates for free universal education, at least for whites. "Common Schools are the glory of our land, where even the beggar's child is taught to read, and write, and think, for himself."[55] They believed that education for the poor and underprivileged was a crucial first step on the ladder of upward social and economic mobility. Indeed, the first institutions to offer basic educational instruction for the masses in the United States were the Sabbath (or Sunday) schools that evangelical churches established in the eighteenth century. Religious education from the Bible was the core component for those schools. The Bible was also used as a textbook for reading and writing. Sunday schools shifted to solely teaching religious instruction following the advent of compulsory state education in the 1870s, when "common" or community-funded schools took over the function of instruction in reading, writing, and arithmetic.

Some antebellum evangelicals also advocated for equal rights for women. Jesus modeled this behavior by addressing women no differently than men, even violating social norms at times to do so, as when he conversed with a woman at a well outside the presence and authority of the head of her household, a major cultural taboo of the time (John 4:1–42). In the subset of letters attributed to Paul that scholars deem to be authentically his, he consistently treats women as equals, referring to some as "co-workers" and describing one as an "apostle," the same designation by which he refers to himself.[56]

A representative early advocate of gender equality is James H. Fairchild (1817–1902), an ordained minister and professor at Oberlin College. Fairchild responded to the question of what constituted a "woman's rights and duties" firmly in the egalitarian gender rights tradition of Jesus and Paul: "the same, in general as those of all other human beings, because she possesses the common attributes of humanity." Fairchild argued as well for women to receive the same wages as men for similar work.[57] The embrace of gender equality was quite radical in the nineteenth century. Contrast that with today's right-wing evangelical churches and denominations, such as the Southern Baptist Convention, that still to this day refuse to support the ordination of women ministers.

Following the Emancipation Proclamation and the end of the Civil War, many evangelicals worked assiduously to repair the rends in America's social and spiritual fabric. This included supporting freedmen's associations and backing emancipated African Americans' efforts to socially and economically integrate into the larger society. Toward the end of the nineteenth century, socially concerned evangelicals shifted their focus to the suffering in the immigrant slums of New York, Chicago, and other large cities, establishing rescue missions, soup kitchens, and settlement houses. The reforms they championed went beyond piecemeal tweaking of existing policies to actual structural reforms, such as the formation of trade unions, child labor laws, housing reform, the equality of women, and fighting political corruption. They sought to fight the depredations of the "robber baron" oligarchic class and rampant exploitation in the workplace by empowering the populace with education offered by common (public) schools open to common folks, thereby broadening and deepening democracy.

By their attention to the needs of the people and their stands against racial injustice, economic exploitation, and political corruption, justice-minded eighteenth- and nineteenth-century evangelicals were trying to be faithful to the biblical dictum of "love your neighbor as yourself." They failed at times to live up to the demands of their faith, which were made more difficult by their relatively socially unenlightened times. Yet they struggled earnestly to inculcate a tenor of justice and social equity into American society. In their wake they left this nation on firmer moral ground with enhanced social ideals to live up to. But for far too many of those in the late twentieth and early twenty-first centuries who embraced the description "evangelical," it has been a very different story.

CHAPTER 2

YOU WILL KNOW THEM BY THEIR FRUITS

*The Strange Fruit of
Right-Wing Evangelicalism*

I N 1959, THE LILY-WHITE board of education in Prince Edward County, Virginia—which includes Farmville, the town of my birth—closed all public schools for more than five years rather than allow black students to set foot in the superior facilities of the segregated white schools. Most white children continued their educations uninterrupted at a state-supported, segregated private academy. A few black children, like my cousins, Doris and Elsie May, were able to leave the state to stay with relatives or family friends and attend the schools in their communities. (My sister and I were fortunate; our family had already migrated north.) But because they were unwelcome in Prince Edward's surrounding counties because their families were not taxpayers, most of Prince Edward County's black children were denied an education for the entire five-year duration of the racially motivated school closures.[1] When the schools finally reopened in 1964, many of the young people had already permanently joined the workforce in farm and field or billet cutting, or were too disheartened to sit in classes with children five years their junior. The tragic result is that most of the black people of that generation in Prince Edward County were never educated beyond grammar school.[2] The segregationists' treachery exacted a terrible toll on their lives, from which many of the county's black residents never fully recovered. Today, Farmville is the poorest town in the state. The typical household income in Farmville is $37,722 a year, little more than half the state median household income of $71,564, far below the national figure of $60,293.[3] No doubt the income level of blacks in the more rural areas of the county falls below that, some quite significantly. This perpetration of evil upon thousands of innocent children was not only the doing of racist politicians serving the racist inclinations of racist constituents. Among its chief spearheaders was Jerry Falwell Sr., who went on to become one of the most politically influential right-wing evangelicals in America.

The immense irony here is that the origins of the social witness of American evangelicalism were rooted in vastly different soil, in what Luke presents as the first public sermon of Jesus's ministry, in which he boldly heralds freedom from both the poverty and the oppression that the policies right-wing evangelicals support wreak upon so many:

> The Spirit of the Lord is upon me,
> because he has anointed me
> to bring good news to the poor.
> He has sent me to proclaim release to the captives
> and recovery of sight to the blind,
> to let the oppressed go free,
> to proclaim the year of the Lord's favor. (Luke 4:18–19)

Indeed, there is every indication that early evangelicals endeavored to take these words of Jesus seriously and to put them into action as best they could. They tried to bring good news to those bereft and economically exploited, to those in need of healing, to those held unjustly and brutalized in the bowels of an inhumane carceral system. Looking back, it is difficult to believe that today's right-wing evangelicals spring from the same historical roots, for in recent years evangelicalism has taken a turn that Jesus would certainly reject. As evangelical scholar Mark Labberton puts it, "the good news of Jesus Christ has been taken hostage by a highly charged, toxic subculture."[4]

A decade or so ago, while reading *The Future of Faith in American Politics* by David Gushee, a distinguished evangelical professor of Christian ethics, I was surprised to come upon a section titled "Black Evangelicals: Jesse Jackson and Obery Hendricks." Although the evangelical culture at that time was not nearly as craven as today's, I'd lived through the bitter, self-righteous, racism-tinged, flatulent harangues of the Moral Majority and the Christian Coalition, so evangelical Christians remained among the last folks that I wanted to be associated with. As I've already averred, in my opinion too few of them take seriously the Bible's call to love our neighbors as ourselves and to "let justice roll down like waters, and righteousness like a mighty stream" (Amos 5:24, NKJV). I have no doubt that Reverend Jackson feels the same.

I have since come to know David Gushee as a good man, a faithful Christian, and a gifted ethicist struggling mightily with the tragic turn his beloved evangelicalism has taken. He has been savaged in evangelical circles for his support of full civil rights for gay men and women and his rejection of right-wing evangelicals' toxic stands against immigrants and Muslims. I realize now that David referenced Reverend Jackson and me because he shares our understanding of the ethical and political demands of the Christian Gospel and the importance of fighting in the public square to fulfill them.[5] But despite David's good intentions, I rejected wholeheartedly his evangelical labeling, not least because of the Christian nationalist and white supremacist stains upon modern evangelicalism. Since 81 percent of evangelicals voted for Donald Trump and most of that number continue to support his hateful, un-Christian words and deeds, the evangelical label is even less welcome to me now.

Among the disturbing differences between evangelicals of the past and right-wing evangelicals today is the latter's attitude toward society's responsibility to America's poor and disadvantaged. They do not attempt to deny the Bible's pervasive insistence that the well-off and those in authority make provisions for the unfortunate poor. Instead, they characterize their opposition to social welfare programs as rooted in skepticism about the efficacy and deleterious effects of federal antipoverty spending, rather than in a refusal to help the poor. But upon closer examination that does not appear to be the case.

When surveys have posed questions specifically focused on addressing the needs of the poor rather than on social-safety-net spending practices, the responses of right-wing evangelicals indicated that the biblical call to care for the poor had little to do with their attitudes. For instance, a 2018 Billy Graham Center poll asked respondents to choose the most important from a list of twelve issues and candidate character traits that determined how they voted in 2016. Among black and Hispanic evangelicals, a candidate's "ability to help those in need" was the second or third most commonly named factor. Of those in particular who voted for Trump, concern for the poor was among their lowest priorities.[6]

Yet, although they are overshadowed in the public consciousness by right-wing evangelicals, there are progressive, even left-wing evangelicals today who hold the Gospel in no less esteem. In fact, in a number of ways these progressive evangelicals have more in common with the justice-minded early evangelicals and, compared to their right-wing counterparts, they are more faithful today to the ethical responsibilities of the Gospel, such as active concern for the poor, the unjustly incarcerated, the economically exploited, and the politically oppressed. Indeed, in 1973 a group of progressive evangelical activists crafted "The Chicago Declaration of Evangelical Social Concern." Ron Sider, a principal author of the document, explains that by writing the declaration he and his fellow activists were "confessing our failure to confront injustice, racism and discrimination against women, and pledging to do better."[7] Put in other words, these progressive evangelicals were both decrying and pledging to work to address right-wing evangelicalism's relative lack of regard for social justice. Progressive evangelical leaders and organizations like Faith in Action, Jim Wallis's *Sojourners,* the Gamaliel Network, the Samuel Proctor Conference, and Rev. William Barber and his Repairers of the Breach are actively working to honor that pledge.

A further irony of right-wing evangelicals is their oft-invoked self-description as the "new abolitionists,"[8] which draws a spurious parallel between their antiabortion crusade and the nineteenth-century movement that sought to free from enslavement living, breathing, tortured, and brutalized human beings. In fact, right-wing evangelicals would have us believe that their entire contemporary movement began as a moral response to the US Supreme Court's 1973 *Roe v. Wade* ruling, which legalized a woman's right to choose. But that is simply untrue. The modern right-wing evangelical movement that sold its soul to Donald Trump did not begin with *Roe v. Wade.* It fundamentally emerged from a racist maelstrom that began to spread in the mid-1960s—a full two years before the *Roe* decision—with the resolute resistance to the Civil Rights Act of 1965 and the Voting Rights Act of 1968 by Republicans and unwavering white-supremacist southern Democrats, known as "Dixiecrats," who were so enraged when the Democratic Congress passed the civil rights legislation that they deserted to the Republican Party, which they found much more amenable to their racial politics. But the racist maelstrom erupted in full earnest in 1970 under the pretext of religious outrage when the Internal Revenue Service established a statute that revoked the federal tax-exempt status of all educational institutions that practiced racial discrimination as a matter of policy. In 1971, in *Green v. Connally,* the US Supreme Court upheld the IRS statute, ruling that racially discriminatory private schools are not entitled to federal tax exemption provided for charitable, educational institutions. It was this ruling that sparked the modern evangelical movement as we know it today. Paul Weyrich, one of the architects of the Religious Right in the 1970s, explained as much. "What galvanized the Christian community," he said, "was not abortion, school prayer, or the ERA [Equal Rights Amendment]. . . . What changed their minds was Jimmy Carter's intervention against Christian schools, trying to deny them tax-exempt status on the basis of so-called de facto segregation."[9] Ed Dobson, a close colleague of Weyrich, affirmed his recollection of the movement's origins. "I sat in the smoke-filled back room with the Moral Majority, and frankly I do not remember abortion ever being mentioned as a reason why we should do something."[10]

Weyrich's surprising admission of the pro-segregation origins of the right-wing evangelical movement refers to its outrage at the government's revocation of the tax-exempt status of Bob Jones University, a deeply conservative right-wing evangelical Christian institution in South Carolina, which staunchly opposed the government's directive to end its segregationist practices. Bob Jones University argued that separation of the races was God's will, and thus it should be allowed to continue its "God ordained" segregationist ways without government penalty. The school became a cause célèbre for right-wing evangelicals, and its defiance against the government's ruling a defining moment for the movement.

Despite its claim to be guided by divine will, in actuality Bob Jones University was a virulently racist institution and an active proponent of white supremacist practices. Its founder, Bob Jones Sr., was a rabid racist who called anti-segregationists "satanic propagandists" and believed, among other myths, that African Americans should be grateful to whites for subjecting their ancestors to the horrors of chattel slavery. Otherwise, he said, "they might still be over there in the jungles of Africa, unconverted." The depth of Jones's racial antipathy was also reflected in his choice of speaker to deliver the keynote address at the school's 1927 groundbreaking: Alabama governor Bibb Graves, a darling of that state's murderous

KKK. As recently as 1998 the university was still defending its prohibition against interracial marriage and, presumably, interracial
dating:

> God has separated people for his own purposes. He has erected
> barriers between the nations, not only land and sea barriers, but
> also ethnic, cultural, and language barriers. God has made peo-
> ple different from one another and intends those differences to
> remain. Bob Jones University is opposed to intermarriage of the
> races because it breaks down the barriers God has established.[11]

Conflating their racism with patriotism and Christian nationalist notions, many evangelicals joined the fight to protect white
supremacy at Bob Jones under the guise of protecting religious
freedom. Perhaps the most prominent segregationist evangelical
of that time was Jerry Falwell Sr., a pastor in Lynchburg, Virginia,
whose Thomas Road Church had established a whites-only K–12
school in 1959, ironically called a Christian academy. In a 1958 sermon entitled "Segregation or Integration: Which?," Falwell decried the 1954 *Brown v. Board of Education of Topeka* ruling:

> If Chief Justice Warren and his associates had known God's word
> and had desired to do the Lord's will, I am quite confident that
> the 1954 decision would never have been made. The facilities
> should be separate. When God has drawn a line of distinction,
> we should not attempt to cross that line.[12]

For Falwell, integration was "the work of the devil." "The true
negro," he contended, "does not want integration. He realizes his
potential is far better among his own race." He further argued
that black people's quest to enjoy equal opportunities, benefits,
and protections under law was an insidious communist plot: "We
see the hand of Moscow in the background."[13] In "Ministers and
Marches," a sermon he preached in 1965 at the height of the civil
rights movement, he cast aspersions on its leaders: "I do question

the sincerity and nonviolent intentions of some civil rights leaders such as Dr. Martin Luther King Jr., Mr. James Farmer, and others, who are known to have left-wing associations." For him, civil rights legislation "should be considered civil wrongs rather than civil rights."[14] He outright accused King of being a "Communist" provocateur, opposed sanctions on South Africa's brutal apartheid regime, and when the courageous nonviolent freedom fighter and Anglican bishop Desmond Tutu was awarded the Nobel Peace Prize, Falwell derided him as a phony.[15] An active purveyor of racist propaganda, Falwell regularly featured hard-line segregationist politicians like Lester Maddox and George Wallace on his syndicated television program *The Old-Time Gospel Hour,* which was broadcast through network affiliates and cable stations around the country.[16] And Falwell was a principal leader, in alliance with numerous Virginia ministers and politicians, including the infamous segregationist senator Harry Byrd, in the Massive Resistance campaign against school integration that closed the Prince Edward County public schools. For five years, they fought tooth and nail in every available court, using every legal strategy they could contrive to keep black children from enjoying the same educational advantages as white children, brutally damaging thousands of innocent lives in the process.

In 1979, Falwell—along with Ed Dobson, Paul Weyrich, and Pat Robertson, the last a prominent evangelist who had founded the Christian Broadcasting Network in 1960—formed the pretentiously named Moral Majority. The Moral Majority was the first of a series of activist right-wing Christian nationalist organizations. It became perhaps the largest and most influential evangelical lobbying group in the United States, strategically mobilizing right-leaning Americans by promoting its social agenda as *the* "Christian worldview," which included support for school prayer and opposition to abortion, gay rights, feminism, the Equal Rights Amendment, and anything they believed militated against "family values," including social welfare programs, which they decried nearly as heartily as they decried pornography and illicit drugs. But however sincere their concern for these issues, looming over them was the goal of imposing on all of American society a Christian nationalist agenda, with its ever-present undercurrent of white supremacy. True to the values of its founders, racism remained a driving subtext of the Moral Majority movement.

The Moral Majority experienced its heyday in the 1980s during the Reagan presidency. It was instrumental in Reagan's election as president. The pollster Lou Harris was convinced that "Reagan would have lost the [1980] election by one percentage point without the help of the Moral Majority."[17] Two days after his January 20, 1980, inauguration, in a gesture of appreciation for their support, Reagan invited Falwell and several fellow evangelicals to meet with him in the Oval Office, the first of many invitations for Falwell, who crowed, "We now have a government in Washington that will help us."[18]

In 1981, Falwell and Tim LaHaye, author of the *Left Behind* book series, founded the Council for National Policy (CNP), described in *Nation* magazine as a secretive organization that "networks wealthy right-wing donors together with top conservative operatives to plan long-term movement strategy."[19] In a 2005 interview, Falwell bragged that the CNP was made up of "four or five hundred of the biggest conservative guns in the country. Ronald Reagan, both George Bushes . . . you name it. There's nobody who hasn't been here."[20] A private 1999 speech to the CNP by George W. Bush is said to have won him the support of right-wing evangelicals, which helped him win the United States presidency in 2000. Interestingly, the content of the speech has never been released by the CNP or by Bush.

At its height, the Moral Majority claimed some four million members. Its political influence and legitimacy relied heavily on Reagan's endorsement of its policy goals. As a result, its influence began to wane when Reagan left the White House. Falwell formally disbanded the organization in 1989, declaring it had accomplished its mission to elect conservative candidates to political office and make evangelical concerns a more prominent part of the nation's social agenda. But it should not be forgotten that for all its high-blown moralism, the Moral Majority was founded on a white supremacist platform of support for the perpetuation of racial segregation in America's educational institutions.

The Moral Majority was succeeded by evangelical groups that continued to embrace its Christian nationalist views and white supremacist underpinnings, differing only in media savvy, organizational structure, and political strategy. Those of particular significance include the Christian Coalition, founded in 1989 by Pat Robertson with the modest original goal of identifying and mobilizing ten pro-life voters in each of America's 175,000 electoral precincts. According to its website, it has since expanded its purview to include the training of Christian activists to "defend America's Godly heritage" through political organizing from local to federal levels and informing voters about timely "pro-family" issues and legislation. Focus on the Family, one of the largest right-wing evangelical organizations, differs from straightforward political advocacy groups like the Christian Coalition. Focus on the Family promotes socially conservative views and "pro-family" public policies through a number of affiliated enterprises, most notably through a daily syndicated radio program that is aired on some two thousand domestic stations, and various other media endeavors. A 1985 spin-off from Focus on the Family, the Family Research Council (FRC), has become one of the most powerful and influential evangelical Christian lobbying organizations in the country.

Since 2006, the FRC has hosted the Values Voter Summit, an annual conference that has become a mandatory stop for conservative Christian leaders and politicians. Consistent with its open Christian nationalism, its racial politics are exclusionary; its website announces that it was founded to promote the "Judeo-Christian worldview" throughout America. Its longtime president, Tony Perkins, is a fierce evangelical voice against immigrants and a staunch defender of the Trump administration's sordid track record on immigration. Perkins has echoed Trump's characterization of immigrants from south of the border as an invading "horde," invoked the Bible in an attempt to defend the administration's anti-immigrant rhetoric as biblically justified ("the right thing," he called it), and advocated the denial of constitutional protections to Muslims.[21] Even prior to Trump's political rise, Perkins had applauded the president of Uganda in a November 26, 2012, tweet for his public support of that country's "Kill the Gays" bill because, Perkins said, he is "leading his nation in repentance." In 1996, he purchased the mailing list of then KKK leader David Duke to use in the campaign of a Louisiana senatorial candidate he supported. In 2001, he was the guest speaker for a Louisiana chapter of the Council of Conservative Citizens, a white supremacist group that advocates against racial intermarriage and whose website once described black people as a "retrograde species of humanity." Perkins addressed the group while standing in front of a Confederate flag.[22]

The largest action group to emerge from conservative and Christian political cultures since the Moral Majority burst into the public square in 2009. In the spring of that year, various political groups arose in boisterous protest against the Obama administration's $787 billion economic stimulus package and comprehensive healthcare proposal, the Affordable Care Act. These diverse groups eventually coalesced into what became known as the Tea Party movement. The primary aims of the coalition included limiting the size of the federal government, reducing government spending, lowering the national debt, and opposing tax increases. Tea Party groups also voiced strong anti-union sentiments, opposed amnesty for undocumented immigrants, and called for tighter border security.

The Tea Party is not a Christian movement per se, but it does include a strong and influential evangelical core membership. A majority of Tea Party respondents (57 percent) identified themselves with the religious right in a 2010 PRRI Survey.[23] This, coupled with the consistency of the movement's interests with right-wing evangelical concerns, points to a strong right-wing evangelical presence in the Tea Party. Unsurprisingly, a 2012 *CBS News* poll found that nine out of ten Tea Party members (89 percent) were white, while just 1 percent was black.[24]

The Tea Party movement was consciously modeled on the famous 1773 Boston protest against British import taxes, but its actions revealed that it was as much, if not more, a protest against Obama's racial identity, what political commentator Fareed Zakaria called "an enraged, utterly obstructionist, Manichean opposition to [Obama's] presidency, and himself personally."[25] At Tea Party rallies, Obama was burned in effigy hanging from a noose, depicted as an "African witch doctor" replete with a bone in his nose and as a mugger holding Uncle Sam in a chokehold, and told to "go home to Kenya" in handheld sign after sign. Even his wife and daughters were subjected to racial slurs and insults. The air at Tea Party gatherings was thick with chants of "We want our country back!" and "Give us our country back!"—as if America had been overrun by a foreign invader. Tea Party doyenne and former Republican vice presidential candidate Sarah Palin epitomized those sentiments with her charge that Obama "is not one of us."[26] Black members of Congress were even spat upon and called derisive racial epithets at Tea Party rallies.[27]

A 2016 Stanford Business study underscored the congruence of Tea Party racial sentiments with those of evangelical Christian nationalists. It found that racial threat and ill will,[28] as well as perceived threats to the dominant status of whites in American society, were powerful motivational factors for Tea Party membership.[29] A 2010 Blair Center–Clinton School survey from the University of Arkansas revealed that Tea Party members overwhelmingly believed that the government has no responsibility for ensuring equality for blacks in employment (84.5 percent), in education (69.3 percent), housing (83.0 percent), and healthcare (81.4 percent). Overall, 62.8 percent of Tea Party respondents agreed that America has gone too far in pushing equal rights for all in this country.[30] These are essentially the same racial attitudes and political concerns held by today's evangelicals. Moreover, a little more than half (52 percent) of white evangelical respondents to a

2015 Public Religion Research Institute (PRRI) poll believe that a nonwhite majority in the US (which is projected to occur by 2045) would be "very bad for our nation." In other words, at least half of white evangelicals believe that maintaining white supremacy is necessary for our nation to be healthy.[31]

The election of America's first African American president in 2008 stirred up a hornet's nest of racism across the country. Then private citizen and political aspirant Donald Trump worked hard to inflame that racism. He obsessively assailed Obama's policies, no matter their merit, attacked Obama's every move with malicious delight, and continually spewed the lie that Obama was a foreign-born "other," an interloping, illegitimate occupant of the American presidency, which was eagerly seized upon by right-wing evangelicals. John Pavlovitz, a North Carolina pastor, characterized the onslaught as unchristian in a widely read blog. "White Evangelicals," he wrote. "You never made any effort to affirm [Obama's] humanity or show the love of Jesus to him in any quantifiable measure. You violently opposed him at every single turn—without offering a single ounce of the grace you claim as the heart of your faith tradition. You jettisoned Jesus as you dispensed damnation on him."[32]

It was in the context of Trump's onslaught of incivility and the Tea Party movement's seething animus for the nation's first black president, buttressed by the Moral Majority's legacy of racism, that the right-wing evangelical movement emerged as it stands today. The Trump campaign and presidency raised racial hatred to a much greater level. In 2019, hate crimes in the US rose to the highest level in more than a decade, with federal officials recording fifty-one hate-motivated killings, the highest number since the FBI began collecting that data in the early 1990s. This includes twenty-two people who were killed in a shooting targeting Mexicans, a frequent rhetorical target of Trump, at a Walmart in the border city of El Paso, Texas.[33] Membership in white supremacist organizations has grown substantially. Tellingly, counties in which rallies were held by Trump, the one extolled by evangelicals as God's chosen, saw hate crimes rise some 226 percent.[34]

But in this recounting there is a crucial point that sorely deserves to be acknowledged, that no matter how ugly the comments spewed at him by right-wing evangelicals, Trump, and Tea Party leaders and supporters, Barack Obama has never returned evil for evil, never responded in kind, never publicly spoken in anger, never resorted to insults or name-calling. His rabid right-wing detractors many times accused him of being an antichrist but, ironically, the truth is that Barack Obama has conducted himself more like a Christian than any of those who so viciously attacked him.

Even with white supremacists praising Trump as their hero, and even with Trump refusing to condemn his supporters' racial hatred, Trump evangelicals like Paula White still deny that Trump and the evangelical cult that has grown around him appeal to racial violence. White denounced the claim that President Trump is a bigot, saying he is "absolutely not a racist." Her proof? "People have known him for many years as a very successful businessman, very successful person. He had never had this title, this tag, this label, this narrative, as racist," said White. "Only when he becomes president, suddenly is this almost out of nowhere."[35]

Not true. During the 2015 primary campaign, South Carolina Republican senator Lindsey Graham described Trump as a "race-baiting, xenophobic bigot."[36] (Graham changed his tune after Trump won the election, claiming that he had "never heard [Trump] make a single racist statement.") Moreover, Trump had been labeled a racist decades before Graham called him out. In 1973, Trump—who was then running the family real estate firm—and his father were sued by the Department of Justice for refusing to let black people live in their buildings, in violation of the Fair Housing Act. Federal investigators found an unquestionable pattern of racial exclusion using a number of schemes. So widely known were the racially discriminatory rental practices by Fred Trump, later taken up by his son Donald, that the legendary folksinger Woody

Guthrie, once a tenant in a Trump building, in 1954 wrote a song, "Old Man Trump," to decry the racism he witnessed.[37]

An employee at a Trump property in Brooklyn admitted to investigators that he was told by the Trumps that "if a black person . . . inquired about an apartment for rent . . . I should tell [the black person] that the rent was twice as much as it really was." The Trumps reluctantly signed a consent decree to refrain from "discriminating against any person in terms, conditions, or privileges of sale or rental of a dwelling."[38]

Even more troubling is his attack on the Central Park Five. In 1989, five teens aged fourteen to sixteen—four black, one Hispanic—were accused of raping and nearly beating to death a white woman jogging in New York's Central Park. Before their trial even began, while they were still presumed innocent, Trump bought a full-page ad in the *New York Times* that screamed "BRING BACK THE DEATH PENALTY. BRING BACK OUR POLICE!"[39] When the five young men were exonerated in 2002 by DNA evidence after unjustly spending as much as thirteen years behind bars, Trump not only refused to apologize, he also suggested they deserved their punishment because, he claimed, they were "guilty of something else" that he never specified.[40] In 2014, they were awarded punitive damages of $41 million for malicious prosecution, pain, and suffering and the tragic loss of their childhood years. In fact, in an op-ed published in the *New York Daily News,* Trump railed against both their exoneration and the settlement, odiously claiming that "settling doesn't mean innocence. . . . My opinion on the settlement of the Central Park Jogger case is that it's a disgrace."[41]

Trump has never come close to similarly denouncing any crime committed by a white person against a person of color, no matter how heinous or how clear their guilt. Yet he granted a pardon to the notoriously racist Arizona sheriff Joe Arpaio *before he was even sentenced* for ignoring a federal order to cease illegally profiling, jailing, and terrorizing Hispanic residents. As journalist Adam Serwer observed in *The Atlantic,* "The specific dissonance of Trumpism—advocacy for discriminatory, even cruel, policies combined with vehement denials that such policies are racially motivated—provides the emotional core of its appeal."[42]

The racism promulgated by Trump during his time in office (and cosigned by the silence of his court evangelicals) is, of course, well known. His words and actions have actively misled white evangelicals to refuse to honor one of the most important Gospel commands of Jesus, more important than any doctrinal tenet contrived in his name: to love their neighbors as themselves. In the place of this central dictum of the good news, Trump's evangelicals carried a pernicious message directly counter to the faith they profess: that it is acceptable to commit transgressions of virtually any kind against other human beings simply because their skin bears a different hue or they speak in unfamiliar tongues. The extent to which Christians enact, support, or tolerate these behaviors is the extent to which they are at war with the Gospel of Jesus Christ. It is of such people that Jesus said, "Woe to you . . . hypocrites! For you lock people out of the kingdom of heaven. You yourselves do not enter, nor will you let those enter who are trying to" (Matthew 23:13).

Jesus said, "You will know them by their fruits" (Matthew 7:16). In the end, fully comprehending the modern right-wing evangelical movement means knowing that its impetus, its defining event, was not love for their neighbors. The lesson of the Good Samaritan was nowhere in their purview. Quite to the contrary, modern right-wing evangelicalism is defined by a shamelessly *un*holy impulse: to protect the perquisites of white supremacy. It demonstrates a greater dedication to that end than to serving the God they claim to love, in whose image all of humanity is created. To this day the Moral Majority and its successor movements have yet to meaningfully repent for their sins against black America with words, much less with deeds. Some right-wing bodies, such as the Southern Baptist Convention, have offered public apologies for supporting slavery. But their unwavering support of the race-baiting Donald Trump renders the few tepid evangelical gestures at repentance highly questionable, if not fully meaningless.

Right-wing evangelicals' complicity in Trump's debasement of American society shamefully paints the Christian Gospel of light, love, and egalitarian justice as an ugly, loveless, exclusionary ideology of domination. Jesus said that each of us will be known by the fruit of our acts and attitudes. The rot of the unholy fruit of Trump's evangelical supporters and apologists has spread across the length and breadth of this nation, portraying evil as good and good as evil. That is their vile and blasphemous harvest. In the name of God.

CHAPTER 3

WHO DO YOU SAY THAT I AM?

*Right-Wing Evangelicals'
Dangerous Misappropriation of Jesus*

WITH A MANE of well-coiffed silver-white hair, John MacArthur has the patrician look of a wealthy WASP lawyer or a successful Wall Street banker rather than the evangelical minister that he is. He is an aristocrat of sorts, however, in that he is one of right-wing evangelical Christianity's most prolific and most widely respected biblical commentators. He has been listed among America's most influential Christian pastors. He hosts an internationally syndicated Christian radio program and has written or edited more than 150 books, two of which have sold over a million copies each. Christians of all stripes, from black Baptist preachers like Rev. William Barber to white Catholic nuns like Sister Simone Campbell, labor day in and day out to heed the call of the prophet Amos to engage in efforts to make a society in which "justice rolls down like waters and righteousness like a mighty stream." One would expect MacArthur to celebrate those heeding the prophet's call. Yet in September 2018, MacArthur published yet another widely read work, a manifesto-style open letter called *The Statement on Social Justice* *and the Gospel.* In it he does a curious thing: he attacks "social justice" as *anti-biblical.* He writes, "We deny that political or social activism should be viewed as integral components of the gospel or primary to the mission of the church."[1]

To date, the document has been cosigned by well over ten thousand evangelical leaders and activists.

The statement takes pains to give the impression of careful scholarship by employing sober prose and spurts of theological jargon. But ultimately, its claims fall short. For instance, it reduces the harsh reality of social and political oppression to mere perception—"a person's feeling of offense"—and stoops to the well-worn, racist dog whistles of "entitlement" and false claims of victimhood: "We reject any teaching that encourages racial groups to view themselves as privileged oppressors or entitled victims of oppression. While we are to weep with those who weep, we deny that a person's feelings of offense or oppression necessarily prove that someone else is guilty of sinful behaviors, oppression, or prejudice."[2]

Further, the document draws a false equivalency between *forced* racial segregation and *voluntary* self-segregation, and between those who practice segregation and those who are victimized by it: "We deny that Christians should segregate themselves into racial groups or regard racial identity above, or even equal to, their identity in Christ."[3] But the central, most wrongheaded claim of the statement is its branding of social justice as somehow impugning biblical truth. "The Bible's teaching," it says, "is being challenged under the broad and somewhat nebulous rubric of concern for 'social justice.'" But the Bible itself tells a different story. Divine concern for social justice permeates the Bible; the political and social activism within the biblical text is integral to the ethics of biblical faith.

Yet incredibly, the statement asserts the opposite: that "concern for 'social justice' presents an onslaught of dangerous, false teachings that threaten the gospel, misrepresent Scripture, and lead people away from the grace of God in Jesus Christ." Unfortunately, this misguided sentiment is by no means an anomaly. In

June 2019 the Southern Baptist Convention convened a national panel titled "The Dangers of Social Justice in Evangelicalism." And in a July 2019 video, declared Tom Ascol, president of the evangelical Founders Ministries, a polity reform group within the Southern Baptist Convention, "I see godless ideologies that have spread across Western civilization over the last decades with a vengeance . . . through the Trojan horse of social justice."[4]

The statement declares that it is Christians' duty to live under "the biblical standard of righteousness." Yet MacArthur's rhetoric does not reflect a fully informed understanding of what that standard is. Indeed, the statement reveals a misunderstanding of the biblical witness at its most fundamental level, a misunderstanding shared by virtually all right-wing evangelical leaders. Social justice is not a Trojan horse for secular ideologies. It is not, as an article by one Georgia pastor charges, "an attack on the sufficiency of scripture."[5] *It is central to the biblical witness.* It simply is not possible to fully understand the teachings of Jesus without a clear understanding of the centrality of social justice to the Bible.

The biblical writers did not articulate a theoretical concept of social justice. What they gave us are markers by which it is to be understood and enacted. These markers have been overlooked, misunderstood, and obscured by modes of reading that stress the spiritual and supernatural while overlooking the biblical books' various social and political settings in life and their implications. Therefore, a bit of unpacking is called for here in order to gain a clear comprehension of the import of social justice in the Bible. Accordingly, we begin with the witness of the Old Testament.

The teachings of the Hebrew Bible, called the Old Testament by Christians, are the unassailable foundation of the teachings of Jesus. Judaism is the religion that Jesus was born into, nurtured in, matured in, his entire existence steeped in. The gospels portray him as an observant Jew with their many references to his dutiful observance of Jewish High Holy Days. Moreover, the gospel of Matthew says that Jesus directly declared his fealty to Judaism and its scriptures: "Do not think that I have come to abolish the law or the prophets; I have come not to abolish but to fulfill" (Matthew 5:17).

Except for a very few verses and phrases, primarily in the books of Daniel and Ezra, the Old Testament is written in Hebrew.[6] Throughout the Old Testament, social justice is signified both conceptually and literally by the pairing of its most frequently used Hebrew conceptual terms, *mishpat* and *tzedekah,* which together also comprise the most often occurring pairing of terms in the entire Bible. *Mishpat,* the Hebrew term for "justice," or "judgment," is arguably the most important conceptual term in the Bible. It is certainly the single most frequently used term. In its various forms it occurs more than four hundred times. A close second is *tzedekah* ("righteousness," that is, "doing what is right" or "putting justice into action"), with three-hundred-plus appearances. The ubiquity of these terms both singularly and collectively gives us a sense of their centrality to the biblical witness.

Mishpat (*mishpatim,* plural) has various nuances of meaning. These include "rights," "vindication," "deliverance," "norm." Its dimension of "judgment" refers to the act of discerning between good and evil, as, for example, "The Lord enters into judgment [*mishpat*] with the elders and princes of his people: It is you who have devoured the vineyard; the spoil of the poor is in your houses" (Isaiah 3:14). Hebrew Bible scholar Temba Mafico observes that "there is strong evidence that attests that originally . . . *mishpat* referred to the restoration of a situation or environment which promoted equity and harmony (*shalom*)."[7] This suggests that the underlying meaning of *mishpat* is *egalitarian* justice.[8] In its most basic meaning, egalitarian justice in the Bible can be understood to signify that everyone in society should have equal rights;[9] that all have a right to fair and equitable treatment in the major spheres of living.[10] This is well expressed in Moses's instruction to the Hebrew community:

> You shall appoint judges and officials throughout your tribes, in
> all your towns that the Lord your God is giving you, and they

shall render just decisions for the people. You must not distort justice; you must not show partiality; and you must not accept bribes, for a bribe blinds the eyes of the wise and subverts the cause of those who are in the right. Justice, and only justice, you shall pursue. (Deuteronomy 16:18–20)

This egalitarian dimension is seen as well in the practical and ethical imperative in Leviticus 19:18 that is quoted by Jesus: "love your neighbor as yourself" (Matthew 22:39). The French philosopher and mystic Simone Weil put it plainly: "The Gospel makes no distinction between the love of our neighbor and justice."[11]

As with *mishpat,* the full meaning of *tzedakah* is also widely misunderstood. *Tzedekah* is usually rendered as "righteousness," in the sense of individual personal piety. Yet there is no term in the Hebrew of the Old Testament for "individual." In fact, the concept of an individual as the center of attention didn't exist as a social norm in the ancient Near East. Thus, the primary focus of *tzedekah* in the Bible is not personal piety. People defined themselves and judged their actions *dyadically,* through the eyes of their communities and the common good, rather than as atomized individuals.[12] And clearly, *tzedekah* is much more than a feeling or an affect. Rather, its focus is social, *ha'am,* "the people"—the community or society. Accordingly, *tzedekah* should be translated as "doing right by others" or "acting with justice." Its unmistakable implication is that people are to interact with others in their communities in ways that are commensurate with justice. That means that the true yardstick of righteousness is the degree of one's active dedication to the well-being of one's neighbors and the common good. The repeated biblical appearances of *tzedekah* in conjunction with verbs testifies to this. For instance, from the book of Isaiah:

A shoot shall come out from the stump of Jesse, and a branch shall grow out of his roots. . . . His delight shall be in the fear of the Lord. He shall not judge by what his eyes see, or decide

by what his ears hear; but with righteousness [tzedakah] he shall
judge the poor, and decide with equity for the meek of the earth.
(Isaiah 11:1, 3–4)

In this sense *tzedekah* has no meaning unless it is connected to
putting justice into action according to the basic ethical standards
of the Bible: actively doing the things that make for a healthy,
peaceful, and morally and ethically empowered society.

What *mishpat* and *tzedekah* both speak to is the imperative
of making fair and just dealings in society the social norm. Thus,
whenever they are paired, the terms signify *social justice,* putting
justice into practice in society. Jewish theologian David Novak
suggests that the pairing can be understood to signify "correct justice." He goes on, "Even better might be *true justice.*"[13] For my
part, I translate the term as *social justice* to foreground its activist,
collectivist dimension. This dimension is heard in the prophet Jeremiah's admonition to the house of King David:

> Thus, says the Lord: Act with *justice and righteousness [social jus-
> tice]*, and deliver from the hand of the oppressor anyone who
> has been robbed. And do no wrong or violence to the alien, the
> orphan, and the widow, or shed innocent blood in this place. . . .
> But if you will not heed these words, I swear by myself, says the
> Lord, that this house shall become a desolation. (Jeremiah 22:3, 5;
> my addition is in parentheses.)

The command to live by the imperative of social justice is
also seen throughout the piety of the Psalms. See, for example,
"Happy are those who observe *justice,* who do *righteousness [so-
cial justice]* at all times" (Psalm 106:3; italics indicate my emphasis and augmentation here and in the verses that follow). The
psalmist left no doubt about the crucial importance of the social justice imperative: "*justice* and *righteousness* [social justice]
are the foundation of his throne" (Psalm 97:2) and "[God] loves
justice and *righteousness* [social justice]" (Psalm 33:5). Again he

writes, "Give *justice* to the poor and the orphan; treat the oppressed and the needy with *righteousness*" (Psalm 82:3). Social justice is so foundational to the prophetic tradition that God declares it through the prophet to be the measure by which people's deeds will be judged:

> See, I am laying in Zion a foundation stone. . . . And I will make justice the line, and righteousness the plummet. (*mishpat* and *tzedekah*; Isaiah 28:16–18)

The Bible especially enjoins the responsibility to practice social justice upon those in positions of authority and governance, because their decisions have the most far-reaching effects in society and can literally mean the difference between life and death. This includes establishing and maintaining just governmental structures and fair and equitable policies of distribution of wealth, resources, respect, status, and authority. Simone Weil calls this "the supernatural virtue of justice," which, she explains, "consists of behaving exactly as though there were equality when one is the stronger in an unequal relationship."[14] The Five Books of Moses tell us that in practical terms this means enacting regulatory protections against obstacles to living a decent life, such as protecting the poor from usurious exploitation;[15] prohibiting perversions of justice, partiality, and bribes in courts of law;[16] regularizing measures of weight, physical length, and both liquid and dry quantity to guard against the poor being cheated;[17] enhancing the requirements for valid legal testimony;[18] sacralizing economic parity by allowing less expensive sacrifices to be made in the temple;[19] and instituting the Jubilee year of land reclamation.[20] It is social justice that Walter Brueggemann describes when he observes that

> the intention of Mosaic justice is to redistribute social goods and social power; thus it is distributive justice. This justice recognizes that social goods and social power are unequally and destructively distributed in Israel's world (and derivatively in any social

context), and that the well-being of the community requires that social goods and power to some extent be given up by those who have too much, for the sake of those who have not enough.[21]

The following inaugural psalm for a newly crowned king articulates the social justice imperative for governance as a biblical ideal, if not a standing norm:[22]

Endow the king with your *mishpat*, O God,
the royal son with your *tzedekah*.
May he judge your people in *tzedekah*,
your afflicted ones with *mishpat*.
May the mountains bring prosperity to the people,
the hills the fruit of *tzedekah*.
May he defend the afflicted among the people
and save the children of the needy;
may he crush the oppressor. . . .
For he will deliver the needy who cry out,
the afflicted who have no one to help.
He will take pity on the weak and the needy
and save the needy from death.
He will rescue them from oppression and violence,
for precious is their blood in his sight. (Psalm 72: 1–4, 12–15,
 NIV with my augmentation)

So where does our brief foray into the Old Testament bring us? Hopefully, to the understanding that because the command for believers to engage in social justice is foundational to the Old Testament, it is also foundational to the Christian Gospel, permanently woven into the DNA of Jesus and, therefore, woven into the DNA of the Gospel. In what the gospel of Luke presents as the first public pronouncement of Jesus's ministry, his choice of words can be seen as a manifesto of sorts, as the first public statement of the core principles of his ministry. And it is unambiguously about social justice:

The Spirit of the Lord is upon me,
because he has anointed me
to bring good news to the poor.
He has sent me to proclaim release to the captives
and recovery of sight to the blind,
to let the oppressed go free,
to proclaim the year of the Lord's favor. (Luke 4:18–19)

The closing statement of his proclamation in Luke 4:21 leaves no doubt that it is a pronouncement of the role he saw for himself in the world: "Today this scripture has been fulfilled in your hearing." Jesus confirms this self-identification when followers of John the Baptist ask him if he is the one they have expected: "Go and tell John what you have seen and heard: the blind receive their sight, the lame walk, the lepers are cleansed, the deaf hear, the dead are raised, *the poor have good news brought to them*" (Luke 7:22, emphasis added).

Notably, in the Luke 4 passage no term for social justice is used. That is because the commandment to act in ways that are consistent with social justice is such a basic ethic of the faith to which Jesus was heir that here, as elsewhere in the gospels, clearly it was taken for granted. The eminent Jewish scholar Abraham Joshua Heschel acknowledges it is "an *a priori* of biblical faith, self-evident, . . . inherent in [God's] essence and identified with [God's] ways."[23] Moreover, in the Bible justice is presented as a defining characteristic of God: "the Lord loves justice" (Psalm 37:28); "the Lord is a God of justice" (Isaiah 30:18); "[God's] work is perfect, and all [God's] ways are just" (Deuteronomy 32:4).

Without calling it by name, Jesus expresses this sentiment in his recapitulation of Leviticus 19:18, "love your neighbor as yourself." Because it calls for the same rights, opportunities, and access to the good things in life for others in society as we seek for ourselves, this verse is a foundational statement of social justice. Heschel explains that ancient Israel "[did] not distinguish between right and duty."[24]

In other words, inextricably paired with the *right* to be treated with justice is the *duty* to treat others with justice. Therefore, active responsible concern for social justice would have been very real for Jesus. This is reflected in a number of his parables. Examples include the parable of the unforgiving servant, which dramatically decries economic exploitation (Matthew 18:23–35), as does the parable of the workers in the vineyard, in which desperate landless workers are totally subject to the whims of a rich landowner (Matthew 20:1–16); the parable of the rich fool and his futile, selfish accumulation of wealth (Luke 12:13–21); and the parable of the dishonest manager, which presents in bold relief how economic dishonesty can be casually treated as normative (Luke 16:1–13). His so-called Cleansing of the Temple, really a planned disruption of temple commerce,[25] is a dramatic rebuke to the legitimacy of the temple economic apparatus (Mark 11:15–19). The narrative of the widow's offering (Mark 12:41–44) highlights the injustice of the wealth gap between the poor and the rich in Israelite society; her poverty stands as a stinging rebuke to a status quo that ignores the many scriptural commands to care for the welfare of widows who, with orphans and immigrant strangers, were among the most vulnerable members of Israelite society.[26]

But the New Testament doesn't only tell us about Jesus's social justice stance. Like the Old Testament, it also has a term used to signify social justice. It is the Greek word *dikaiosune*. As with the narrow traditional rendering of *tzedekah* as pious personal righteousness, standard translations of the gospels from the Greek in which they were originally written take a similarly narrow approach to *dikaiosune*, also rendering it as "righteousness" in the sense of personal moral piety. Yet as students of biblical Greek know, *dikaiosune* also has the more expansive interpersonal meaning of *justice*, i.e., right action done in community and society, how people should conduct themselves in their treatment of others in society. In that *dikaiosune* has this social dimension, it should also be understood as connoting *social justice*. With this in mind, "Blessed are those who hunger and thirst for righteousness"

(Matthew 5:6) can be read as "Blessed are those who hunger and thirst for *social justice*" (emphasis added here and in the following verses). Similarly, "But seek first the kingdom of God and his righteousness, and all these things will be added to you" (Matthew 6:33, ESV) can be read as "Seek first the kingdom of God and its *social justice* and all else will be added to you." Jesus informing John the Baptist that he must be baptized "to fulfill all righteousness" can also be understood as meaning that he must be baptized in order "to fulfill all *social justice*" (Matthew 3:13–15). In the same way, "Blessed are those who are persecuted for *righteousness'* sake" (Matthew 5:10) can be read as "Blessed are those who are persecuted for the sake of *social justice*," that is, for trying to make social conditions more just. Ethicist Nicholas Wolterstorff offers a helpful explanatory comment. "My own reading of human affairs," he writes, "is that righteous people are either admired or ignored, not persecuted; people who pursue justice are the ones who get in trouble."[27]

What did social justice mean to Jesus? A clear-eyed reading of the gospels reveals that it meant a more equitable access to wealth, resources, security, authority, and power. The gospels portray relief for the impoverished masses in Israel to be his primary concern. We know this because *he spoke about poverty and the impoverished more often and more passionately than any subject except God.* His concern was so great that he spoke of the poor even in the sublime heights of the Beatitudes: "Blessed are you who are poor, for yours is the kingdom of God" (Luke 6:20).

It is estimated that between the vagaries of weather and climate, the taxes paid to their Roman overlords, and mandatory religious obligations, some 95 percent of the people of Israel were poor, with hunger widespread.[28] Rabbinic writings tell of bands of homeless poor people roaming the countryside,[29] so desperate that when the poor tithe was distributed they sometimes stampeded like cattle.[30] The sad observation of a second-century rabbi could just as easily have been made in Jesus's day a century earlier: "the daughters of Israel are comely, but poverty makes them repulsive."[31] So great was the poverty and hunger that the gospel portrays the expectant mother of Jesus thanking God that among the acts of salvation to come from the Messiah in her womb was that he would "[fill] the hungry with good things" (Luke 1:53). The gospels record Jesus feeding the hungry on several occasions. He intoned to those without enough food to eat, "Blessed are you who are hungry now, for you will be filled" (Luke 6:21). He even acknowledged the people's hunger as he taught them to pray for "daily bread" (*arton epiousion*, Matthew 6:11), the dietary staple of the poor.

In metaphors, parables, and direct assertions Jesus issued denunciations of inequitable treatment and the traditions and structural barriers that stood in the way of people's material well-being.[32] He said, "Woe to you who are rich. . . . Woe to you who are full now" (Luke 6:24–25) and "It is easier for a camel to go through the eye of a needle than for someone who is rich to enter the kingdom of God" (Matthew 9:24). He commended a rich tax collector for pledging to give half of his fortune to the poor and repay fourfold anyone he might have defrauded (Luke 19:1–10). There is the poignant parable of the haughty rich man who ignored the desperation of a beggar "covered with sores" and ends up in hell (Luke 16:19–26). And, again, in the parable of the sheep and the goats he declared that people who do not respond to the hunger, thirst, and nakedness of those in need "will go away into eternal punishment" (see Matthew 25:31–46).

Jesus railed against the rich without compromise or qualification. But because his social justice pronouncements concerning poverty and wealth are so extreme, they are usually ignored or dismissed as quaint and unrealistic. But when viewed in the context of Jesus's setting in life, what might appear as quaint or unrealistic in actuality offers valuable ethical guidance.

It is true that Jesus judged all material riches as immoral, without exception. But his pronouncements had a different meaning in his time and place. They reflect a perspective that cultural anthropologists call "limited good," a cultural worldview prevalent in ancient Near Eastern peasant societies that held that every material good was in finite supply.[33] Late antiquity was a world of rudimentary technology with no real economies of scale. Upward socioeconomic mobility was almost nonexistent. Most persons were peasants, virtually powerless against the vagaries of nature and the will and whim of the powers that be. In such a setting the notion of the world as containing only a finite amount of goods was a fully reasonable conclusion. As anthropologist George M. Foster explains, "Broad areas of peasant behavior . . . suggest that peasants view . . . their total environment—as one in which all of the desired things in life . . . exist in finite quality and are always in short supply."[34] Given their belief in a limited amount of available goods and resources in the world, coupled with the cultural belief that, because everyone was created in the image of God, everyone was entitled to their own fair share of those goods, it was a small step to the conclusion that anyone who accumulated more wealth than others did so by unjustly depriving their neighbors of their own rightful portion. Thus, all accumulations of wealth beyond that of others in their communities were considered unjustly gained by greed, deceit, exploitation, or theft. As cultural anthropologist Bruce J. Malina explains, "That every rich person is a thief or the heir of a thief was a truism based upon the perception of limited good. If all goods are limited and people were created more or less on equal footing, then those who have more must have taken it from those who now have less."[35] That is why Plato (428–348 BCE) declared, "The very rich are not good,"[36] and eight centuries later the indictment of St. Jerome (Eusebius Sophronius Hieronymus, ca. AD 347–420) could be even more biting: "Every rich person is a thief or the heir of a thief."[37]

Because of the immense technological advances since Jesus's time, his indictment of every rich person and *all* accumulations of riches as sinful and unjustly gained does not hold in today's world. One can become rich in technologically advanced societies with their economies of scale from innovations and inventions without stealing from others. But that doesn't change the moral and ethical character of Jesus's sayings; he still railed against ill-gotten wealth that is unjustly obtained and maintained. So, when Jesus's words are applied to today's world of technological and industrial advance, they carry the same character of judgment and indictment against greedy, dishonest, unscrupulous, unjust economic elites as they did in his day. In other words, no matter the time or the setting, wealth is unjust for Jesus whenever it is gotten and used in an unjust fashion, or for unjust ends, or when it is greedily accumulated and not shared with those in need. In a real sense, Jesus offers a profound judgment of America's capitalist ethos.

Moreover, Jesus's sense of social justice was quite politically radical. He mounted bold public demonstrations against the temple economic apparatus and its money changers. He fed thousands of poor people which, on at least one occasion, moved an assembled crowd to commit the seditious act, punishable by death by Roman law, of attempting to crown him king in a land already ruled by Caesar (John 6). He fearlessly denounced the agents of the temple's reigning status quo as a "brood of vipers" (Matthew 23:33), "whitewashed tombs" (Matthew 23:27), and excoriated them as enemies of God: "You are from your father the devil" (John 8:44). He even highlighted the exploitation of landless workers (Matthew 20:1–16).[38]

The New Testament gospels testify that Jesus's deep concern for the plight of poor people was ever present. Today he would be considered a radical, perhaps even a socialist, for preaching good news to the poor and woes to the rich; for explicitly and implicitly denouncing the unjust, inequitable distribution of wealth and abuse of economic power in his homeland; for staging disruptive public demonstrations against an exploitive, nonresponsive political-religious establishment at the central site of their power (Mark 11:15–19); and for traveling his country for three years disturbing the status quo. It is important to note, however, that his radical stances were not just political in nature. The gospels attest that prior to beginning his ministry of activism, Jesus spent an extended period in the wilderness engaged in spiritual ministrations that included solitude, fasting, meditation, and contemplation.[39] The gospel of Luke makes clear that there was a direct relationship between his spiritual preparation and his activism, for it is only after his extended wilderness sequestration that he publicly declared the messianic ("anointed") role he was to play in the lives of his people (Luke 4:16–18). Thus, the social radicality of Jesus was a function of his holistic spirituality. That is to say that his *vertical* spiritual relationship with God defined his *horizontal* spiritual relationship with humanity. The point at which the vertical and the horizontal spiritualities meet and interact is what we may call *holistic* spirituality. It is his holistic spiritual attunement that fuels the activist urgency of his social and political ministry.

For right-wing evangelical Christians, it is the foregrounding of their evangelical identity in opposition to other modes of Christian belief—especially progressive Christianity—that is important almost to the point of constituting a political litmus test. They routinely largely regard anyone who does not subscribe to their beliefs to be morally unfit for political office. It does not matter how much others attempt to love their neighbors or respond to the needs of the weak and vulnerable; for evangelicals, anyone who does not condemn same-gender-loving people, oppose a woman's right of sovereignty over her own body, or reject the government's responsibility to care for the welfare of those in need is not a worthy person. Yet nowhere did Jesus suggest dogmatic religious litmus tests as necessary requirements for following him, or even for going to heaven; not once in his Gospel pronouncements does he say that God would judge anyone based upon adherence to any particular creed. In fact, in the entirety of the gospels he says virtually nothing about what to believe. What he did teach were *ethical* precepts about serving and honoring God by treating our neighbors in ways consistent with the just and loving will of God or, as I have articulated it elsewhere, *treating the people's needs as holy.*[40]

Jesus's words in Matthew 25:31–46 testify that what ultimately determines whether people are bound for heaven or condemned to hell is not what they do in the privacy of their bedrooms, or the regularity of their attendance at church or synagogue, or their degree of diligence in performing table blessings and bedtime prayers, not even what they profess to believe. According to Jesus here, what determines whether a person's path leads to heaven or to hell is the way they treat others: whether they have endeavored in their own ways, no matter how large or small, to remove obstacles to the satisfaction of others' real needs; whether they have tried to ease the systemically imposed suffering of those unjustly held in the hellish depths of prisons, and so on. In other words, people will be judged by whether they have endeavored to live lives leavened by the divine imperative of social justice, again, as articulated in the parable of the sheep and the goats:

> Then he will say to those on his left, "Depart from me, you who are cursed, into the eternal fire prepared for the devil and his angels. For I was hungry and you gave me nothing to eat, I was thirsty and you gave me nothing to drink, I was a stranger and you did not invite me in, I needed clothes and you did not clothe me, I was sick and in prison and you did not look after me. . . . Truly I tell you, whatever you did not do for one of the least of these, you did not do for me." Then they will go away to eternal punishment, but the righteous ["the just"] to eternal life. (Matthew 25:41–46, NIV)

Even though Jesus clearly predicated divine judgment upon being responsive to the needs of the poor and the vulnerable, evangelicals rarely cite those teachings. On the few occasions that they do quote Jesus's pronouncements about the poor, they invariably cite Mark 14:7: "For you always have the poor with you." The context of this verse is an unnamed woman's desire to anoint Jesus's calloused feet with expensive oil. Jesus's response is a rebuke to what he takes to be the disciples' feigned concern for the poor. But right-wing evangelicals construe it instead as a declaration that concern for the poor is unimportant, even wasted, because efforts to reduce poverty are doomed to fail. (Sometimes appended to it is the dubious logic that if God wanted poverty ended, God would have ended it.) But, as is so often the case, they fail to quote the entire verse because it does not suit their purposes. What they leave out not only conveys the actual point Jesus is making; it also is an indictment of their failure to address the needs of the poor and vulnerable and their contrivance to camouflage it with expressions of false concern: "And you can show kindness to them whenever you wish; but you will not always have me." The irony is that this verse can also be read as a direct indictment of right-wing evangelical leaders' and politicians' opposition to social-safety-net policies so desperately needed by many millions of America's poor and vulnerable.

Another passage used by right-wing evangelical leaders and politicians to justify their disdain for social welfare policies crafted to help America's needy poor, which includes the working poor, is 2 Thessalonians 3:10 ("Anyone unwilling to work should not eat"). This verse is part of the apostle Paul's instruction to the Christians in the Greek city of Thessalonica about how they should respond to those who considered themselves too spiritually evolved to engage in the mundane act of working to support themselves. Instead it is used by evangelicals as an ill-intentioned blanket depiction of recipients of public assistance (most of whom are children and others unable to work) as lazy and unwilling to support themselves, which they then use to justify cutting public welfare funding. One such malefactor is right-wing evangelical representative Jodey Arrington of Texas, who cited this verse in a mean-spirited ploy to indict recipients of the Supplemental Nutrition Assistance Program (SNAP—formerly the Food Stamp Program) as "freeloaders," while ignoring both that this view is implied nowhere in Paul's statement and, more important, that many recipients are "the least of these" in American society: homeless, sick and disabled, unemployed or working poor, including many military veterans.[41]

Right-wing evangelicals have evolved what might be called a "Jesus personality cult" that is obsessed with the person of Jesus as spiritual savior rather than with the principles for justly living in the world that he taught and died for. It is because of their near obsession with the person of Jesus as spiritual savior of the world that they miss the politically radical dimension of his ministry. The message he proclaimed was holistic; it called for change not only in individual hearts but also in the economic and political conditions that affected the life chances of people in *this* world. He called for a radical redistribution of authority and power, goods and resources, so all people might have lives free of political repression, enforced hunger and poverty, and undue insecurity. We see this in the Lord's Prayer instruction to his disciples to pray for the coming of God's kingdom and God's will—instructions that directly imply supplanting the oppressive rule of Rome with God's kingdom, which, as we saw above, is characterized in the Bible as founded and imbued with social justice. In this sense, even the seemingly benign entreaties of the Lord's Prayer reflect Jesus's radicality, for even the mere suggestion of introducing another kingdom—spiritual or secular—into Rome's imperial domination of Israel constituted the capital crime of sedition, the punishment for which under Roman law was . . . the horror of crucifixion.[42]

The only conclusion to be drawn from these considerations is that right-wing evangelicals' misunderstanding of Jesus is deeply problematic, both theologically and politically. It is a problem *theologically* because it diminishes the empathic boldness of Jesus and the radicality of his teachings. It is problematic *politically* because it has misled evangelical believers into supporting policies that actually penalize the very people—the poor and vulnerable—that the Gospel says should be the subjects of their loving care. It is this misunderstanding of the Bible's social justice imperative that accounts for right-wing evangelicals' essentially anti-gospel domestic policy stances, with which they actively oppose virtually every social and political program that would aid those most in need. Their support in 2020 for the Trump administration's budget proposal is a good example. The proposal all but declared war on the well-being of America's poor and vulnerable by seeking to

- add millions to the ranks of the uninsured by repealing the Affordable Care Act (ACA) and cutting $777 billion over ten years from Medicaid and Affordable Care Act subsidies, ending protections for people with preexisting conditions.
- cut assistance that helps struggling families afford the basics, including food and rent, by drastically reducing SNAP (food stamps) by $220 billion or 30 percent over ten years, cutting basic Social Security assistance for people with disabilities, reducing supports to poor families with children through Temporary Assistance for Needy Families (TANF), cutting public housing assistance and raising rents for millions of low-income households receiving rental assistance.
- increase income inequality and widen racial disparities by permanently extending the 2017 tax law's lopsided tax cuts that confer most tax benefits on high-income taxpayers and heirs to very large estates. These tax cuts for the rich coupled with cuts in aid to the needy are projected to significantly worsen income inequality.[43]

It is not an exaggeration to say that without the imperative to build a more just and humane world in accordance with the moral and ethical structures of the Bible, the ministry of Jesus Christ would have little meaning. Certainly it would contain little that could be construed as good news for the poor or liberation for the oppressed. Yet the right-wing evangelical elites either fail to comprehend this basic truth or willfully turn a blind eye to it. At any rate, for whatever reason, they do not teach it to their flocks. They do not acknowledge the biting critiques of structural injustice in Jesus's message or his passion to change the unjust social, economic, and political structures in which he lived. They seem simply to want nothing to do with the political radicality of Jesus. They might allow that Jesus was a *spiritual* radical who sought only to bring people into better personal relationships with God. But as we have seen, the chief focus of Jesus and the gospels is the welfare and salvation of the entire community. That sensibility is dramatically foregrounded in the gospel of Luke's account of the devout old Simeon, who encountered the infant Jesus and his parents in the Jerusalem temple while spending his last days there in prayer, not for his individual salvation but rather for the comfort and salvation of his entire people (Luke 2:25–35).

In the final analysis, the inextricable bond between social justice and biblical faith is affirmed in both the Hebrew Bible and the gospels again and again. Sadly, right-wing evangelical leaders such as John MacArthur and those under their sway do not acknowledge this. The great tragedy here is that because these evangelicals do not understand the basic political dimension of God's vision for the world, they cannot fully understand God's message to humanity. And if they do not fully understand the message of God to humanity, they cannot fully understand the message borne by Jesus, the one who came into the world in God's name. As a consequence, we have thousands of believers cosigning distorted interpretations of biblical meaning like MacArthur's *Statement on Social Justice and the Gospel.*

The tragic consequence of evangelicals' propagation of a domesticated, apolitical Jesus is this: that the power of the Gospel to address unjust, exploitive, soul-crushing structures in our society is robbed of its full might. In its place, right-wing evangelicals have chosen to make an idol of the American state. They chose to elevate to near-messianic status an immoral, dishonest, functionally non-Christian man as president of the United States. In doing so, right-wing evangelicals have militated against the foundational social justice imperative of the very Bible they claim to hold so dear. For the justice-minded evangelicals of the past who understood that loving our neighbors means working to build a loving and equitable society for all, surely today's right-wing evangelicalism would be strange fruit indeed.

CHAPTER 4

A NEW COMMANDMENT I GIVE YOU: THAT YOU LOVE ONE ANOTHER

Right-Wing Evangelicals, Homosexuality, and Marriage Equality

IN APRIL 2014, a young woman was attacked in broad daylight on a Michigan street by an angry group of men who cursed and hurled ugly epithets at her, knocked her to the ground, and beat and kicked her until they tired of it. She was left writhing on the sidewalk, purple bruises covering her torso, her face distorted and swollen. The cause of their hate-filled attack? The men recognized her from her locally televised wedding a few days earlier—to a woman.[1]

Nowhere in the four gospels does Jesus speak of homosexuality or make any statement that can even be construed as alluding to it. And when Paul's few apparent references to homosexuality are examined in their original koine Greek language and for their function in Paul's theology and call to discipleship, exactly what he has in mind is not clear. The same with the handful of Old Testament passages that seem to prescribe death for all men everywhere and in every age who engage in homosexual relations. When their ancient Hebrew terminology and setting in life are critically examined, those referred to in these passages are similarly brought into question. Yet right-wing evangelicals, indeed, Christians of many stripes, condemn and reject same-gender sexual intimacy as stridently as they condemn murder. Some are less strident, claiming to "hate the sin, but love the sinner." But even less strident denunciations still condemn homosexuals as residing outside the will of God. In this chapter we will examine the most oft-cited reasons for the condemnation of homosexuality and the beliefs and assumptions that underlie them.

Homosexuality and all behaviors that do not conform to traditional notions of gender expression have been stigmatized, penalized, and criminalized since the earliest days of the American experience, although some Native American societies have responded in a more humane fashion. Early European explorers reported that among the Crow people "men who dressed as women and specialized in women's work were accepted and sometimes honored; a woman who led men into battle and had four wives was a respected chief."[2] The *Original Journals of the Lewis and Clark Expedition* (written between 1804 and 1810) reported, "Among the Mamitarees if a boy shows any symptoms of effeminacy or girlish inclinations he is put among the girls, dressed in their way, brought up with them, & sometimes married men."[3] But such humane acceptance of difference was not the case among Euro-American settlers. In the American colonies, with few exceptions, the penalty for sodomy, or same-gender sexual relations, was capital punishment. In 1779 the Virginia legislature even rejected Thomas Jefferson's efforts to reduce the punishment to castration.

In some parts of the world, sodomy remains punishable by death. In 2014, Uganda declared homosexuality a capital crime with the avid support of several prominent American evangelical preachers, including Tony Perkins, head of the evangelical Family Research Council, and Scott Lively of the California-based Abiding Truth Ministries. In *The Pink Swastika*, the widely debunked polemic he coauthored with Kevin E. Adams, Lively went so far as to argue that "homosexuals [are] the true inventors of Nazism and the guiding force behind many Nazi atrocities."[4]

As late as 1962, homosexuality was a felony in every state in the US, punishable by lengthy prison terms, often prescribed with hard labor. However, in that year the Model Penal Code, which was developed by the American Law Institute to promote uniformity among the laws of the various states, removed the criminalization of consensual same-gender sexual relations from its recommended statutes. In the following years many states accepted the Model Penal Code's suggestion to decriminalize sodomy. Those that didn't reduced their penalties. In 1969 patrons of the Stonewall Inn, a gay bar in New York City, battled police after what they characterized as years of rousting and mistreatment. This incident, which came to be known as the Stonewall Rebellion, served to bring the issue of gay rights to heightened national attention. In the wake of the rebellion and ongoing efforts by the gay rights movement, little by little homosexuality began to become less stigmatized. More positive depictions of gay men and lesbians appeared in books and movies. Even television censors relaxed their strictures, allowing depictions of homosexuality in popular television shows like *All in the Family*. In 1973, the American Psychiatric Association removed homosexuality from the Diagnostic and Statistical Manual of Mental Disorders (DSM), in effect ruling that it was no longer considered by professionals to be a psychological abnormality.

These social changes raised alarms among conservative Christians, but especially among right-wing evangelicals, who took the lead in countering them. In 1977, Anita Bryant, a born-again Christian and a former Miss America runner-up, founded Save Our Children to repeal an ordinance passed in Miami–Dade County, Florida, that made it illegal to discriminate against homosexuals in housing, employment, and social services. Bryant was supported in her campaign by the National Association of Evangelicals, with its three-million-plus members, and by major evangelical figures

Pat Robertson, Jim and Tammy Bakker, and Jerry Falwell. Bryant unleashed a campaign of strident attacks on Miami's gay community. She claimed to have proof that gays were "trying to recruit our children to homosexuality." To the Cuban community she said, "It would break my heart if Miami would become another Sodom and Gomorrah, and you would have to leave again," raising the specter of a society so debauched and out of control that they might have to return to Castro's Cuba to escape it.[5] Falwell declared to a Miami rally that defenders of the antidiscrimination bill were tantamount to a gang of murderers. "I want to tell you," he railed, "we are dealing with a vile and vicious and vulgar gang. They'd kill you as quick as look at you."[6] Save Our Children took out a full-page ad warning that defeat of their attempt to repeal the bill would result in an "epidemic of pornography,"[7] despite the fact that studies show overwhelmingly that rates of sexual abuse and pedophilia among gays is no greater than heterosexuals, and perhaps less.[8]

The efforts of Save our Children and its allies were successful; six months after it was passed, the antidiscrimination law was repealed by a landslide. From there, Bryant announced a national campaign to repeal all laws that protected the rights of gay people in America. As the legal scholar Geoffrey R. Stone observes, "The Victory in Dade County generated momentum for a new, religion-based, anti-gay movement."[9] Bryant vowed to "carry our fight against similar laws throughout the nation that attempt to legitimate a lifestyle that is . . . perverse and dangerous to the sanctity of the family, dangerous to our children," and "dangerous to our survival as one nation, under God."[10] Her use of the term *lifestyle* cast homosexuality as a decadent, antisocial choice that is anathema to every acceptable more of American life. Within two years, legislation enacted to protect gays from discrimination had been repealed in cities across the nation.[11]

Anti-gay efforts continued, but as we will see in chapter 5, in the 1970s and 1980s, the major issue animating right-wing evangelicals became the US Supreme Court's *Roe v. Wade* ruling that legalized abortion nationwide. Evangelical leaders' fervent antichoice rhetoric, their strident accusations that pro-choice advocates were "child murderers" and the like, coupled with the support of friendly occupants in the Oval Office in Ronald Reagan and later George H. W. Bush, kept the right-wing evangelical masses energized and their fundraising efforts well remunerated.

But this changed in 1992 with the election of Bill Clinton. Throughout his campaign Clinton had made no secret of his support for *Roe*. On that and other issues, it was clear that he would not be the ally of right-wing evangelicals that Reagan had been. Moreover, with the fall of the USSR they couldn't use the fear of communist expansion to keep their followers up in arms. Right-wing evangelicals found themselves in dire need of a new foil to catalyze their followers in their quest to dominate America society. When Clinton was able to get Congress to pass the Don't Ask, Don't Tell law in 1993, which protected gays in the nation's military from discrimination, right-wing evangelicals found the issue they sought to rally the faithful. In 1992 in the state of Colorado James Dobson of Focus on the Family successfully mounted a hard-fought campaign for an amendment to the state constitution that banned all legislative protections for gays in the state, but in 1996 the amendment was struck down by the US Supreme Court. When Vermont legalized civil unions for gays in 2000, evangelicals grew increasingly worried that the next step could be something they could not have fathomed even a few short years before: fully legalized marital rights for same-sex couples. They were right.

On June 26, 2015, the US Supreme Court handed down a ruling that evangelical Christians deemed to be of such sinful magnitude that many fearfully prayed for America to be spared from the divine wrath they were certain had been unleashed. It is on that date that the court decreed, in *Obergefell v. Hodges,* that every state in the union must extend to same-sex couples the same right to lawfully marry as is enjoyed by all other Americans of legal age. "The right to marry is a fundamental right inherent in the liberty of the person," wrote Justice Anthony Kennedy for the majority, "and

under the Due Process and Equal Protection Clauses of the Fourteenth Amendment couples of the same sex may not be deprived
of that right and that liberty." Justice Kennedy then articulated the
essence of the marital state itself. "No union is more profound than
marriage, for it embodies the highest ideals of love, fidelity, devo-
tion, sacrifice and family," he wrote. "In forming a marital union,
two people become something greater than once they were." And
apparently most Americans held similar sentiments. According to
a June 30, 2015, CNN poll, 59 percent of Americans agreed with
the decision.[12]

But not so with right-wing evangelical Christians. Six out of
ten fully opposed the ruling. They believe that homosexuality is
unambiguously condemned in the Bible as hopelessly sinful, start-
ing with the Genesis story of Sodom and Gomorrah. For them the
very idea of marriage equality and same-gender intimacy is such
an affront to what they call "traditional" biblical marriage—between one man and one woman—that they condemn it vigorously at every turn, often in vile and insulting terms. Trump court
evangelical Robert Jeffress has remarked that homosexuality "is
so degrading that it is beyond description."[13] Many of his evangelical colleagues agree. Some are moved to advocate the outright
murder of gays, like the evangelical pastors who applauded the
tragic 2016 mass shooting at a gay nightclub in Orlando, Florida, which took forty-nine lives and left many others gravely injured. A Fort Worth, Texas, pastor said of the victims, "These 50
[sic] sodomites are all perverts and pedophiles, and they are the
scum of the earth, and the earth is a little bit better place now. . . .
There are still several dozens of these queers in ICU and inten-
sive care. Tonight, I'll pray that God will finish the job that that
[shooter] started."[14] A Georgia pastor tweeted, "I see them as get-
ting what they deserved!" (Ironically, that pastor was convicted in
2018 of eight counts of child molestation and sentenced to life in
prison.)[15] A pastor in Sacramento spewed this hatred to his congregation: "Hey, are you sad that 50 [sic] pedophiles were killed
today? No . . . I think that's great. I think that helps society. I think

Orlando, Florida's a little safer tonight. . . . The tragedy is that more of them didn't die."[16]

President Jimmy Carter is a born-again evangelical, but by no means is he a right-winger. In a 2018 *HuffPost Live* interview, he took pains to defend marriage equality: "I think Jesus would encourage any love affair if it was honest and sincere and was not damaging to anyone else, and I don't see that gay marriage damages anyone else."[17] To which evangelical leader Franklin Graham responded, "Former President Jimmy Carter . . . is absolutely wrong when he said Jesus would approve of gay marriage. Jesus didn't come to promote sin, He came to save us from sin. The Bible is very clear. God destroyed the cities of Sodom and Gomorrah because of homosexuality."[18]

Graham here turns to the classic anti-gay biblical argument that the destruction of Sodom and Gomorrah was punishment for rampant homosexuality. The problem, however, is that the Bible does not say that God destroyed those cities because of homosexuality. If we take a closer look at the story of Sodom and Gomorrah and the handful of other biblical passages upon which evangelicals base their denial of equal status in the human family to their gay brothers and sisters, it becomes clear that either the meanings of those passages are either too ambiguous from which to draw a final conclusion or—despite popular belief—*they do not refer to homosexuality at all.* Opponents of same-gender sexual intimacy read the handful of ambiguous biblical passages about homosexuality as if their meaning is plain, even though they are reading them thousands of years after they were written in ancient forms of foreign languages without any idea of the intricacies of translating texts and determining their biblical meaning.

First, it is important to recognize that the people of biblical antiquity had no idea of homosexuality as an identity, an orientation, or a lifestyle. In fact, there is no word in either biblical Hebrew or biblical Greek that corresponds to *homosexuality* in the sense that we use it today. In fact, the Bible is almost totally uninterested in it. To the degree that the ancients might have referred to same-gender sexual relations at all they would have had in mind only individual acts, not overarching identities or "lifestyles." In addition, the term *homosexuality* was not even coined until the latter half of the nineteenth century. And the first use of *homosexual* in any English translation of the Bible did not occur until 1946, with the publication of the Revised Standard Version.

Turning to the story of Sodom and Gomorrah in the book of Genesis (19:1–11), we read that a group of men of Sodom insisted that God's servant, Lot, send out from his home his three male visitors (who, unbeknownst to the locals, were actually angels) so they could collectively "know (*yada*) them"—that is, engage in sexual relations with them.[19] Lot strenuously resisted their demand. At one point he even offered his virgin daughters instead (!), but the men were bent on gang-raping Lot's male visitors. This is a galvanizing story—men seeking to rape other men. What is so often missed, however, is that at no point does the text even imply that the men in the offending crowd were anything other than marauding heterosexuals who for some reason sought to sexually brutalize and humiliate Lot's guests. Yet for two millennia the crowd in this passage has been erroneously presented as a gathering of *homosexual* men, which is supposedly an indication that *homosexuality* was rampant in Sodom. This misunderstanding has resulted in Sodom and Gomorrah being presented as Exhibit A in the case against the right of gay people to exist.

But a closer look at the Bible itself tells quite a different tale. Whereas the biblical narrative presents no reason for the destruction of Sodom and Gomorrah other than general wickedness, other biblical references identify the towns' fatal transgressions as greed, unscrupulousness, and domination of others, not homosexuality. Not one reference even implies homosexuality. The book of Ezekiel (16:49) says that Sodom's sins were "pride, excess of food, . . . prosperous ease" (in other words, greed), and that it "did not aid the poor and needy." Throughout the Old Testament, failure to help those in need is considered a sin because the arid lands could be so hostile. The prophet Jeremiah gives the same

general reasons for Sodom and Gomorrah's wickedness as Ezekiel (Jeremiah 23:14). And in the gospel of Matthew, Jesus himself implies that Sodom was destroyed for its callous inhospitality
(Matthew 10:14–15). The New Testament Letter of Jude does ascribe Sodom's destruction to sexual licentiousness, but here again,
the text makes no specific reference to homosexuality: "Likewise,
Sodom and Gomorrah . . . indulged in sexual immorality and
pursued unnatural lust" (Jude 7; literally, "went after the flesh").
Hebrew Bible scholar Jon D. Levenson cites a rabbinic tradition
in the Mishnah, a second century CE written compilation of the
oral tradition of Jewish law, that the sin of Sodom was its pervasive
and selfish inhospitality, which the Mishnah characterizes with a
saying: "What is mine is mine; what is yours is yours."[20] Commentator Jay Michaelson suggests that homosexual rape is simply the
backdrop of a story written to emphasize both the commission of
violence and the violation of hospitality norms: "Homosexual rape
is the way in which [the Sodomites] violate hospitality—not the
essence of their transgression. Reading the story of Sodom as being
about homosexuality is like reading the story of an ax murderer as
being about an ax."[21]

Perhaps an even more telling indication of how the story was
understood in antiquity is the lack of writings connecting the destruction of Sodom and Gomorrah with same-sex relations until it
appears in a text by the first-century CE Jewish philosopher Philo
(ca. 20 BCE–ca. 50 CE), some six hundred years or so after the book
of Genesis was finalized.[22] And that interpretation does not appear
to have been cited with any measure of consistency until the sixth
century CE, some 1,300 years after Genesis was written. Like the
biblical writers, the early church father Origen of Alexandria (ca.
184–ca. 253 BCE) associated Sodom's sin with inhospitality, not
homosexuality.[23] Similarly, for St. Jerome (ca. 347–420) in the fifth
century CE, the sins of Sodom were pride and decadence—again,
not homosexuality.[24] It is difficult to escape the conclusion that
using the ancient story of Sodom and Gomorrah as justification
for homophobia today has no credible basis in the Bible. The Bible

condemns many things about Sodom and Gomorrah, but homosexuality is not one of them.

There are only a couple of other direct references to gay sex in the Old Testament (lesbianism is never mentioned). The context of each of these is the Hebrews' (later called Israelites) immigration into the land of Canaan, an entrenched, highly organized social milieu that already had well-established polytheistic religious customs. As newcomers, there would have been much pressure on the Hebrew minority, with their still-evolving social and religious traditions, to assimilate into the Canaanite religious culture. Deuteronomy 6:10–12 reflects the concern that the Hebrews might be seduced by the Canaanites' more advanced societal infrastructure:

> The Lord your God has brought you into . . . a land with fine, large cities that you did not build, houses filled with all sorts of goods that you did not fill, hewn cisterns that you did not hew, vineyards and olive groves that you did not plant—and when you have eaten your fill, take care that you do not forget the Lord, who brought you out of the land of Egypt, out of the house of slavery. (Deuteronomy 6:10–12)

In response, Moses stipulated a number of laws, prohibitions, and liturgical prescriptions in Yahweh's name to compel the Israelites to resist the dominant Canaanite practices. One Canaanite religious practice those laws appear to have been crafted to address was the Canaanite ritual of male priests honoring their goddesses by dressing like women, assuming social roles associated with women, and—in some cases—even undergoing voluntary castration.[25] In response to the apparent attraction of this ritual practice (the fact that men practiced it suggests there were perquisites attached to it), Moses declared cross-dressing to be an abomination, an "abhorrent" practice in the sight of God (Deuteronomy 22:5). Many take this verse to apply to homosexuality. Although the meaning of the stricture might appear self-evident, it is not as clear as it seems.

The Hebrew term rendered in virtually every English translation of the Bible as "abomination" or "abhorrent practice" or the
like, is *toevah* (plural, *toevot*). But in the Bible *toevah* is not a practice that God abhors in itself; it is something abhorred because it
transgresses the Hebrews' cultural and religious boundaries, thus
presenting a threat to the cultural and religious integrity of Israelite existence. This is reflected in the fact that of its 103 occurrences
in the Old Testament, *toevah* is almost always associated with
some non-Israelite practice, form of worship, or idolatry. This can
be seen clearly in Deuteronomy 18:9–12:

> When you come into the land that the Lord your God is giv-
> ing you, you must not learn to imitate the abhorrent practices
> [*toevot*] of those nations. . . . For whoever does these things is
> abhorrent [*toevah*] to the Lord; it is because of such abhorrent
> practices [*toevot*] that the Lord your God is driving them out be-
> fore you.

This is further elucidated in Leviticus: "But you shall keep my
statutes and my ordinances and commit none of these abominations [*toevot*], either the citizen or the alien who resides among you
(for the inhabitants of the land, who were before you, committed
all of these abominations [*toevot*], and the land became defiled)"
(18:26–27). Jay Michaelson points out that six verses in Deuteronomy "further identify idolatry, child sacrifice, witchcraft, and other
'foreign' practices as *toevah*."[26] They are considered abominations
(*toevot*) because they are alien to the practices of Israel. The only
major exception to this is the book of Proverbs, in which *toevah* is
used twenty-one times to refer to various "ethical failings."[27]

Nonetheless, what the preponderance of the occurrences of the
term *toevah* indicates is that although in this passage cross-dressing
was the subject of divine disapproval as an offense to the budding Israelite religion and culture, the passage and the meaning of
toevah ("abomination") indicates that it was not issued as a universal admonition. It was addressed only to Israelites. They are its

only concern. This is very important. It is abhorrent only for the people of Israel. The witness of the Bible does not say that it is a universal sin; rather, as a non-Israelite practice, it is abhorrent simply because it threatened the integrity of Israelite culture and religion.

A further Canaanite practice that offended the integrity of Israelite religious sensibilities was what is erroneously called male and female ritual "temple prostitution." In actuality, this practice consisted of sexual activity performed as part of religious worship, seemingly for the purpose of appeasing gods of fertility. This, too, the Hebrews were forcefully admonished to avoid: "None of the daughters of Israel shall be a temple prostitute" (*qedeshah,* literally "a female holy or consecrated one," that is, a woman who engaged in Canaanite temple sexual rites); and "none of the sons of Israel shall be a temple prostitute" (*qadesh*), their male counterpart in those rites (Deuteronomy 23:17). It is in the same context of concerns about Hebrew absorption into Canaanite religious practices, at least in part, that the following commandments were issued: "You shall not lie with a male as with a woman; it is a *toevah*" (Leviticus 18:22) and "If a man lies with a male as with a woman, both of them have committed a *toevah;* they shall be put to death" (Leviticus 20:13). In addition, a much more practical consideration might also have been at play in these latter passages: a concern of the Hebrew minority that same-gender sexual relations could hinder the growth of their labor force, which is the lifeblood of labor-intensive agricultural societies. It was also a threat to the population growth needed to maintain the Hebrews' security and autonomy.

For thousands of years these ancient pronouncements have been treated as timeless biblical laws, yet they were specifically codified—reflecting the lack of appreciation of the complexity of human sexuality that prevailed in antiquity—to protect Hebrews from adopting the *toevot,* or foreign practices, of the dominant culture that surrounded them. One of the most telling confirmations that the primary purpose of these pronouncements was to ensure the

Israelites' fealty to the Hebrew God in the face of external temptations is found in Leviticus (19:1–2): "You shall be *qadosh*," ("holy"; literally "set apart") "as I myself am holy." This further attests that these biblical strictures were specifically issued to the Hebrews. The Jewish scholar Jacob Milgrom, in his recapitulation of remarks he delivered to his synagogue about Leviticus 18:22, supports this reasoning, which is also applicable to every Old Testament verse that is purported to condemn same-gender sexuality: "This biblical prohibition is addressed only to Israel. Compliance with this law is a condition for residing in the Holy Land, but not elsewhere. Thus, it is incorrect to apply it on a universal scale."[28]

These strictures in Leviticus and Deuteronomy are the only references to homosexuality in the entire Old Testament. Not a word in Proverbs or the Psalms. The prophets Amos, Micah, and Isaiah, among others, rail with great outrage against every social and moral transgression in Israel, yet not one mentions anything about same-sex relations. When Old Testament passages that traditionally have been understood to condemn what we today call homosexuality are considered in their proper social and historical contexts and translated with an appropriate degree of rigor, it becomes clear that their meanings are simply too ambiguous to support with any measure of certainty the claim that homosexuality is considered by the Bible to be a sin.[29] And, as we noted above, there is no mention of lesbianism in the Old Testament at all. But what we do find is the story of the love between David and Jonathan, son of King Saul.

In the first of two biblical texts attributed to the prophet Samuel, we are told that "the soul of Jonathan was bound to the soul of David . . . and Jonathan made a covenant with David, because he loved him as his own soul," and that Jonathan sealed their covenant of love by giving gifts to David (1 Samuel 18:1–4). Later, David and Jonathan are described as "kissing each other and weeping" at their separation (20:41). After Jonathan's untimely death, David cries out to him, "Your love for me was wonderful, surpassing the love of women" (2 Samuel 1:20).

Here we have a biblical story of a great love between two men that is said to be even dearer to them than the love of the opposite sex. Now, we cannot claim with any degree of certainty that this account narrates a sexual relationship between David and Jonathan. For centuries men in many cultures have routinely kissed the cheeks of other men in both greeting and brotherly affection; perhaps that is the kind of kiss these biblical figures shared. And because of the entrenched patriarchy that then reigned, the friendship and camaraderie between men was often of greater importance than with women, whom they considered their social inferiors. Still, should the love between these men be considered any less beautiful, would it descend from sacred to profane, become worthy of disgust or even of death, if we were to learn that the physical contact between Jonathan and David really did go beyond mere kissing? It is a worthy question, if for no other reason than the biblical narrative of the love between David and Jonathan attests—in sacred scripture, no less—that love between two people of the same gender can be as deep and as holy as any other love.

It is the same when we consider the four gospels and whether the condemnation of same-sex love finds support in the sayings of Jesus. Nowhere in the four gospels does Jesus speak of homosexuality or make any statement that can be construed as alluding to it. The only two New Testament passages that might be interpreted as condemning homosexuality are found in the letters of the apostle Paul. In his letter to the church in Rome, Paul writes,

> For this reason God gave them up to degrading passions. Their women exchanged natural intercourse for unnatural, and in the same way also the men, giving up natural intercourse with women, were consumed with passion for one another. Men committed shameless acts with men and received in their own persons the due penalty for their error. (Romans 1:26–27)

Paul speaks of "degrading passions" in this passage, but he is not referring to homosexuality or lesbianism as we understand them, because in antiquity there was yet to evolve the concept of homosexual *identities* and *orientations*. Homosexual acts were seen as just that—discrete homosexual *deeds,* not characteristics of an identity or a "lifestyle." Rather, "degrading passions" can imply purely lustful, orgiastic acts considered outside the pale of "acceptable" sexual behavior; wanton sexual adventure or wild engagement in unconventional sexual acts for titillation alone. It could even refer to prostitution. What one prominent late-nineteenth-century psychologist considered "unnatural" sexual desires and practices can give us a sense of its possible meanings.

In *Sex and the Constitution,* the legal scholar Geoffrey Stone quotes the description of "unnatural, perverted sex" offered by an E. C. Spitzka: "(1) an absence of sexual desire; (2) an excess of sexual desire; (3) sexual desire at an 'abnormal time of life'; and (4) sexual desire that 'is not of such a character as to lead to the preservation of the species.'"[30] Paul could have in mind any of these acts, yet we cannot be sure what he meant. Moreover, because in antiquity the notion of homosexual identities as such did not yet exist, it must not be missed that when Paul speaks of those who exchange what is "natural" for what is "unnatural," he would have been condemning certain sex acts by *heterosexual* men and women—the only sexual identity that was culturally imaginable at that time—that had no motivation except lust or some variety of what Spitzka calls "unnatural, perverted sex." Therefore, because the exact meaning of Paul's use of "degrading passions" is not clear and because there are a number of plausible meanings for the term, his condemnation in Romans 1:26–27 cannot with any measure of certainty or integrity be considered a blanket condemnation of same-gender love and sexual intimacy per se. In fact, Paul is not describing love or emotional intimacy at all, only certain unnamed "shameless acts" between consenting heterosexual men and women that he considers subsumed by "degrading passions."

In Romans 1:26, Paul uses the phrase "gave them up." This phrase is translated from *paradidomi,* the same word used in Matthew 17:22 to describe Jesus being "given up" or "handed over" to the Romans by the Sanhedrin. But how could people be given up or handed over to become homosexuals? The preceding verses provide the answer:

> Therefore, God gave them up in the lusts of their hearts to impurity, to the degrading of their bodies among themselves, because they exchanged the truth about God for a lie and worshiped and served the creature rather than the Creator, who is blessed forever! Amen. (Romans 1:24–25)

The answer, then, is that Paul would not have meant that they were "given up" to homosexuality because, again, sexual practices were not yet thought to be indicative of a sexual identity. What those he condemned were "given over" to was what Paul considered immoral, degrading sexual behavior associated with some form of idol worship ("worshiped the creature"), such as the Artemis fertility cult mentioned in Acts 19:35 or, in the case of Jewish believers, perhaps because they had effectively renounced biblical faith. In the final analysis, then, what Paul is renouncing is lewd, lascivious behavior. Jay Michaelson puts it succinctly: "Paul's meaning here is that the Romans turned their backs on God, and as a result were *given over* to various forms of immorality, including sex that Paul understood as unnatural"[31] (my emphasis).

Also, it should not be overlooked that here Paul has made an argument from nature by declaring what is natural and what is not. Yet, if Paul's millennia-old argument about human nature is worthy of consideration, why should more recent insights into the nature of human sexuality be ignored? Although the evidence is far from conclusive, there are reputable scientific studies that indicate that same-gender sexual attraction and identification may well have genetic origins. According to geneticist Andrea Ganna at the Broad Institute of MIT and Harvard, "the largest survey to date for genes associated with same-sex behavior," a study of nearly half a million subjects from the United States and Great Britain, has concluded that people's genetic makeup could account for as much as 25 percent of same-gender sexual behavior, but it gives no guidance for addressing the conundrum of determining whose homosexual behavior is a natural expression of their genetic makeup and whose is not.[32] In addition, there is much anecdotal evidence to support a conclusion that the sexual identity of lesbian, gay, and bisexual people develops in childhood. I have known persons, some within my own extended family, who clearly identified with the opposite sex, even exhibiting their mannerisms, years before puberty. I have seen several gay youths grow up in households surrounded by macho role models, yet they always seemed to identify with the feminine long before they were old enough to have a sense of themselves as sexual beings. I realize that anecdote is not evidence, and thus far, relatively little empirical study of the possibility of homosexual genetic makeup has been conducted, but these indications are significant enough to warrant consideration.[33] Moreover, a recent development seems worthy of note. After decades of teaching that being gay was never natural but rather a mindset that could be modified, McKrae Game, founder of Hope for Wholeness, the nation's premier evangelical-Christian gay conversion therapy program, announced in 2019 that he himself is gay and always has been gay. In effect, he offered himself as Exhibit A that gay conversion therapy is a sham and that some human beings naturally come into this world—that is, they are created by God—naturally oriented toward homosexual attraction.[34] Gay conversion therapy, also known as "reparative" and "sexual reorientation" therapy, has been shown to have seriously harmful consequences, from anxiety and severe depression to suicidal tendencies.[35] Despite the possibility of such harmful consequences, in November 2020, a federal appeals court in Florida overturned a ban on gay conversion therapy in the city of Boca Raton.[36]

The other passage in the New Testament that is used to indict homosexuality as a sin is found in Paul's first letter to the Christian community in the Greek port city of Corinth. But unlike in

Romans, in 1 Corinthians Paul does not offer an argument. Instead he makes an assertion:

> Do you not know that wrongdoers will not inherit the kingdom of God? Do not be deceived! Fornicators, idolaters, adulterers, male prostitutes [*malakoi*], sodomites [*arsenokoitai*], thieves, the greedy, drunkards, revilers, robbers—none of these will inherit the kingdom of God. (1 Corinthians 6:9–10)

Malakoi, the plural form of the Greek term translated here as "male prostitutes," literally means "soft," pejoratively connoting "effeminate." Most behaviors that were ridiculed or condemned as "soft" in late antiquity were not sexual in nature as, for example, in the apparent sarcastic description of fine clothing in Matthew 11:8. Because women were considered weak, with less self-control than men, the term generally signified weakness and the absence of self-control. David Frederickson specifically translates *malakoi* as "those who lack self-control."[37] Observes Dale B. Martin, "When used as a term of moral condemnation, the word still refers to something perceived as 'soft': laziness, degeneracy, decadence, lack of courage."[38] Contends Matthew Vines, "Being 'soft' in a sexual sense meant that a man was self-indulgent and enslaved to his passions."[39] Although its exact meaning for Paul is unclear, it is possible that he uses the term to refer to male child prostitutes or effeminate men, or perhaps to a combination of both, such as "effeminate call-boys," as Robin Scroggs argues.[40] Robert A. J. Gagnon concludes that for Paul, *malakoi* signified "passive partners in homosexual intercourse, the most egregious case of which are those who intentionally engage in a process of feminization to erase further their masculine appearance and manner."[41] All of these learned speculations are worthy of consideration to some extent, perhaps some more than others. But the reality is that when all is said and done, we cannot be sure what Paul means by this term. As Matthew Vines points out, like most of the other behaviors listed in 1 Corinthians 6, *malakoi* can simply be understood as the sin of "excess or exploitation."[42]

Arsenokoitai, the term variously translated as "sodomites" and "sexual perverts," as far as we know, is Paul's invented compound of the Greek terms *arsen,* "male," and *koites,* "have sex," or "male bedders," as Robert A. J. Gagnon translates it.[43] Apparently the term was rarely used in Greek literature after Paul, but of its surviving uses it most often seems to refer to economic exploitation, not same-gender sexual behavior,[44] although citing its use in a second-century Christian letter, *To Autolychus,* Dale B. Martin suggests that the term might refer to "economic exploitation by some sexual means."[45] Thus, like *malakoi,* the meaning of *arsenokoitai* is also not clear today. Yet it does seem to refer to some form of homosexual relationship, possibly exploitive in nature. It is notable that Paul chose to use the term *arsen,* "male," which could connote a young male, rather than *aner,* which unambiguously means "man." Therefore, for Paul *malakoi* could refer to youths who are sexually exploited and *arsenokoita* to refer to grown men who exploit them. But this interpretation raises the question of why an abused youth would be denied inclusion in the kingdom of God for having been abused. Perhaps in Paul's strict morality he somehow understood both the *malakoi* and the *arsenokoitai* to be blameworthy for their sexual relationships, in which case he would be blaming victims for their own victimization. Robin Scroggs offers another suggestion, that *malakoi* are sacred sex workers like the *qadeshim* in Deuteronomy 23:17, but boys rather than men, and *arsenokoitai* are the men who frequent them.[46] John Boswell argues that *malakoi* refers to those who masturbate and *arsenokoitai* are "active male prostitutes, who were common throughout the Hellenistic world in the time of Paul."[47]

At any rate, what is apparent in all of this is that today the meaning of these terms for Paul and the nature of the relationships he describes with them simply is no longer clear. When this is coupled with the lack of evidence of any known concept of a homosexual identity or orientation in antiquity, it becomes even more evident that we cannot conclude with any degree of certainty that what Paul condemned in his letters is what we today would call gay sex. Given the high degree of scholars' uncertainty about Paul's meanings, he could have just as well had another meaning in mind that has been lost in the fog of antiquity.

It is easy to dismiss the discussion of these ambiguities of meaning as obtuse and needlessly technical. But those who are true and sincere lovers of their neighbors and who claim the Bible as their guide in life should be willing to step outside their comfort zones to at least consider these observations to ensure that they are not wrongly judging as sinful the natural sexual dispositions of millions of their brothers and sisters who, just like them, are created in the image of God. For in the final analysis, the ambiguity and uncertainty surrounding Paul's meaning of these two terms are too great to be used to determine any human being's fate, acceptance, and happiness.

Next, we come to the gospels and Jesus Christ. Nowhere in any of the four gospels does Jesus mention or even allude to same-sex relations. As we saw in the previous chapter, what he does declare in the parable of the sheep and the goats (Matthew 25:31–46) is that the primary way every person will be judged as worthy of heaven or of hell—no matter what their personal *beliefs* might be—is not by whom they love or choose to share their lives with but rather by whether they have lived righteously, trying to serve those in need and labored to establish justice in the land. In the final analysis, there is nothing in the words of Jesus anywhere in the gospels that gives even the smallest sense that anyone will be judged by whom they choose to love, as long as they *do* choose to love.

This brings us back full circle to the controversial question of whether the union between members of the same gender is a biblical sin. The term *traditional marriage* is used by evangelicals to challenge the right of gay people to sacralize their bonds of affection. Yet, as biblical scholars, cultural anthropologists, and social scientists of various disciplines have acknowledged for generations, throughout history there has been a wide range of marital arrangements that different cultures have considered traditional if not sacred. And in the last four decades, reputable church historians, like the late Yale historian John Boswell, have uncovered and laboriously translated ancient records that indicate that same-sex marital rites were performed in the early post-apostolic Christian Church.[48] Of course, it is by no means certain that these same-gender marriages included sexual intimacy. It is entirely possible that these documents represent nonsexual, same-gender marital bonding for the purpose of uniting different groups, clans, or countries for purposes of power, authority, and resources or simply to sacralize platonic friendships.[49] In addition, there is no indication that these same-sex unions represent a widespread practice. But what matters is that whether these unions were sexual in nature or not, they were still recognized and sanctioned by the ancient church as biblically ordained. There is no evidence that these marriage rituals were ever considered traditionally normative. Still, their existence challenges the claim that there is one biblically ordained tradition of marriage sanctioned by the church. The evidence of post-apostolic same-gender marriages belies that.

When talking about marriage, conservative Christians of all stripes use the word *traditional* to mean "singularly legitimate." In fact, rather than indicating a single, God-ordained, "traditional" mode of marriage, the Bible speaks of a number of kinds of marital relationships without condemnation or presenting any of them as singularly traditional. In the Bible there is polygamy; concubinage (an arrangement of sexual relationship in which a woman lives with a man but has lower status than his wife or wives); there is Abraham impregnating Hagar, the slave of his wife, Sarah, at Sarah's behest; there is Jacob marrying the sisters Rachel and Leah simultaneously and also impregnating the female slave of each. Moreover, in the gospel of Luke (20:27–44), Jesus speaks without criticism or judgment about Levirate marriage, which holds that if a man dies childless, his widow was compelled to marry his eldest living brother so she might bear a child—preferably a son—in the name of her dead husband. If the eldest brother died without giving her a child, she was to marry the next eldest brother. If he should die without fathering a child with her, then she was to marry the next eldest, and on down the line of male siblings until she either bore a child or ran out of brothers. None of these arrangements are any longer acceptable in Christendom, but that does not change the fact that the Bible speaks of them without a hint of condemnation and without designating any one particular marital practice as "traditional" or normative.

In other words, the contention that there is only one biblically ordained mode of marriage is simply not supported by the Bible. Of course, there are various cultural notions of traditional marriage, such as polyandry and group marriage, that hold sway in some societies. There is nothing intrinsically wrong with cultures extolling certain marital practices as traditional for themselves. Indeed, as long as they are not harmful, coercive, or destructive, there can be much to commend various cultural traditions of marriage, if only to support social stability. However, *widespread social acceptance of a cultural practice as "traditional" is not the same as being biblically sanctioned.*

No doubt many are sincere in their belief that homosexuality and same-sex marriage are biblical sins. But their belief can withstand rational scrutiny only if they ignore all the critical considerations that biblical scholars have raised to the contrary. For as we have seen, the biblical passages used to support the claim that homosexuality is a sin are simply too ambiguous, and the supporting evidence too slim and much too open to dispute to be used as the determining factor of even one person's happiness and life chances, much less the lives of untold millions.

I've never understood why it is a scandal that two people who plan to spend the rest of their lives in loving communion would seek to consecrate their love in the name of God. Despite the Catholic Church's open stance against same-sex marriage, Pope Francis shared a similar sentiment. He courageously declared in a 2020 documentary, "Homosexuals have a right to be a part of the family. They are children of God and have a right to a family. Nobody should be thrown out, or be made miserable because of it."[50]

Several years ago, I was on the faculty of a theological institution in New Jersey. There I had a colleague whom I admired and greatly appreciated. I always marveled at the depth of his quiet spirituality and warmth, his willingness to give of himself to assist others, his faithfulness to teaching and supporting his ministerial students. After working with him for about a year, I learned that he was gay when another colleague asked about his partner. I later learned that he and his partner, an equally beautiful human being, had lovingly lived together for almost four decades. What was I to do with the new information about this man? Was I to look at him differently now that I knew he was gay? Should that have devalued the beautiful spirit about which I'd marveled and found so inspirational? If neither his great generosity of spirit nor his dedicated service to the church of Jesus Christ nor the longevity of his loving bond offered enough guidance for how I should respond to him, there did remain for me the standard by which Jesus said we will all be judged and, in turn, the standard by which we are to judge others: the parable of the sheep and the goats (Matthew 25:31–46). By that measure this loving, giving, faithfully self-sacrificial man was worthy of all the respect and consideration I could give him, no matter whom he shared his life with.

Nowhere in the Gospel does it say anything about whom we should and should not love, only that we *should* love. The Jesus whom evangelicals claim as their savior decreed, "A new commandment I give you: Love one another" (John 13:34). Yet, shamefully it is true that very few gay people feel loved by evangelical Christians, who have proven to be quite selective and mean-spirited about whom in the human family they consider worthy of their love. And the false olive branch of "I don't hate the sinner; I just hate the sin," with which many evangelicals justify their rejection of homosexuals, is ultimately a loveless utterance, because it dismisses as sinful the very being of those who have an affinity for intimacy within their own gender. To paraphrase the Gospel of Jesus Christ:

How can you claim to love God whom you have not seen, but not love the children of God you see every day, people like you who seek only to love and to be loved?

In this chapter we have considered every passage in the Bible that is used to condemn same-sex intimacy as a sin. But no matter how one understands this handful of passages, no matter what they believe, nothing gives anyone the right to make gay men and women objects of hatred, ridicule, violence, and exclusion. Such mistreatment of anyone, no matter who they might be, violates to its very depths the Gospel's call to love and care for one another. That is to say that no one can demonize homosexual people and follow the teachings of Jesus Christ too. The two are mutually exclusive. If right-wing evangelical Christians really understood the Gospel of Jesus Christ, they would understand this as well. And the vicious attack on that young Michigan woman for consecrating her love for another woman in the sight of God might well have never happened.

CHAPTER 5

I HAVE OTHER SHEEP NOT IN THIS FOLD

*Right-Wing Evangelicals and the
Demonization of Immigrants and Muslims*

T**HEY FLED BECAUSE** they had to. Life in the land of their birth had become too cheap. Their children's bellies were rarely full and death always seemed near. So each family prayed for traveling mercies, secured babies at their mothers' breasts, hoisted overstuffed bundles upon their shoulders, spat bitter farewells on the harsh ground of their suffering, and fled upon the only means of transport that was theirs: their own tired feet and a few jerry-rigged carts. Pregnant women caressed their fullness, infants squirmed beneath their parents' weighty fears, sunbrowned youths in their turn carried the elders too spent to walk. Then they left, a ragtag rabble of the hungry, the fearful, the bedraggled, all daring to hope.

Already malnourished when they left, the desperate column limped along for miles unmeasured, their lips parched, their stomachs angry, the hard sun burning their necks and faces. On the way some were born, some were buried, some became so sick they

begged to be left behind. Tears and blood were shed in like measure. Yet they pushed on despite blistered feet, cramping muscles,
and screaming bellies, each day unfurling a new calendar of hurts,
all to seek a land of milk and solace they were not certain they
would ever enter.

This is not the tale of embattled refugees and asylum seekers
from Mexico. Nor is it about the "caravan" of safe-haven seekers
from Guatemala or Honduras in 2018, although it could be. No,
it is a recounting of an event whose name is the same in every
tongue. Indeed, it is the root event of the Judeo-Christian faith:
the Exodus of the oppressed Hebrews from their hell in Egypt in
their quest for a land in which they might find their rest and sink
their roots.

The Exodus is the root event of biblical faith because it is the
first time the God of the Bible intervened in history on behalf of a
people rather than to individual *persons* like Abraham and Lot. But
why? It certainly was not because they held an acceptable common
faith—the Hebrews were not an ethnicity per se. Rather, they were
an oppressed class that had little in common but their humanity
and the depth of their suffering,[1] as is reflected in their turn to
worship tribal deities the moment Moses turned his back to com-
mune on the mount with God. The Exodus story tells us that God
interceded because the Hebrews' oppression offended God's finely
drawn sense of justice:

> The Egyptians became ruthless in imposing tasks on the Israel-
> ites, and made their lives bitter with hard service in mortar and
> brick and in every kind of field labor. They were ruthless in all the
> tasks they imposed upon them. . . .
>
> Then the Lord said, "I have observed the misery of my peo-
> ple who are in Egypt; I have heard their cry on account of their
> taskmasters. Indeed, I know their sufferings, and I have come
> down to deliver them from the Egyptians.'. . . The cry of the Is-
> raelites has now come to me; I have also seen how the Egyptians
> are oppressing them. (Exodus 1:13–14; 3:7–9)

In other words, the Exodus, the root event of the Judeo-Christian tradition, is a *liberation event* that freed the Hebrews from political oppression. But the deliverance of the Hebrews not only made them free. It also made of each sojourner a *ger*.

The Hebrew term *ger* (plural, *gerim*) occurs in the Bible some ninety-two times. Although in many translations it is rendered as "stranger" or "alien," its meaning is essentially synonymous with "immigrant"—someone in a locale, region, or country that is not native to them. A related term, "resident alien" (*ger toshav*), signifies an immigrant who has already put down roots and set up permanent residence in a society. In the final analysis, though, both are immigrants; one is simply more settled than the other. In this sense, most residents of America are themselves, or are descendants of, a resident alien (*ger toshav*) of some sort.

The Hebrews' acknowledgment of the divine grace that attended them throughout their flight from Egypt is the reason for the high compassion for immigrants that runs throughout the Bible.

> The Lord brought us out of Egypt with a mighty hand and an outstretched arm . . . into this place and gave us this land, a land flowing with milk and honey. So now I bring the first of the fruit of the ground that you, O Lord, have given me. You shall set it down before the Lord your God and bow down before the Lord your God. Then you, together with the Levites and the aliens who reside among you [*gerim toshvim*], shall celebrate with all the bounty that the Lord your God has given to you and to your house. (Deuteronomy 26:8–11)

Just as extending hospitality to immigrants is one of the Bible's highest ethics, conversely, refusing hospitality to immigrant strangers is among its major sins, for denial of hospitality posed a real danger to travelers between the widely dispersed settlements that dotted the arid plains. It also disrupted the traditional reciprocal relationships that were so crucial to the health and cohesion of peasant societies in antiquity.[2]

Showing hospitality to immigrants is such an iron-clad commandment that the book of Malachi, the last book of the Old Testament, carefully included the abuse of immigrants in its roster of transgressions reviled by God (in the examples that follow, for illustrative purposes I replace the NRSV's terms "alien" and "stranger" with "immigrant." The passages' meanings remain unchanged):

> Then I will draw near to you for judgment; I will be swift to bear witness against the sorcerers, against the adulterers, against those who swear falsely, against those who oppress the hired workers in their wages, the widow and the orphan, against those who thrust aside the *immigrant*, and do not fear me, says the Lord of hosts. (Malachi 3:5, my emphasis; NRSV, "alien")

The Bible further commands believers to extend to immigrants the same civility and respect with which they are commanded to treat each other:

> For the Lord your God . . . loves the *immigrants,* providing them food and clothing. You shall also love the *immigrant,* for you were *immigrants* in the land of Egypt. (Deuteronomy 10:17–19, my emphasis; NRSV, "stranger")

. . . including the same rights under the same canons of justice that apply to the native born:

> There shall be one law for [both] the native and for the *immigrant* who resides among you. (Exodus 12:49, my emphasis; NRSV, "alien")

But extending hospitality to immigrants is more than an exercise in good manners and civility. It also entails taking steps to provide an adequate subsistence until they are able to provide for themselves:

You shall allot it as an inheritance for yourselves and for the *immigrants* who reside among you and have begotten children among you. They shall be to you as citizens of Israel; with you they shall be allotted an inheritance among the tribes of Israel. In whatever tribe *immigrants* reside, there you shall assign them their inheritance, says the Lord God. (Ezekiel 47:22–23, my emphasis; NRSV, "aliens." Also see Leviticus 19:10.)

Furthermore, the Bible insists that it is incumbent upon society to provide regulatory protections to shield vulnerable immigrants from exploitation:

Do not exploit ['ashaq] a hired worker who is poor and needy, whether that worker is a fellow Israelite or *an immigrant* residing in one of your towns. (Deuteronomy 24:14, my translation and emphasis. Also see Exodus 23:12–13.)

It is seldom acknowledged, but providing material support for immigrants until they can support themselves is one of the principal reasons tithing was established:

When you have finished setting aside a tenth of all your produce in the third year, the year of the tithe, you shall give it to the Levite, *the immigrant,* the fatherless and the widow, so that they may eat in your towns and be satisfied. (Deuteronomy 26:12, my emphasis; NIV, "foreigner." Also see 14:28–29.)

The importance of hospitality to immigrants in the biblical tradition is seen in the book of Job. One of the ways Job tried to justify himself to God as a righteous man was by testifying that he had offered shelter to immigrants:

The *immigrant* has not lodged in the street; I have opened my doors to the traveler. (Job 31:32, my emphasis; NRSV, "stranger.")

However, the responsibility to immigrants is not one-sided. For their part, immigrants must honor all laws of their host locales and avoid acts that would offend the justice of God:

> But whoever acts high-handedly, whether a native or an *immigrant*, affronts the Lord, and shall be cut off from among the people. (Numbers 15:30, my emphasis; NRSV, "alien")
>
> Assemble the people—men, women, and children, as well as the *immigrants* residing in your towns—so that they may hear and learn to fear the Lord your God and to observe diligently all the words of this law. (Deuteronomy 31:12; NRSV, "aliens." Also see Numbers 15:30; Exodus 12:19; Leviticus 17:10; 20:2; 24:16.)

But it is not only Old Testament edicts that reflect divine concern for immigrants, although that should make no difference to Christians; after all, the writings of the Old Testament were the only Bible Jesus knew. The importance of showing generosity to immigrants is also reflected in the New Testament. In 1 Peter, believers are characterized as "aliens" and "strangers" (*xenoi*, Greek) in the sense of immigrants in a new land of faith: "Beloved, I urge you as aliens and exiles . . ." (2:11). The Letter to the Hebrews even offers a metaphysical reason for treating immigrants with kindness: "Do not neglect to show hospitality to strangers, for by doing that some have entertained angels without knowing it" (13:2). And among the actions in the parable of the sheep and the goats that Jesus said will land both believers and unbelievers in hell, we must not overlook that he pointedly included refusing hospitality to an immigrant:

> Then they also will answer, "Lord, when was it that we saw you hungry or thirsty or a *stranger* [*xenos*] . . . ? Then he will answer them, "Truly I tell you, just as you did not do it to one of the least of these, you did not do it to me." And these will go away into eternal punishment. (Matthew 25:44–46; my emphasis)

The deliverance of the suffering Hebrews from oppression and bondage is celebrated in poem and prose, in song, stage, and screen. It is commemorated every year as the high holy Jewish holiday Passover. Yet the modern-day exodus to America to escape dangerous and intolerable living conditions, rapacious taskmasters, murderous gangs, sexual assault, sexual trafficking, and the intolerable human toll of internecine warfare is given neither credence nor compassion by right-wing evangelical elites and their followers, as if the Bible has never spoken. They simply do not seem to care that the immigrants from south of the border whom they so sorely malign more often than not are fleeing the darkness of extreme poverty and unbridled violence at the hands of criminals and corrupt governmental forces alike. Or that Muslims are fleeing war-ravaged lands unable to maintain order or deliver crucial services or protect them from cruel subjugation by both radical Islamists like ISIS and the Taliban and from devastating, heartless destruction by the forces of the Syrian government.

Because of right-wing evangelicals' professed regard for the Bible, with its ubiquity of admonitions to support immigrants, one would expect them to be immigrants' greatest champions. Instead, they are among immigrants' greatest foes. Despite their faith claims and supposed fidelity to the Bible, the reality is that with few exceptions right-wing evangelical elites and their followers overwhelmingly support the US government's inhospitable, inhumane treatment of immigrants that is being waged on a monstrous scale. Apparently, evangelicals' disdain for people of color and religious "others" trumps even the authority of the Bible. In fact, by their own admission, the majority of evangelicals simply do not care what the Bible says about immigration. Incredibly, a 2015 poll revealed that nine out of ten evangelicals admit that "the scripture has no impact on their views toward immigration reform."[3] And white evangelicals in particular are even more opposed to immigration reform, holding more negative views about immigrants and caring for the poor and the vulnerable than any other religious group in America.[4] The Pew Research Center found in 2018 that 68 percent of white evangelicals believe that the United States "does not have a responsibility to accept refugees" even when lives are at stake.[5] In a January 2018 *Washington Post*–ABC poll, 75 percent of white evangelicals responded that "the federal crackdown on undocumented immigrants" is a positive development, presumably including cracking down on those fleeing starvation, torture, and death.[6] In other words, the desire to ensure that neither succor nor solace is extended to immigrants, most of whom are black and brown, is more important to evangelical elites and their followers than the authority of the Bible they claim to love. It is difficult to reach any other conclusion, for the Bible's teachings on this subject are much too clear and straightforward to be misread. It seems much more likely that evangelicals *purposely* misinterpret the Bible in this way because it suits their white supremacist biases and Christian nationalist aspirations.

We can get a sense of this casual misappropriation of the Bible in the assertions of a white evangelical Christian woman in small-town Alabama who was interviewed by *Washington Post* reporters in 2018. "Love your neighbor," she claims, really means "love your *American* neighbor." Likewise, for her "welcome the immigrant stranger" means "welcome the *legal* immigrant stranger." And "the least of these" that Jesus speaks of in the parable of the sheep and the goats (Matthew 25:31–46) she claims are actually "*Americans,* not the ones crossing the border" (emphasis in the original).[7]

Indeed, the anti-immigrant attitudes and policies supported by evangelicals today have a striking affinity with those openly fueled by racism and xenophobia in nineteenth-century America. In the 1840s, both the thousands of Chinese immigrants seeking refuge in America from the Opium Wars and the thousands more seeking to find work in the newly discovered California gold fields were confronted with an insuperable wall of racial hostility. Worse, Chinese immigrants were blamed for the economic depression of the 1870s. Rampaging white mobs indiscriminately attacked them, destroyed their property, and murdered eighteen Chinese men in one of the largest mass lynchings in American history.[8] The upsurge of racial resentment culminated in the racist Chinese Exclusion Act of 1882 and several related laws that denied citizenship to Chinese immigrants already living in the United States and banned from our shores all others of Chinese nationality who sought to grace them.

Seeking to enter this country without going through the proper channels is illegal, but that is no excuse for demonizing immigrants as "rapists and murderers," in Donald Trump's notorious words, or for treating them as criminals inexorably driven to crime and violence by native instinct. By any measure, the federal government's treatment of immigrants is inhumane and it is indefensibly anti-biblical. It proffers the despicable lie that border security and compassion are mutually exclusive. But people of moral decency must never allow compassion to be pushed aside when people's lives and well-being are at stake.

President Ronald Reagan was a hero to evangelicals because he appeared to share their values and their biases. In 1980, as a presidential candidate in a primary debate with George H. W. Bush, he rejected the idea of a border fence between the United States and Mexico.

> Rather than talking about putting up a fence, why don't we work out some recognition of our mutual problems, make it possible for them to come here legally with a work permit, and then while they're working and earning here they pay taxes here. And when they want to go back, they can go back, and they can cross. And open the border both ways by understanding their problems.[9]

Reagan has long been criticized as a racist.[10] His racism was on full display in a recently released audiotaped conversation with Richard Nixon in which Reagan calls African diplomats "monkeys . . . still uncomfortable wearing shoes."[11] Nonetheless, Reagan believed that welcoming immigrants into America (although presumably not Africans) was so important that in his last speech as president he left it as a sort of final testament.

> I think it is fitting to leave one final thought. . . . It's the great life force of each generation of new Americans that guarantees that America's triumph shall continue unsurpassed into the next century and beyond. . . . This, I believe, is one of the most important sources of America's greatness. . . . This quality is vital to our future as a nation. If we ever closed the door to new Americans, our leadership in the world would soon be lost.[12]

But today's right-wing evangelicals either have forgotten or have chosen to ignore their vaunted hero Reagan's testament to the importance of immigrants in America. The rhetoric of evangelicals like James Dobson, Franklin Graham, Jerry Falwell Jr., and Robert Jeffress instead legitimizes the dehumanizing border policies of the Trump administration in the name of protecting their version of American culture. In his July 2019 newsletter Dobson wrote,

> Without an overhaul of the law and the allocation of resources, millions of illegal immigrants will continue flooding to this great land from around the world. Many of them have no marketable skills. They are illiterate and unhealthy. Some are violent criminals. Their numbers will soon overwhelm the culture as we have known it, and it could bankrupt the nation.[13]

One journalist pointed out how such portrayals serve to normalize the immorality of the mistreatment of immigrants: "The characterization of migrants at the border as disease-carriers, criminals, swindlers, and uneducated provides further legitimization that these are the type of people that American culture must be protected from."[14]

Supporters of the draconian "zero tolerance" (read "zero compassion") policies that the government and its court evangelicals declare to be so crucial to the everyday security of this nation ignore an important fact: that by far most incidents of terrorism are *not* committed by immigrants. They are committed by white males who are either US citizens or legal residents, and therefore, no fence or ban could possibly protect other residents from them.[15] But more to the point, immigrants, both documented and not, have been shown to be much more law abiding than native-born Americans. Among the studies that attest to this is the US government's 2008–2014 Secure Communities program. The Secure Communities program was implemented in three thousand US counties for the purpose of identifying and deporting noncitizens with criminal convictions. Ultimately, some 250,000 people were deported under the program. Yet, a study of the program's results concluded that it "led to no meaningful reductions in the FBI index crime rate. Nor has it reduced rates of violent crime—homicides, rape, robbery, or aggravated assault." The study's conclusion "calls into question the long-standing assumption that deporting non-citizens who commit crimes is an effective crime-control strategy."[16] Studies with similar conclusions were already known and available years before Trump made the specious claims that his right-wing evangelical supporters echo as if they are Holy Writ. Their willingness to ignore facts and figures indicates quite strongly that the impulse to demonize brown-skinned immigrants is more important to Trump's evangelicals than truth or reality.

Historically, Christians have been wary of Muslims since the medieval Christian Crusades to capture Jerusalem from Muslim control (1096 and 1271 CE). Since the terrible loss of life on 9/11 at the hands of Islamist extremists, that wariness has become indiscriminate antipathy toward all Muslims, all of whom are now regarded as potential terrorists seeking to reduce Christian America to ashes. Shamelessly taking yet another page from the Chinese Exclusion Act, candidate Trump purposely raised anti-Muslim sentiments to a fever pitch in 2016 with his announcement that as president he would protect America from terrorism by imposing a total ban on all Muslims from entering the United States. Under the false veneer of biblical morality, right-wing evangelical

Christian leaders parroted this corrosive anti-Muslim rhetoric, spewing avalanches of anti-Islamic malevolence. Franklin Graham called Islam "a religion that calls on its soldiers to shout 'Allahu Akbar' ['God is Great'] as they behead, rape, and murder in the name of Islam."[17] John Hagee, another Trump court evangelical, has contended that America is the target of Islamist terrorists because we are a democratic country: "[Muslims] hate us because we are free. They hate us because it is their religious duty to hate us. They are trained from the breast of their mother to hate us."[18]

As a result, almost three-quarters of right-wing evangelicals (72 percent) supported the Trump administration's ban against Muslim immigration—more than any other group.[19] This demonization of Muslims by right-wing Christians—who, these days, have the loudest political megaphone of all Christian believers in America—has led to Muslim children being bullied in grammar schools, Muslim women being assaulted in public for wearing their traditional *hijab* head covering, murders of Muslim innocents—even murders of those, like Sikhs, who were *thought* to be Muslims.[20] Riz Ahmed, the Muslim actor best known for his role of Bodhi Rook in the motion picture *Star Wars: Rogue One,* voiced a widely held fear among Muslims after he was detained at an airport by Homeland Security in April 2019 because of his name: "It's really scary to be a Muslim right now, super scary. I've often wondered, 'Is this going to be the year when they round us up, if this is going to be the year they put Trump's registry into action. If this is going to be the year they ship us all off?'"[21]

I noted in chapter 2 that the number of reported hate crimes more than doubled in counties that hosted 2016 Trump campaign rallies, and in 2018 religious, racial, and ethnic hate crimes—especially against Muslims—reached a sixteen-year high.[22] Despite this pattern of unholy violence, the professed right-wing evangelical followers of the Prince of Peace have made few concerted efforts to stem the rising tide of hatred or to reach out to Muslim communities for dialogue and understanding. Not only do evangelicals fail to seek out respectful dialogue with Muslims, they also oppose those who do. In February 2019 when Pope Francis and Grand Imam Ahmed Al-Tayebb of Egypt's influential Al-Azhar University issued a joint declaration "in the name of God who has created all human beings equal in rights, duties and dignity," evangelical elites immediately rejected their claim of universal humanity.[23] In 2015, right-wing evangelicals had already hounded a tenured political science professor, an African American woman, from the faculty of evangelical Wheaton College because she suggested that Christians and Muslims share a common God.[24]

Yet the unassailable reality is that, as with Christianity, the vast majority of Muslims are peace-loving worshippers of the same God of Abraham as Christians. And like all persons of goodwill throughout the world, the vast, overwhelming majority of Muslims are hardworking folks who simply seek to raise healthy families and live decent, peaceful lives. Moreover, the Qur'an, the holy book of Islam, extolls the virtues of Judaism's Torah and the New Testament Gospel, calls Christians their fellow "people of the book," and holds Jesus in the highest regard, mentioning his name some seventy-one times, even affirming his virgin birth. The violent Islamic extremists who ignore their holy book's pronouncements and commit acts of murder and terror in its name are but a tiny sliver of the three billion worldwide adherents to the Islamic faith. The extremists who profess to be Muslims are no more representative of the Islamic faith than the murderous factions of the KKK and alt-right extremists are representative of Christianity. Yet evangelicals demonize and sow fear of Muslims as if they are all terrorists in waiting, while ignoring the transgressions of murderous Christian fringe elements. In a monograph for the School of Advanced Military Studies, Major Frederick D. Wong of the US Army warned, "Americans readily identify Muslim extremism as a viable threat to America. However, they ignore or remain unaware of Christian extremism in the same context, despite the similarities in ideology that advocate violence against Americans."[25]

But as much as evangelical leaders and their followers demonize Muslims, because of geographical proximity most of their ire is directed toward Latin American immigrants, especially Mexicans. They support the US government's illegal efforts to herd asylum seekers back across the border into Mexico while their immigration claims are evaluated, a clear violation of federal law and the rules of the United Nations High Commission on Refugees (UNHCR), of which the United States is a signatory. Incredibly, they even supported President Trump's expressed desire to revoke birthright citizenship for the American-born children of undocumented immigrants. That these measures are illegal or impractical seemed not to matter.

Similarly, nearly nine in ten (85 percent) regular, church-going Trump supporters applauded his proposed wall at the Mexican border, despite—or perhaps because of—its toxic racist implications. In contrast, only 78 percent of Trump supporters who do not attend church regularly approve of the wall. This suggests a damning reality: that evangelicals who support Trump are those most willing to ignore their Bible's commands to treat immigrant strangers humanely.

US immigration policies have reached an unbelievable crescendo of barbarity by systematically separating children from their parents, even babes in arms.[26] Pope Francis's denunciation of the practice went straight to the heart of the matter. "It goes against natural rights," he declared. "It's something a Christian cannot do. It's cruelty of the highest form."[27] Yet, incredibly, separating children from their parents was official policy from the start. "If you are smuggling a child then we will prosecute you, and that child will be separated from you as required by law," announced right-wing evangelical attorney general Jeff Sessions at a May 2018 law enforcement event in Scottsdale, Arizona. "If you don't like that, then don't smuggle children over our border."[28] Not only have children been separated from their parents, but at the time of this writing no clear process has been put in place to ensure that children will be reunited with their families.[29] In October 2020, lawyers appointed by a federal judge to reunite separated immigrant families announced that they have been unable to locate the parents of 545 immigrant children, a human tragedy of unfathomably cruel proportions.[30]

In his 2018 State of the Union address, President Trump declared, "Let us reaffirm a fundamental truth: all children—born and unborn—are made in the holy image of God." Yet, in no way have the Trump administration's policies honored God's name or treated the lives of children as holy. Scholar Eddie Glaude Jr. describes the sickening actual reality of "children in cages with mucus-smeared shirts and soiled pants, . . . fourteen-year-old girls forced to take care of two-year-old children they do not even know, . . . sleep-deprived babies in rooms where the lights never go off, crying for loved ones who risked everything to come here."[31]

As was often the case, the Trump administration did quite the opposite of its claims. As Glaude laments, immigrant children were held like animals in actual chain-link cages,[32] their captivity cruelly compounding their psychoemotional wounds from the events and conditions that originally forced them and their families to leave behind all they had and knew. The UNHCR reported that "no less than 58 percent of the 404 children [it] interviewed were forcibly displaced because they suffered or feared harms that indicated a potential or actual need for international protection."[33] Nonetheless, videos surfaced of immigrant children being dragged, manhandled, and cruelly abused by those charged with their care and protection.[34] A lawsuit filed by the Center for Human Rights and Constitutional Law charged that migrant children held in government custody were sometimes handcuffed for extended periods (one boy testified that he was handcuffed for ten days), involuntarily drugged to the point they could not walk, stay awake, or maintain their physical or mental health.[35] A physician with Catholic Charities Humanitarian Respite Center reports that necessary medication was confiscated from children. "Somebody's going to get hurt, if they haven't already." He added, "Or frankly, someone could die."[36] As of this writing at least six children are known to have died from lack of adequate medical care. Many more children have been deeply damaged both psychologically and physically, some perhaps permanently. In her summary of an in-depth interview with Coleen Kraft, a physician and president of the American Academy of Pediatrics, journalist Kristine Phillips reported,

> Such a situation could have long-term, devastating effects on young children, who are likely to develop what is called toxic stress in their brain once separated from caregivers or parents they trusted. It disrupts a child's brain development and increases the levels of fight-or-flight hormones in their bodies, Kraft said. This kind of emotional trauma could eventually lead to health problems, such as heart disease and substance abuse disorders.[37]

After a congressional tour of the US Customs and Border Protection holding facilities, New Mexico congressman Ben Ray Lujan declared the children's holding cells "inhumane." In a medical declaration obtained by ABC News, physician Dolly Lucio Sevier wrote of the children, some as young as two-and-a-half months old, being held in the Ursala US Customs and Border Protection facilities in McAllen, Texas, "The conditions within which the children are held could be compared to torture facilities."[38] Dana Sabraw, a district court judge appointed by George W. Bush, ruled in *Ms. L. v. U.S. Immigration and Custom Enforcement; et al.,* "The facts set forth before the court portray reactive governance—responses to address *a chaotic circumstance of the government's own making*"[39] (emphasis added). Texas congressman Al Green called the facility "unbelievable." Said Green, "The [American Society for Prevention of Cruelty to Animals] would not allow animals to be treated the way human beings are being treated in this facility. To tolerate what I have seen is unthinkable."[40] Even more unthinkable: in March 2020 in the wake of the COVID-19 crisis, thousands of immigrant children were still being held in government immigrant detention centers so devoid of protective measures that a federal judge decried them as "hotbeds of contagion."[41] In an August 2020 press release, the International Rescue Committee warned that "tens of thousands" of immigrants in the United States, including children, were being held in "unsanitary conditions amidst suspect and potentially 'superspreading' levels of COVID infection in ICE detention centers."[42]

Despite the claims of Trump's evangelicals that he is a dedicated Christian, clearly his administration was not guided by the multitude of biblical passages that enjoin compassion, equal justice, and radical social, economic, and political inclusion of immigrants. Apparently he relied on the very problematic teachings of right-wing evangelical preachers instead. In a Bible study guide entitled *What the Bible Says About Our Illegal Immigration Problem,* the White House Bible study guru, Ralph Drollinger, argued that the Bible commands that "the nations" be kept separate by means of "borders and boundaries" claiming, "God's Word says He frowns on illegal immigrants."[43] Drollinger's teaching is false and specious and irrelevant to modern border policies, given that national boundaries were neither well defined nor rigidly enforced in biblical antiquity. He supports his anti-immigration ideology with a nonsensical extrapolation from the story about the Tower of Babel in Genesis: "'Come, let us go down, and confuse their language there, so that they will not understand one another's speech.' So the Lord scattered them abroad from there over the face of all the earth" (Genesis 11:7–8). It is a patently ridiculous misreading of the biblical text, for if Drollinger's specious interpretation was correct, it would mean that God has intended for people of different ethnicities and speakers of different tongues to never interact or converse with each other.

This is not biblical Christianity. It is right-wing ideological Christianity, in which the teachings of the Bible are twisted, distorted, and used selectively to support right-wing evangelical ends. In a 2018 interview, Tony Perkins of the Family Research Council further promotes that ideology by conflating the Bible's pronouncements on immigration with his own right-wing politics with the false claim that the Bible calls for "assimilation of immigrants." He remarked, "In fact, in almost every instance you read in the Old Testament about taking in the poor, immigrant and stranger, it is then that they have an obligation to operate by your customs and laws. It's the assimilation, it's the rule of law."[44] As we saw earlier, the Bible does enjoin reciprocal rights and responsibilities upon immigrants, but it never compels them to assimilate to their host culture, religion, or society—it mandates only that they be respectful and observant of its customs, laws, and strictures. If they seek to settle in the land and fulfill appropriate social responsibilities, they are to be allowed to live in peace as resident aliens.

The magnitude of the Trump administration's abusive and reactionary immigration policies suggests not simply occasional lapses in judgment and humane impulses. Rather, it signals an evil, abusive system. If a definition of evil is harming innocents by design or by purposely turning a blind eye to their suffering, then right-wing evangelicals are consciously supporting a *system* guilty of gross evil committed against children, the most innocent of all innocents. This evil was demonstrated in bold relief in June 2019 when the Trump administration went before an incredulous ninth circuit of the US Court of Appeals to argue that *it shouldn't be required to give migrant children toothbrushes, soap, and somewhere to sleep other than cold concrete floors.*[45] But the systemic evil doesn't just victimize children. In June 2019, Vice President Mike Pence visited the US Border Patrol station in McAllen, Texas. There he witnessed four hundred men too closely jammed into a holding pen to sleep or even sit. The men, who said they had been unable to shower or brush their teeth in weeks, emitted what a reporter accompanying Pence described as a stench so "horrendous" that some guards wore face masks. Yet in the face of such human suffering and inhumane treatment, Pence, a professed evangelical follower of the compassionate Jesus Christ, held up the facility as a model of competence and proficiency. "What we saw today," he declared with impious hypocrisy, "was a facility that is providing care that every American can be proud of."[46]

The barbarity of the government's treatment of immigrants is shamefully compounded by its use of corporately owned private prisons, the sole concern of which is ever-expanding profitability. As early as 2014, the American Civil Liberties Union issued a major report decrying that migrants housed in private prison facilities are subjected to shocking abuse, including overcrowding, unclean living conditions, sexual abuse, and increased use of isolation cells.[47] Observed Emily Ryo, an associate professor at the University of California's Gould School of Law, "The industry is in the business of expanding the system so they can make more money off holding more immigrants than can be [humanely] confined."[48] Apparently, those conditions remain unabated. Incarcerated immigrants continue to complain that their holding cells are so cold that they refer to them as *hierleras,* "iceboxes."[49]

Because of this history of abuse and troubling safety records of private prisons, in 2016 the Obama Justice Department ruled that the federal Bureau of Prisons could no longer contract with any private prison corporation for any reason. Soon after taking office, President Trump—the "born again" champion of evangelicals—rescinded the order, whose sole purpose was to protect the vulnerable. This freed the corporate prisons to once again engage in their inhumane, dangerous practices. As of this writing, nineteen private prisons are being paid to house some eighteen thousand migrants, or about 41 percent of the approximately forty-four thousand being held by Immigration and Customs Enforcement (ICE). As of early 2019, ICE had paid at least $807 million to private prisons.[50]

Immigrants to the United States have been demonized as interlopers with no right to seek solace on our soil. For President Trump, the asylum seekers are not women, children, and men in crisis but "some of the roughest people you've ever seen, people that look like they should be fighting for the U.F.C."—the Ultimate Fighting Championship.[51] But we who respect the dignity of our fellow beings must reject such outrageous mischaracterizations and ask ourselves why anyone would abandon homes, land, livelihood, possessions, family, and community to travel by foot for hundreds of danger-ridden miles with babes in arms and children in tow, to arrive at a hostile country's border with no guarantee of acceptance, if not to escape real danger and desperate hardship. In early 2019, *New York Times* columnist Nicholas Kristof interviewed immigrants from Central America who recounted the suffering and death that has driven so many to emigrate north. A Honduran woman lamented, "Food doesn't grow here anymore. That's why I would send my son north." Drought and soil-stripping winds have destroyed successive corn crops, leaving farming families totally bereft, with no choice but to watch their children die of starvation and lack of simple medicines, like penicillin. One woman mourned, "Because I had no money, my children died."[52]

The truth is that the United States bears a good deal of responsibility for the conditions these immigrants are trying to escape. Most come from countries where the US government has carried out major military, political, or economic interventions. In a sense, this immigration northward is a "journey of the colonized to the seat of the colonizer," as Nobel laureate Toni Morrison put it.[53] For instance, for the million people who became permanent residents of America in 2017, eight of the top ten countries or regions of origin have experienced major US interventions: Cuba, the Dominican Republic, El Salvador, Guatemala, Haiti, Mexico, the Philippines, and Vietnam.[54] The interventions include various military incursions, some coupled with commandeering central banks and expropriating huge sums from those countries, as in the case of Haiti. Then there are the drastic financial economic interventions. Among the most deleterious are the rapacious "austerity" measures imposed upon poor borrowing nations by the International Monetary Fund and the World Bank, of which the United States is a major patron.[55] Those who take seriously the declaration of Jesus that "you will know the truth, and the truth will make you free" (John 8:32) must acknowledge this truth: that this nation's sins against most asylum seekers are twofold: we have harmed them with foreign policies that have undermined their countries' security and economic stability, then injured them further by subjecting them to unconscionable abuse, turning them away when they have fled to our borders to escape the chaos and insecurity that our nation has helped to create.

For centuries, scholars have speculated about who Jesus had in mind when he declared, "I have other sheep that do not belong to this fold. I must bring them also, and they will listen to my voice. So there will be one flock, one shepherd" (John 10:16). Whatever the scholars' conclusions, it is important to note that this verse gives no indication that Jesus's sheep were restricted to a particular region or religious belief. One of the most outstanding traits of Jesus's ministry was his acceptance of everyone. He neither demonized nor turned his back on anyone in need—not the Roman colonizers of his people (Matthew 8:5–13); nor women unaccompanied by men, a serious taboo in that culture (John 4:1–26); nor the tax collectors who were roundly disdained by most Jews as traitors (Luke 19:1–10); not even a leprous Samaritan (Luke 17:11–19).[56] Because virtually all of Jesus's teachings are about serving God by serving our neighbors, "other sheep that do not belong to this fold" could well mean anyone who would accept the ethical demands of his message and strive to live lovingly and justly, no matter their origin or religion. This would include those who have sacrificed their freedom and their very lives to serve their neighbors, yet are not professed Christians, like Mahatma ("Great Soul") Mohandas Gandhi and Nelson Mandela.[57] Martin Luther King put it this way:

> I think Jesus was saying [with this verse], . . . "I have people dedicated and following my ways who have not become attached to the institution surrounding my name. I have other sheep that are not of this fold. And my influence is not limited to the institutional Christian church." I think this is what Jesus would say if he were living today concerning this passage.[58]

That is why right-wing evangelicals' refusal to treat immigrants of different faiths and nationalities as fellow children of God is a terrible affront to the Gospel they profess to love: because they callously reject and sometimes seek to destroy those Jesus so lovingly embraced. Their disdain for the welfare of immigrant women, children, and men has also blinded right-wing evangelicals to the ominous consequences for our own country, foreshadowed by our government's hard-line policies toward immigrants. In their antipathy to immigrants, right-wing evangelicals are poised, as the saying goes, to "cut off their nose to spite their face." That is, the inhumane, unbiblical policies they so wholeheartedly endorse are shutting the door to the large numbers of immigrants that have always been needed to sustain America's economic health. Because the death rate in America exceeds its birthrate, without a significant influx of immigrant labor, millions of jobs may go unfilled.[59] For example, it is estimated that without immigration America's economic growth from 1990 to 2014 would have been 15 percent lower.[60] Nor do evangelical leaders inform their followers that the erosion of the human rights of anyone within our borders ultimately leaves all Americans vulnerable to the depredations of political wolves of every stripe. Toni Morrison gives a sense of the danger that is posed by our nation's departure from decency. In 1995 she penned an incisive essay that projected, with great prescience, our downward descent from a democratic state to a fascist regime. Her observations are alarming, because virtually every step she charts on the path to fascism is present in America's current treatment of its asylum seekers and immigrants. According to Morrison, a country on the road to fascism will exhibit these practices:

1. Construct an internal enemy, as both focus and diversion.
2. Isolate and demonize that enemy by unleashing . . . overt and coded name-calling and verbal abuse.
3. Employ ad hominem attacks as legitimate charges against that enemy. Enlist and create sources and distributors of information who are willing to reinforce the demonizing process. . . .

4. . . . Monitor, discredit, or expel those that challenge or destabilize processes of demonization and deification. . . .
5. Subvert and malign all representatives of and sympathizers with this constructed enemy.
6. Solicit . . . collaborators who agree with and can sanitize the dispossession process.
7. Pathologize the enemy in scholarly and popular mediums. . . .
8. Criminalize the enemy. Then prepare, budget for, and rationalize the building of holding areas for the enemy—especially its males and absolutely its children.[61]

By their advocacy of policies that treat Muslims and immigrants of color like they are children of some other, lesser god, right-wing evangelical Christians are fully complicit in the erosion of the moral core of American society. Each step on the road to fascism is being trod before our eyes, largely because those who claim to revere the Gospel of Jesus Christ commit the monumental sin of refusing to accept all their neighbors as their equals in the household of God. They have suspended their Gospel affections toward those who come to our borders seeking decent lives for themselves and their loved ones. One observer put their actions into Gospel context:

Refugees aren't generalities or stereotypes. They are suffering children with desperate parents struggling to find a better life. And for those who survive the dangerous struggle and enter the U.S., their children are taken away and tortured. . . . Families are being torn apart forever. Intentionally. This is one of the most stark, clear choices a Christian can make: Defend torture of children, or support Christ. You can't do both. You cannot be a Christian and support what the government is doing to families and children.[62]

One wonders how America's right-wing evangelicals live with their choice to support such inhumane treatment of anyone, much less children, some of whom are babes in arms. It is a most monumental failure of Christian imagination not to realize that their Lord and Savior could never countenance such atrocities. Any Christian leaders who do not actively oppose this onslaught on humanity as a grievous sin against the demands of their faith commit an outrage of unfathomable proportions against the Gospel of Jesus Christ and every canon of decency that we know.

CHAPTER 6

YOU SHALL NOT ADD TO THE WORD WHICH I COMMAND YOU

Right-Wing Evangelicals, Abortion,
and the Meaning of "Pro-Life"

FROM THE OUTSET, I want to be clear that the purpose of this chapter is not to pass moral judgment on the painfully divisive issue of abortion. Both pro-choice and antiabortion advocates offer arguments that deserve much greater consideration than I can offer here. Nor is my purpose to question or challenge the sincerity of the everyday people who hold dear those positions. Rather, this chapter seeks to examine the accuracy and veracity of right-wing evangelical leaders' claims that the Bible prohibits abortion— claims with which they continually evoke roiling outrage among their followers—and the ways those claims are crafted to serve their political agenda.

Since the 1990s, right-wing evangelicals have treated the issue of abortion as more important than any issue in American public life—with the exception, perhaps, of homosexuality and gay marriage. Neither America's highly questionable recent wars and horrendous loss of life in the Middle East nor the governmental missteps and knowing misinformation that have caused the needless deaths of countless Americans from COVID-19 have raised the ire of right-wing evangelicals as much as abortion. In a real sense, right-wing evangelicals are treating the interests of the unborn as more consequential than the welfare of those already birthed and grappling with the struggles of life. To a great degree this explains their overwhelming support for the presidency of Donald Trump despite his often shockingly un-Christian behavior: it is because during his campaign he belatedly claimed to be an opponent of abortion and vowed to overturn *Roe v. Wade.*

The opponents of the US Supreme Court's 1973 *Roe v. Wade* ruling have characterized it as a capitulation to libertinism or a gross governmental devaluation of human life, if not government-sanctioned murder. The National Association of Evangelicals railed hard against the ruling, asserting it made it legal "to terminate a pregnancy for no better reason than personal convenience or sociological considerations."[1] But in reality, rather than personal convenience, what is most at stake for most women are real-life consequences. Abortion was first made illegal in the United States with the passing of the Comstock Act in 1873. But rather than ending the practice, the Comstock Act simply drove it underground, forcing women to resort to abortifacients and crude devices. The sad consequence was septic abortions, hemorrhaging, and obstetrical infections that frequently resulted in death. Despite the danger, a number of factors continued to drive women to seek abortions. A particular factor was economic anxiety. The desperation of the Great Depression, for example, led to nearly one million abortions in the early 1930s.[2] As doctors eventually began to understand the relationship between clandestine abortions and maternal mortality, they began to push for legalizing abortions in cases in which the mother's health was threatened. In 1961 the American Law Institute suggested that abortion should be legalized when a pregnancy is the result of rape or incest, endangers a woman's physical or mental health, or when a serious fetal deformity is suspected.[3] That same year, the National Council of Churches passed a resolution advocating much the same. The birth defects caused by a 1964 rubella epidemic and the anti-nausea drug thalidomide added to the debate consideration of quality of life after birth.[4] In a 1965 CBS television program, Walter Cronkite reported that there was an "abortion epidemic" in America of some one million abortions per year.[5] These on-the-ground realities—combined with the lobbying efforts of medical practitioners, women's rights groups, and choice advocates—eventually led to the nationwide legalization of abortion on demand by the US Supreme Court in *Roe v. Wade.*

Today, right-wing evangelicals' near obsession with abortion has caused them to overlook most other crucial issues of social concern. However, this is an anomaly in the history of American evangelicals. As we saw in chapter 2, evangelicalism has not always been the one- or two-issue faith that it is today. This is powerfully illustrated in the concerns of the Sixth General Conference of the Evangelical Alliance in 1873. John Fea points out that it included sponsored sessions devoted to "the labor problem, the importance of upholding the separation of church and state, religious liberty, temperance, Sabbath reform, the family, Christian unity, world religions, the dangers of wealth and materialism, the role of education in society, the care of the sick, the industrial revolution, and crime, . . . even a session on cruelty to animals."[6] He further notes that "not only did the speakers at the conference address the social problems of the day from a biblical perspective, but they also discussed the social and economic structures that lead to these ills."[7]

As the evangelical scholar Randall Balmer observes, "Both before and for several years after *Roe,* evangelicals were overwhelmingly indifferent to the subject."[8] A 1970 poll of clergy in the Southern Baptist denomination, the nation's largest evangelical denomination, found that 70 percent of their members "supported abortion to protect the mental or physical health of the mother, 64 percent supported abortion in cases of fetal deformity and 71 percent supported abortion in cases of rape."[9] In 1971 the Southern Baptist Convention passed a resolution calling for legislation "that will allow the possibility of abortion under such conditions as rape, incest, clear evidence of severe fetal deformity, and carefully ascertained evidence of the likelihood of damage to the emotional, mental, and physical health of the mother."[10] In fact, for years after the 1973 legalization of abortion by *Roe v. Wade,* the vast majority of evangelical Christian leaders offered neither complaint nor opposition to the ruling. For its part, the Southern Baptist Convention reaffirmed its 1971 resolution in 1974 and again in 1976. W. A. Criswell—the influential right-wing seg-regationist, former president of the Southern Baptist Convention, and pastor of the denomination's largest church—commented at the time of the *Roe* ruling, "I have always felt that it was only after a child was born and had life separate from its mother . . . that it became an individual person. It has always, therefore, seemed to me that what is best for the mother and for the future should be allowed."[11] A full two years after the ruling, Pat Robertson, now an unyielding denier of women's sovereignty over their own bodies, was still relegating abortion to "a strictly theological mat-ter," meaning it warranted neither public discussion nor policy consideration.

In fact, abortion did not become an issue of significant discus-sion for right-wing evangelicals until the late 1980s. In his book *Thy Kingdom Come,* Randall Balmer relates that it was in the 1980s that leaders like Paul Weyrich, cofounder of the right-wing think tank the Heritage Foundation and coiner of the term *moral ma-jority,* then decided to elevate abortion into a mobilizing issue. This antiabortion stance would well serve right-wing evangelicals' political goal of dominating the American body politic, as dis-cussed in chapter 2. Abortion was elevated to its present level of concern in 1990, when a gathering of leading right-wing Chris-tians met in private to chart a master strategy to dominate Amer-ica's social and political terrain. According to Balmer, among the heavyweight attendees were Weyrich; Ralph Reed, then execu-tive director of the Christian Coalition; and Richard Land, then president of the Ethics and Religious Liberty Commission of the Southern Baptist Convention. After much discussion, the group concluded that the next step in their strategy would be to build upon evangelicals' still-simmering anger at the government's Bob Jones University antisegregation ruling by focusing what they termed the US Supreme Court's "liberal" *Roe v. Wade* decision. In this way an issue that for years had raised little alarm among evangelicals was transformed into a full-blown issue of vociferous religious contestation.

Since then, right-wing evangelicals have employed highly inflammatory rhetoric to press their point, calling abortion "murder," demonizing both women seeking abortions and medical personnel who perform them as "murderers" and "baby killers"—rhetoric that has resulted in arson, assault, and the actual murders of doctors and nurses. Some right-wing evangelicals have gone so far as to use the term *holocaust* to describe abortion and the laws that protect the right to have one. Even President Trump falsely—and ghoulishly—weighed in by equating abortion with infanticide. "The baby is born, the mother meets with the doctor, they take care of the baby, they wrap the baby beautifully," he said. "Then the doctor and mother determine whether or not they will execute the baby."[12] So strident and angry are the anti-abortion sentiments of right-wing evangelicals that when Al Mohler, president of the Southern Baptist Theological Seminary, honored Representative John Lewis, the late civil rights icon, in a tweet, he was criticized by his peers because Lewis had steadfastly defended a woman's right to choose. A Texas pastor tweeted, "To bestow honor upon one whose political positions funded and endorsed the killing of millions of innocent babies is shameful leadership." An Indiana pastor issued a tweet excoriating Mohler because, he said, Lewis had "a 100% baby-slaughter record" and consistently voted "to advance the slaughter of the pre-born."[13]

A major part of right-wing evangelicals' "pro-life" strategy has been to claim as an unquestioned biblical truth that fetuses—actually one-cell zygotes—are persons who are imbued with souls at the moment of conception. The significance of this is that, if true, it would make the act of aborting a fetus at any point in its development the equivalent of killing a stranger walking the street. They support this claim by citing select scriptural passages that they allege make their case. Some of the most often employed include, "For it was you who formed my inward parts; you knit me together in my mother's womb" (Psalm 139:13); "Indeed, I was born guilty, a sinner when my mother conceived me" (Psalm 51:5); "Now the word of the Lord came to me saying, 'Before I formed you in the womb I knew you, before you were born I set you apart'" (Jeremiah 1:5, NIV); "When he who had set me apart before I was born . . ." (Galatians 1:15, RSV); and "When Elizabeth heard Mary's greeting, the baby leaped in her womb. . . . 'As soon as the sound of your greeting reached my ears, the baby in my womb leaped for joy'" (Luke 1:41, 44, NIV).

To be sure, these passages are expressive and poetic, but they do not make the point that antiabortion advocates claim they do. The verses from the Psalms (139:13 and 51:5) and Paul (Galatians 1:15) are their writers' spiritual musings about their own births, not statements about biological origins or the point at which a fetus becomes a person with a soul. As Episcopal priest Kira Schlesinger observes, "It is highly unlikely that the author of Psalm 139 wrote . . . to address when life begins or the moral status of a fertilized egg, zygote, or fetus."[14] The Jeremiah passage, so compelling and beautiful, is simply God's declaration of the divine hand in Jeremiah's prophethood. Like the passages from the Psalms, it says nothing about biology or soul endowment. And the Lukan passage narrates a special miracle, not a normal occasion of birth. Neither does it say anything about personhood. Biblical scholar Richard B. Hays, though no pro-choice advocate, says of this Lukan passage, "To extrapolate from this text . . . a general doctrine of the full personhood of the unborn is ridiculous and tendentious. . . . [It] cannot be used to prove any particular claim about prenatal personhood, nor does it have the issue of abortion in any way in view."[15] In fact, not one of these passages says anything about when a fetus is considered to be a person; even their claims about being known before birth only point to divine foreknowledge of the circumstances of their births and what they would become in life, which is simply testament to God's omniscience. In the final analysis, these passages speak only to the biological reality of a developing fetus prior to birth.

Yet by strategically interpreting the Bible to define fetuses as actual children, evangelical leaders have managed to recast legalized abortion from a theological issue mainly of significance to those who share their beliefs into a looming political issue they characterize as the government-sanctioned murder of children. Evangelical scholar R. C. Sproul declared, "The *Roe v. Wade* decision . . . is the nadir of American jurisprudence, the moment of the state's greatest failure to be a state."[16] The sincerity of their personal beliefs notwithstanding, right-wing evangelical leaders have purposely raised these points with the expectation of increasing rank and file right-wing ire at "liberal" elected officials—that is, any elected officials that do not accept their agenda—as a way of increasing their own political influence. So far, their calculation has proved to be correct. For several decades evangelical elites have quite successfully misled multitudes of the faithful to believe that abortion is the most pressing Christian issue in the public square—more important than addressing childhood poverty, gun violence, widespread hunger and homelessness, the trafficking and abuse of children, and the millions upon millions of Americans without healthcare. They have used the issue to discredit their political opponents as immoral advocates of child murder and have successfully made opposition to abortion a virtual litmus test of Christian political bona fides. But their sycophantic support of a sitting president who ordered children to be caged without the least glimmer of remorse reveals that their moral outrage begins and ends with their own group interests.

In reality, the Bible never once directly mentions voluntary abortion. What it does say clearly suggests that the death of a fetus is not equivalent to the death of a living, breathing human being and thus must not be treated that way. The one biblical passage that comes closest to addressing the issue is Exodus 21:22–23, which is part of a section of laws dealing with recompense for damage caused by violence:

> When people who are fighting injure a pregnant woman so that there is a miscarriage, and yet no further harm follows, the one responsible shall be fined what the woman's husband demands, paying as much as the judges determine. If any harm follows, then you shall give life for life.

The biblical penalty for causing a pregnant woman to abort a fetus, albeit involuntarily, is a monetary fine, as long as she is otherwise unharmed. But if the woman is seriously injured, the punishment is *lex talionis,* "eye for eye, tooth for tooth" (Exodus 21:24). No matter the claims to the contrary by "pro-life" evangelicals, the difference is indisputable: the lone biblical passage that addresses aborting a fetus states that unborn fetuses and living human beings are to be valued differently. In other words, it says that the life of a pregnant woman is more valuable than what is in her womb. Those who argue against abortion even when a woman's health is at stake seem to overlook this. Thus, rather than supporting the claim that abortion is a heinous biblical sin, this passage actually does the opposite: it demonstrates that those who call abortion murder and revile providers of abortion as murderers are lacking biblical sanction for their inflammatory charges. In essence *they are attributing claims to the Bible that the Bible itself does not make.*[17]

There is one other passage in the Bible that touches on abortion, if in a different way. Of the 613 laws in the Old Testament, it is the only one that needs God's intervention to be fulfilled.

It is seldom cited, presumably because of its controversial nature, but the book of Numbers (5:11–31) specifies that if a husband suspects that his pregnant wife has been unfaithful, "the man shall bring his wife to the priest" (5:15) to discern whether that has occurred. The priest is to give the accused woman some "bitter water" to drink, then "the priest shall make her take an oath" (5:19) and perform an unspecified "curse" over her. Then "he shall make the woman drink the water of bitterness that brings the curse" (5:24). The text provides that "if she has defiled herself and has been unfaithful to her husband, the water that brings the curse shall enter into her and cause bitter pain . . ." (5:27). If her pregnancy is the result of adultery, the passage goes on to promise that God will punish her infidelity *by aborting the fetus in her womb:* "and her womb shall discharge" (5:27).

This passage methodically codifies actions husbands are to initiate that could result in the abortion of their wives' pregnancies. Although God performs the act, the husband initiates the process and is a willing participant, yet he receives no cautionary moral advice and certainly no condemnation for his role. Because here God uses abortion as the means of exposing the wife's unfaithfulness, the unborn is reduced to an instrument of evidence, if not retribution. Thus, similar to the judgment in Exodus, this biblical passage places a lesser value on the fetus than on its mother.

Moving to the period of the early church, as we know from the letters of the apostle Paul (ca. 5–64 or 67 CE), his missionary journeys took him to some of the seediest and most notorious towns and ports in the Mediterranean basin. The Greek city of Corinth, the site of at least two of Paul's missions, was a major seaport that was widely known to be a nest of vice and prostitution. In these settings the abortion rate for unwanted pregnancies would have been significant. Chroniclers such as Dionysius of Halicarnassus (60–7 BCE) indicated that abortion was so widespread in Rome—another of Paul's destinations—that the authorities had to take stern measures to keep it from significantly reducing Rome's population.[18] In his letters, Paul addresses numerous actions and attitudes that he considered to be morally sinful or worse, but there is no mention of abortion. Neither is it mentioned in the gospels or anywhere in the New Testament, although it is condemned in the *Didache* (also known as The Lord's Teaching Through the Twelve Apostles to the Nations) and in the Epistle of Barnabas, both late first- or early second-century extrabiblical writings little known or consulted in the long history of the church. There are numerous other extant writings and proclamations, dating from the early church into the beginnings of modernity and beyond that take varying positions on when abortions are considered permissible and the punishments and condemnations that should be administered when they are not. But there is relatively little mention of abortion as a major topic of social or religious significance, and certainly nothing like a consensus on the moment a zygote or fetus gains a soul. Some through the centuries have considered *ensoulment*—the development of a soul and personhood—not to occur until the moment of birth. In her personal diary, the former first lady Barbara Bush described what she understood as an experience of ensoulment at the birth of her daughter, Robin, who tragically died in childhood,

> Judging from both the birth and death of Robin Bush, I have decided that that almost religious experience, that thin line between birth, the first breath that she took, was when the soul, the spirit, that special thing that separates man or woman from animals + plants entered her little body. I was conscious at her birth and I was with her at her death.[19]

Others have considered ensoulment to happen at the quickening (when the mother first feels movement in her womb), and still others, like many of today's evangelicals, hold that ensoulment occurs in the zygote at the moment of conception. Adding to the lack of unanimity is that some of the most prominent authorities on Christian doctrine and teachings in the history of Christendom are essentially silent on abortion or do not take unequivocal stands on it.

For instance, Augustine of Hippo (354–430) is widely considered the greatest of all Christian thinkers. His classic *City of God* remains a staple in theological studies. His writings are voluminous, yet his treatment of abortion is almost terse: "The law does not provide that the act [abortion] pertains to homicide, for there cannot yet be said to be a live soul in a body that lacks sensation." The implication is clear: a fertilized egg does not have a soul and is not yet a person. If one follows Augustine, however, at a later, unspecified stage of fetal development when it can evince a response to sensual sensations, perhaps in the third trimester, the fetus might then be considered a live soul.

Thomas Aquinas (1225–1274), a Dominican monk, is also considered one of Christendom's greatest theologians and philosophers. Pope Benedict XV (1854–1922) held Aquinas's teachings in such high regard that he declared, "This [Dominican] Order . . . acquired new luster when the Church declared the teaching of Thomas to be her own." In his *Summa Theologica,* Aquinas wrote, "The intellective soul [true person] is created by God at the completions of man's coming into being."[20] Thus, like Augustine, Thomas Aquinas did not seem to consider abortion to be murder until perhaps the third trimester, when a fetus typically becomes viable. It is at this point that both thinkers apparently believed fetuses were imbued with souls.

In the final analysis, what does this all mean? That nothing in the Bible or in the history of Christendom justifies right-wing evangelicals' divisive obsession with abortion—except, perhaps, their obsession with subjecting American society to their own willful vision of themselves as judges astride every aspect of American society.

We have taken the time to examine right-wing evangelicals' claims about the Bible and abortion because the politicization of their contentions has extremely serious implications for America's body politic. With their incendiary rhetoric they have divided American society, with no room for real dialogue or mutual understanding. Tragically, the antiabortion obsession of right-wing evangelical leaders has distracted believers from engaging in what the Gospel identifies as their paramount responsibilities: extending love, care, assistance, and support to the poor and the needy, the elders and the infirm, the vulnerable and the suffering; to the marginalized, the alone and forgotten; to the immigrant strangers in our midst.

Their obsession with abortion has even induced them to claim as their champion a president whose words and deeds have made a mockery of the very faith they claim to hold dear.

According to a 2019 Pew Research Center poll, 61 percent of Americans say *Roe v. Wade* should remain the law of the land in all or most cases; only 38 percent believe it should not be lawful. But it is also the case that not everyone who supports *Roe* is actually comfortable with abortion. Some outright do not believe in abortion, but neither do they believe they have the right to control the body of another. Right-wing evangelicals do not have the right to impose their belief on the entire American populace, which is replete with diverse questions, concerns, and considerations that are every bit as sincere as their own. If they could successfully influence America's jurists to repeal *Roe v. Wade,* that would result in the recriminalization of almost all pregnancy-ending procedures in many states, exposing women who undergo abortions and the doctors and midwives who provide them to serious legal penalties. Moreover, because the most extreme antiabortion foes lobby for its recriminalization with no exceptions, repeal of *Roe v. Wade* could result in the deaths of untold numbers of women whose health and very survival are threatened by a full-term pregnancy. The historian Leslie J. Reagan puts it plainly: "Making abortion hard to obtain . . . will return us to the time of crowded septic abortion wards, avoidable deaths, and the routinization of punitive treatment of women by state authorities and their surrogates."[21]

For all the seeming righteousness of its claims, right-wing evangelicals' "pro-life" stance does not hold all human life in equal measure, for their concern for life essentially wanes at birth. They raise no hue and cry for policies to assist new mothers and their babies—great numbers of whom are in dire need of support of all kinds—with anything near the energy and dedication they expend for the rights of the unborn, and they show little interest in the civil rights and screaming needs of those already struggling in the world. The bottom line is that right-wing evangelicals really are not at all "pro-life" in any large sense. They simply are abortion obsessed.

There are approximately three thousand verses in the Bible that are concerned with social justice and the common good, with taking care of the poor and the immigrant, with the indiscriminate extension of kindness and compassion. If evangelicals were really "pro-life" and not just obsessed with the unborn, they would be similarly filled with righteous indignation over the massive social injustices that bedevil our nation and our world. If they were really pro-life, they would be actively anti-war, anti–death penalty, and anti–police terrorism and brutality; they would fight to abolish poverty and misogyny and patriarchy, all of which distort and destroy the quality of human lives and communities. If they were really pro-life, they would have long ago erupted in outrage that almost four years after the 2017 devastation of Hurricane Maria the inhabitants of Puerto Rico still have not received adequate aid to salve their ongoing suffering. If right-wing evangelicals were really pro-life, they would be similarly outraged that six years—six years!—after the water supply in the largely poor and black city of Flint, Michigan, was contaminated by unconscionable official misconduct, many of the city's children are showing resultant signs of ill health and neurological damage, and the city's water is still not safe to drink. If they were truly pro-life, they would be so horrified by the rash of gun violence and school shootings that they would promptly cancel memberships in the gun-crazy National Rifle Association and forcefully insist upon much stronger measures to control gun sales and ownership. And if they really, truly were pro-life, if they truly believed in loving their neighbors, they would eschew their intractable self-righteousness, embrace a spirit of humility, and acknowledge that simply because they believe that something is the only immutable truth does not necessarily make it so, and that the moral conclusions they extrapolate from unrelated biblical texts are not the only way biblical morality can be reasonably and sincerely understood.

The hard reality is that if right-wing evangelicals were as concerned for the well-being of women seeking abortions as they are for their unborn fetuses, they would be willing to use some of the considerable energy and the billions of dollars they commit to lobbying activities against abortion and homosexuality to instead support and fund social structures, organizations, and agencies to remove a primary reason women elect to have abortions: the prospect of their being consigned to lives of poverty and unremitting struggle as the result of bearing a child for whom they cannot adequately provide.[22] They could use their considerable clout to support governmental policies that could help mitigate the economic circumstances and lack of infrastructural support that compel so many women to seek abortions. Acknowledging the inevitable economic disparity in the availability of abortions that would be wrought by repealing *Roe v. Wade,* former first lady Barbara Bush asked, "What do I feel about abortion? Having decided that the first breath is when the soul enters the body, I believe in Federally funded abortion. Why should the rich be allowed to afford abortions and the poor not?"[23]

With their name-calling and incendiary rhetoric, right-wing evangelicals have foreclosed any real dialogue with those who seek abortions and those who support a woman's right to choose. Despite the love and care for others that the Gospel commands, the approach of right-wing evangelicals is largely devoid of compassion and empathy. They demonize women who elect to end pregnancies, many of whom have been forced to make the most difficult, heartrending decisions of their lives. Although some women consider abortion a simple procedure with few moral implications,[24] for others it can be a sad and tragic choice. Moreover, there are many reasons women choose to end pregnancies. They include the psycho-emotional inability to cope with the rigors of pregnancy and childbearing, fears for their physical health, the looming trauma of a fetus diagnosed with health conditions that require financial and emotional resources the woman doesn't have, grinding poverty with no prospect to provide even a healthy child with the essentials of a decent life, abandonment by the man who impregnated her, a pregnancy that is the result of rape or incest, and, very importantly, a lack of family and community support systems. Yet those who make the decision to have or to perform legal abortions, even for the most humane or exigent reasons, are often demonized in the name of God, stalked, viciously attacked, and even murdered in retribution for what their antichoice opponents choose to grossly mischaracterize as the King Herod–like mass murder of innocents.

Rob Schenck is an evangelical minister and former "pro-life" activist who left the antiabortion movement after thirty years to become an advocate for women's sovereignty over their own bodies. In a widely read *New York Times* op-ed, this former insider to the movement challenged the hypocrisy of the term *pro-life:*

> What is "pro-life" about putting a woman in a situation where she must risk pregnancy without proper medical, social and emotional support? What is "pro-life" about forcing the birth of a child, if that child will enter a world of deprivation and insecurity, to say nothing of the fear, anxiety and danger that comes with poverty and a lack of educational and employment opportunities? . . . I can no longer pretend that telling poor, pregnant women they have just one option—give birth and try your luck raising a child, even though the odds are stacked against you—is "pro-life" in any meaningful sense.[25]

Those who take seriously the call of Jesus to love our neighbors must ask the Christians whose unyielding abortion obsession imbues our society with such division and rancor: How can you care so deeply about the unborn, yet show so little compassion and concern for the children of God who are already here?

CHAPTER 7

THOU SHALL NOT MURDER

The Unholy Alliance Between
Right-Wing Evangelicals and the NRA

O N A WINTRY NIGHT in February 2018, hundreds of worshippers crowded into a suburban Pennsylvania church. The women wore bridal white; the men, dark hued suits. Upon each head perched a ceremonial crown. Clearly, this was to be no ordinary worship service. Other than their God, the gathering had but one focus: a public and worshipful declaration of marital vows. Some came to repeat the words that had consecrated their unions in years past, while others had come to begin new lives together. Given the occasion, one might have expected to see boutonnieres and bouquets, but there were precious few flowers. Instead of bouquets, dozens of the faithful cradled AR-15 assault-style rifles, weapons designed for the sole purpose of tearing human flesh.

After the pastor proclaimed the marital bonds of the gathered to be eternal, he prayed the love of God upon them, the love of each upon the other, and exhorted all to love and serve their singular God. But he was not finished; he had other prayers and blessings to dispense. In a building dedicated to the Prince of Peace, the pastor proceeded to bless their guns—and their use of them—with a martial supplication suffused with startling irony: he prayed for "a kingdom of peace police and peace militia where the citizens, through the right given to them by almighty God to keep and bear arms, will be able to protect one another and protect human flourishing."[1] Surely the notion that gun ownership is a divine right would seem bizarre to Jesus Christ, even more because it was consecrated in his name. Yet equally bizarre is that among right-wing evangelicals today, the right to own a firearm is virtually a Gospel tenet.

According to a 2017 Pew Research report, white evangelicals are more likely to own a gun than any other religious group, more than even the average American, with the willing consent of their religious leaders.[2] Robert Jeffress, the Texas pastor and unrelenting supporter of President Trump, says he welcomes guns in his church because their presence makes him feel more safe. "I'd say a quarter to a half of our members are concealed carry. They have guns, and I don't think there's anything wrong with that," he said. "They bring them into the church with them."[3] Jerry Falwell Jr., the former president of evangelical Liberty University, urged students to apply for gun permits as if it is a biblical duty. With the same urgency, he encouraged them to hone their skills at the school's firing range. But how did the ownership of firearms—weapons that can destroy a life in mere seconds—come to be considered a sacred right?

Enter the National Rifle Association. The NRA—today a vociferous advocate for the unimpeded ownership of guns and a powerful political force—was founded in 1871 on the heels of the Civil War "to promote and encourage rifle shooting on a scientific basis."[4] Its main mission was teaching soldiers to shoot straight. (Union army Civil War records indicate that only one of each one thousand rifle shots fired hit a Confederate target, prompting Union army general Ambrose Burnside, eventually the first NRA president, to lament, "Out of ten soldiers . . . only one . . . can hit the broad side of a barn.")[5] Originally that was the NRA's only role; it had no lobbying or advocacy function. The NRA did not even begin to inform its members about firearm-related legislation until 1934. A study by Adam Winkler, a constitutional lawyer, found that before 1959 there were few articles in law reviews or journals that engaged the Second Amendment, and none argued that the Second Amendment protected an individual's right to own guns. But in 1960, the first law review article appeared that asserted that claim.[6] Soon after, the individual's constitutional right to bear arms became a virtual NRA mantra. Beginning in the 1960s, their flagship publication, *American Rifleman*, began to feature articles that pressed the issue, prompting legal scholars to take a closer look at the Constitution's guarantees. In 1975, the NRA began directly lobbying lawmakers on behalf of the interests of gun makers and gun owners. Winkler notes that between 1980 and 1999 there was a flood of law review articles arguing that individual gun ownership is a civil right guaranteed by the Constitution.[7]

However, that position was widely challenged. In 1991, retired chief justice Warren Burger described the gun civil-rights argument as "one of the greatest pieces of fraud—I repeat the word 'fraud'—on the American public by special interest groups that I have seen in my lifetime."[8] But such assessments did not stop individual gun rights advocates from declaring their stance to be the standard model of constitutional interpretation. The close relationship between the NRA and evangelicals goes back only to the 1970s, yet evangelicals today accept this "standard model" as if it is the Gospel itself. This was largely due to one man, a right-wing evangelical Christian named Harlon Carter.

From 1950 to 1957, Harlon Carter headed the US Border Patrol, an agency of the US Labor Department. He joined the NRA board in 1951. A staunch right-wing evangelical and an archconservative gun hard-liner, Carter opposed all controls on gun ownership, even background checks for gun purchasers. In 1976, after a quarter century on the NRA board, he resigned his membership to protest the organization's support of what, in retrospect, were moderate gun control measures, as well as its firing of seventy-four employees who also held the same hard-line anti-gun-control stance. But in 1977, Carter and a thousand members of the activist groups the

Second Amendment Foundation and the Citizens Committee for the Right to Keep and Bear Arms overwhelmed the organization's annual meeting and changed its bylaws, thus allowing the insurgents to vote out much of the established leadership and elect Carter executive vice president and CEO.

It was under Carter's leadership (the NRA presidency is largely ceremonial, effectively making the vice president its highest-ranking executive) that the NRA's close relationship with evangelicals began. From that time, references to God in NRA rhetoric and literature occurred with greater frequency. By the end of the 1970s, the NRA had shifted its emphasis from arguing that individual gun ownership is a constitutional right to its current stance that it is a "God-given" right. Wrote Carter in *American Rifleman* in 1979, "Our NRA Members stand foremost in the struggle to protect and preserve all our God-given, constitutional and long-accepted . . . right of the people to keep and bear arms."[9] In a 2008 speech, former five-time NRA president Charlton Heston went further, declaring that the guns themselves were holy. "Sacred stuff," he said, "resides in that wooden stock and blue steel."

Reflecting its close ties to right-wing evangelicals, the NRA holds an annual prayer breakfast that serves to imbue gun ownership with a veneer of Christian religiosity. At the NRA's twentieth annual prayer breakfast in 2018, Joe Gregory, a top donor to the organization, offered an invocation that compared proponents of gun control legislation to biblical-era tyrants and oppressors: "We humbly ask you to direct and bless our efforts against those who would seek to take away those freedoms, . . . deliver us from despots of tyranny."[10] At the right-wing 2018 Conservative Political Action Conference, Wayne LaPierre, the executive vice president, CEO, and public face of the NRA since 1991, invoked divine favor upon the organization's stance that gun ownership is a right, "not bestowed by man [i.e., the US Constitution], but granted by God to all Americans as our American birthright."[11] The current NRA president, Carolyn Meadows, has declared that she fights against gun control measures because, she said, as "a Christian" it's her job to "save" America.[12] This conflation of God, guns, patriotism, and basic human freedom has become the constant refrain of NRA rhetoric. Right-wing evangelicals have adopted it whole cloth.

Every year nearly 115,000 people in the United States are shot in murders, assaults, suicides, suicide attempts, unintentional shootings, or by police intervention; and each year more than 33,000 people die from gun violence, 2,600 of whom are children. Among the twenty-two highest-income countries, the United States accounts for more than 90 percent of all gun deaths of children under the age of fifteen. On average, fifty women are fatally shot each month by intimate partners. Since 1968, more than 1.5 million Americans have died in gun-related incidents; this is a higher death count than Americans killed in all US wars combined.[13] Not to be forgotten is the staggering economic cost of American gun violence: "A recent [2006–2014] Johns Hopkins study of 704,000 people admitted to emergency rooms for treatment of firearm-related injuries over a nine-year period found that emergency room and inpatient charges alone accounted for $2.8 billion each year. This all adds up to a crisis of human life on an epic scale."[14] Yet the supposedly "pro-life" right-wing evangelicals continue to support the NRA's mission to increase the number of guns in America while actively seeking to weaken regulations that might save lives.

Despite the carnage, right-wing evangelicals argue that gun deaths have nothing to do with gun laws and availability; for them it is the evil of sinful hearts that is the problem. "As long as we continue to only . . . look at God on a Sunday morning, and kick him out of the town squares and our schools the other six days of the week, what do we expect?" challenged Texas lieutenant governor Dan Patrick.[15] (Patrick does not address the question of how an omnipresent God is kicked out of anywhere.) In a now-deleted Facebook post, Ohio state representative Candice Keller blamed "transgender, homosexual marriage, and drag queen advocates" and "the Dem Congress" for causing mass shootings.[16] Staunch Trump evangelical Robert Jeffress contends that "laws . . . can never eliminate evil—only Christ can transform a person's heart," by which he means that stronger gun control laws and fewer guns on the street will make no difference.[17] Right-wing evangelicals also argue that if guns were not available, sinful hearts and overwrought spirits would find another way to kill. But laws can save lives. For example, access to guns increases the risk of death by suicide by 300 percent.[18] The fact that gun suicides are concentrated in states with high rates of gun ownership and accessibility demonstrates that the availability of guns *is* the issue. But right-wing evangelicals are not simply *wrong* about this. They are also *disingenuous.* Their obsession with repealing the *Roe v. Wade* and *Obergefell v. Hodges* abortion and marriage equality rulings shows that they don't believe in simply transforming hearts to bring social change. They absolutely do believe in advocating for laws—when those laws give them what they want.

But what does gun ownership have to do with the Gospel? Alyssa Milano, the actress turned activist, raised just that question. In a September 2019 tweet, she asked, "Can someone cite which passage of the Bible God states it is a god-given right to own a gun?" Calling on a verse much cited in defense of gun ownership, Ted Cruz, the right-wing evangelical United States senator from Texas, responded to Milano in a tweet by quoting Exodus 22:2: "If a thief is caught breaking in at night and is struck a fatal blow, the defender is not guilty of bloodshed." This is yet another example of right-wing evangelicals' misleading use of the Bible, because what Cruz offers as conclusive biblical proof that the ownership and use of a deadly weapon are divinely sanctioned, actually has a serious constraint attached to it: if that right is exercised during daylight hours, which is meant to imply a less threatening scenario, it is to be considered murder. If this passage is to have ongoing meaning that is not held captive to primitive settings, the constraint it prescribes must be updated to reflect the social developments and technological advances of every successive epoch. In our time, such a constraint would consist of sensible gun control laws, which, I would argue, include revisiting the "stand your ground" laws that too easily legitimate the use of deadly force.

Since right-wing evangelicals talk about a God-given right to gun ownership, one would expect a much clearer attestation of it in the gospels. But the sayings of Jesus that evangelicals typically employ to support their claim are ultimately no more germane than Cruz's. Among the most often cited is "the one who has no sword must sell his cloak and buy one" (Luke 22:36). However, this verse is an outlier among the gospel sayings of Jesus—not only is it not supported by any of his other teachings, it is also contradicted by his own words: "For all who take up the sword will perish by the sword" (Matthew 26:52), a proclamation much more in line with his ethics of peace and love of neighbors. Another of the sayings of Jesus regularly cited by gun proponents, "I have not come to bring peace, but a sword" (Matthew 10:34), is undoubtedly a metaphorical description of the radical disruption of the status quo that he foresaw for his ministry. It cannot be an exhortation for bearing weapons and violent revolution, because the Gospel's undisputed message is one of peace and nonviolence.

Not only do evangelicals wrongly cite the words of Jesus in support of gun ownership, they also ignore scriptural passages that express the divine desire for fewer deadly weapons. The book of Isaiah, for instance, articulates a divine vision of worldly peace in which weapons of death will be beaten into farm implements (Isaiah 2:3–4). Yet champions of gun ownership strive for the opposite: *more* deadly weapons in circulation. Some are so hell-bent on using the biblical witness to support their thirst for guns that they portray Jesus in ridiculous ways to associate his teachings with deadly firearms, as in a popular bumper sticker: "Jesus would still be alive if he'd had an AR-15." But despite the pains the NRA and right-wing evangelicals take to convince the nation that unrestricted gun ownership is a divine right, they do not seem to believe this claim themselves, because on numerous occasions the NRA has argued *against* unrestricted gun ownership.

In fact, for much of the twentieth century, the NRA lobbied for and coauthored legislation closely similar to the modern legislative measures that the association now attacks as unconstitutional and a denial of God-given rights. In the 1920s, the National Revolver Association—then the arm of the NRA responsible for handgun training—actually proposed gun regulations that were subsequently adopted by nine states. Included in those regulations was a ban on the sale of firearms to noncitizen immigrants, which was perhaps its main selling point. The apparent purpose of this restriction was to keep guns out of the hands of Italian immigrants, who were considered an undesirable element because of the presence of the Mafia and the Sicilian Black Hand gangs. The NRA also assisted President Franklin Roosevelt in drafting the first federal gun control laws, the 1934 National Firearms Act and the 1938 Gun Control Act. Karl T. Frederick, then president of the NRA, testified in support of the National Firearms Act in a 1934 congressional hearing, "I have never believed in the general practice of carrying weapons. I do not believe in the general promiscuous toting of guns. I think it should be sharply restricted and only under licenses."[19]

The NRA continued to support gun control for the next thirty years. In 1967, however, it initially opposed California's Mulford Act, which was crafted to prohibit all public carrying of loaded guns. The legislation was a response to the Black Panther Party's lawfully conducted armed patrols of Oakland, California's black neighborhoods to discourage mistreatment and brutality of the city's black residents at the hands of the Oakland police force. The NRA's initial reasoning was that it was too restrictive to pass a law for all Californians simply to contain the actions of a few. But in May 1967, the Black Panther Party staged an armed protest against the Mulford Act at the California State Capitol, sporting 12-gauge shotguns, .357 magnums, and .45-caliber handguns. Although carrying loaded guns in public had long been legal, the spectacle of armed blacks calling for other blacks to arm themselves was too much to stomach for the lily-white NRA membership. Following the armed Black Panther demonstration, the NRA reversed its position virtually overnight to support the bill after all. It was successfully passed in 1967. Although in reality it was whites who were most heavily armed and responsible for most gun-related deaths, the NRA betrayed its mission to stand against additional gun control measures due to white people's fear of armed blacks walking the streets. The degree of the NRA's hypocrisy is evident when it is considered that it had never sought to limit gun access in response to the murderous KKK and other violent white supremacists: not during the wholesale killing of blacks during the period of Reconstruction, not during the Red Summer of 1919 when scores of black World War I veterans in uniform were gunned down, not even during the civil rights movement, when the KKK declared open season on blacks seeking only to exercise their constitutional right to vote. Harlon Carter had long argued that allowing the acquisition of guns by violent criminals and the mentally ill is the "price we pay for freedom."[20] But when blacks sought to exercise their right to own guns, for the NRA the right to own and bear arms suddenly was neither fully constitutionally guaranteed nor God granted. To the NRA, blacks arming themselves—even for self-defense—was too high a price to pay for that "freedom."

Americans and Their Guns, a history of the NRA published in 1967, asserted that at that time the NRA was "not affiliated with any manufacturer of arms or ammunition or with any jobber or dealer who sells firearms and ammunition."[21] But that is no longer the case. Josh Sugarmann is the executive director of the Violence Policy Center, a gun-control advocacy group that studies the firearms industry and its ties to the NRA. In a National Public Radio interview in 2018 he explained that the National Rifle Association today is essentially a trade support arm for a gun industry that is constantly trying to find new customers as their base of aging white males dies off: "They work to exploit any opportunity to sell guns. . . . Today's National Rifle Association is essentially a de facto trade association masquerading as a shooting sports foundation."[22]

At least thirty gun manufacturers pay the NRA tens of millions of dollars yearly through what its website touts as its Corporate Partners program. The sponsorship program offers various named levels of corporate contributions, ranging from $25,000 to $9,999,999.

The program seems to essentially be a quid pro quo arrangement for lobbying services rendered. Among its partners are some of the largest firearm manufacturers, including Smith & Wesson, Bushmaster Firearms International (manufacturer of the Bushmaster assault rifle), Beretta USA, Springfield Armory, and Sturm, Ruger & Co.; also, gun accessories vendors MidwayUSA and Brownells. A significant number of senior firearm manufacturing executives also belong to the NRA's Golden Ring of Freedom, which requires a $1 million *personal* donation to the organization.[23]

The Golden Ring of Freedom appellation reflects the NRA narrative that buying guns is a sign of patriotism in the face of some unidentified, faceless, looming tyranny. "Our Second Amendment is freedom's most valuable, most cherished, most irreplaceable idea," said LaPierre in 2012. "When you ignore the right of good people to own firearms to protect their freedom, you become the enablers of future tyrants whose regimes will destroy millions and millions of defenseless lives."[24] His statement seems to be a conscious evocation of Thomas Jefferson's famous 1787 declaration, which is quoted quite liberally by right-wing extremists and gun-owning zealots: "The tree of liberty must be refreshed from time to time with the blood of patriots and tyrants." One would expect the NRA's right-wing evangelical partners and supporters to at least gently push back against such valorizations of gun violence, yet their silence is conspicuous and quite telling.

Not only has the NRA benefited from false interpretations of biblical passages, bald appeals to patriotism, and hundreds of millions of dollars in corporate largesse and quid pro quos, it has also benefited from devious tactics like the deliberate spreading of falsehoods specifically crafted to induce panicked gun buying and also to increase the paid NRA membership rolls.

A prime example of this is the widespread alarm the NRA raised during the 2008 presidential election, claiming that Barack Obama was determined to take away the people's guns. "Never in NRA's history have we faced a presidential candidate—and hundreds of candidates running for other offices—with such deep-rooted hatred of firearm freedoms," LaPierre wrote. This rhetoric comported well with the widely touted right-wing charges that Obama was a foreign born, secret Muslim sympathizer bent on destroying America's way of life. He also charged—again, falsely—that Obama had a ten-point plan to "change the Second Amendment," although LaPierre knew full well that no president has that power.[25] Indeed, LaPierre raised such alarm that few panic-stricken gun buyers stopped to think about how ridiculous his claims were. Yet at no time during his entire term of office did Obama make any effort that could even remotely be considered as confiscatory. In fact, gun manufacturing and gun ownership flourished during Obama's presidency, according to the National Shooting Sports Association, a gun industry trade group. Employment within the industry grew by 87 percent, wages increased by 142 percent, and the total economic impact of the industry grew by 169 percent.[26] Apparently, this growth encouraged LaPierre to continue his incendiary rhetoric. In 2016, in a message to the eighty thousand plus NRA members, LaPierre tried to cause another round of panic gun buying by leveling the same falsehood-riddled charge at presidential candidate Hillary Clinton. "If she could," he wrote, "Hillary would ban every gun, destroy every magazine, run an entire national security industry right into the ground, and put your name on a government registration list, . . . and we'll all be kissing our Second Amendment freedom goodbye. . . . You can kiss your guns goodbye."[27] LaPierre had made similar charges against Bill Clinton, comparing his administration to Stalinist Russia and federal officers to "Nazi storm troopers."[28] Political commentator Jared Yates Sexton recalls, "He declared, 'The final war has begun,' and claimed he'd glimpsed documents detailing government plans 'to eliminate private firearms ownership completely and forever.'"[29]

The NRA conscientiously capitalizes on its close ties to evangelicals with fear-based, apocalyptic rhetoric. In an article by LaPierre titled "Stand and Fight" in the February 2013 edition of *America's 1st Freedom*, the NRA's official journal, he virtually guaranteed the collapse of American society in stark apocalyptic terms: "There likely won't be enough money to pay for police protection," he wrote. "Hurricanes. Tornadoes. Riots. Terrorists. Gangs. Lone criminals. These are perils we are sure to face—not just maybe. It's not paranoia to buy a gun. It's survival."[30] This fear-based rhetoric is toxic and morally abhorrent, but strategically brilliant. Not only does it heighten fears of disaster in the general populace, it also fits perfectly with evangelicals' premillennial "end times" expectation that terrible calamities and social chaos will signal the Second Coming of Jesus.

After grabbing his readers' attention with strident appeals to paranoia in "Stand and Fight," LaPierre segued into his marketing pitch by equating the "responsible behavior" of buying guns with protecting American freedom, apparently meaning protecting America from the first African American president:

> Since the election [of Barack Obama], millions of Americans have been lining up in front of gun stores . . . exercising their freedom while they still have it. . . . Millions of Americans are using market forces like never before to demonstrate their ardent support for our firearm freedoms. That's one of the very best ways we can Stand and Fight. . . . We will buy more guns than ever.[31]

In this way the NRA rhetorical strategy purposely exploits racism and racial fears. One journalist wrote of the 2015 NRA video *How to Stop Violent Crime,*

> I watched it in full and found it to be racist, offensive, and based entirely on untruths. All the key code words popularized by Fox News were included in the script: "thug," Chicago as a "Third World nation," "criminal gangbangers, etc., . . ." [but] "one "thug" is conspicuously left out of the NRA's video: Dylan Roof, the gunman who murdered nine African-American congregants in a [Charleston, South Carolina] prayer meeting. . . . NRA leaders like LaPierre know fearmongering about black youth works wonders in terms of selling more guns.[32]

When LaPierre talks about the threat of riots, terrorists, and gangs, he is consciously conjuring the specter of violent people of color, primarily black men. The perception of African American males as overwhelmingly criminal is so entrenched in society that "talking about crime is talking about race."[33] Yet, one is hard-pressed to see any sign of a pushback from right-wing evangelicals against the NRA's poorly veiled dog-whistle racism, which apparently comports quite comfortably with the retrograde racial attitudes of the masses of right-wing evangelicals.

Instead, evangelicals parrot the NRA's misuse of the Bible and its hyperbolic propaganda despite that organization's hypocrisy, its willingness to jettison its foundational principles for malicious racial reasoning, its abiding cynicism, and its voluminous false-hoods. But far worse, their support of the NRA's conflating of the Christian cross with gun ownership is nothing short of blasphemy. The cross represents salvation, love, and willingness to be faithful to God, no matter the consequences. Granted, guns can be instruments of love, as when protecting innocents from deadly harm. But overwhelmingly, guns do not protect innocents. Instead, many millions die unnecessarily because of them: infants, teens, spouses, elders, men and women just living their lives. There is simply no legitimate way that the self-serving and, ultimately, deadly claims of the NRA can be reconciled with the witness of the Bible and Gospel of Jesus Christ.

There are 393 million guns in America, more than one for every person in this country. If the only issue was gun ownership, that would be enough. But for gun manufacturers, that will never suffice; they will never stop reaching for greater profits, no matter the human cost. This is the unholy bargain right-wing evangelicals have made with their support of the NRA.

Despite the unfathomable pain and harm caused by the wide availability of guns in this country, by fighting so hard for unlimited gun rights with no background checks, no waiting periods, and unhampered access to deadly assault rifles, evangelicals show more concern for their individual agendas and desires than for the safety of the communities that nurture them. Right-wing evangelical Christians loudly extoll the dubious virtues of the Second Amendment but seem to little remember that somewhere in the annals of their faith is the Second Commandment: "Thou shall not kill." In any reasonable interpretation, "Thou shall not kill" also means "Thou shall not in any way facilitate killing" by making instruments of death so readily available to so many. As they fight for a right that is not God given and is only implied in the Second Amendment, these evangelicals must be reminded that the Second Commandment is not the Second Request. They in fact have a biblical responsibility to fight for reasonable gun control laws that will save the lives of untold numbers of children of God. In this time of virtually unfathomable gun carnage in America, this is one of the most pressing ways right-wing evangelicals can finally prove that they are fully pro-life, not just antiabortion, and at least begin to express the love for the neighbors outside their own racial and ideological tribe that their Savior requires of them.

CHAPTER 8

THE WORKMAN IS WORTHY OF HIS KEEP

*The Unholy Alliance of Big Business
and Right-Wing Evangelicals*

I N APPRECIATION OF the service and sacrifices borne by America's
World War I veterans, a grateful Congress passed the World War
Adjusted Compensation Act of 1924, which granted $1,000 "bo-
nus" pension certificates to the veterans (the equivalent of $18,000
today), which were redeemable in 1945. But when the Great Depression hit in 1929, with its shockingly high unemployment and
lack of public assistance, desperate veterans requested their bo-
nuses immediately. Their pleas went unanswered. Finally, in May
1932, three hundred determined veterans journeyed to the nation's
capital to demand immediate redemption of their bonus certificates, which for many, if not most, meant the difference between
hunger and full bellies, homelessness and adequate shelter. By July
of that year, some 43,000 Bonus Marchers and their families had
descended on the capital and built more than two dozen camps—
the largest with 15,000 people. They ran these camps with organizational discipline like a bona fide city, vowing to stay until their
demand was met.

In July, Congress voted down a bill to grant the veterans' petition. Adding insult to injury, Congress also directed that their campsites be dismantled and the protestors forcibly moved. They refused. President Herbert Hoover, fearing a riot after two veterans were killed during an armed police eviction gone awry, ordered General Douglas MacArthur to lead a full military assault against the encampments, replete with tanks, cavalry, tear gas, and infantry with fixed bayonets. A baby and a twelve-year-old boy were killed, and hundreds were injured. The Bonus Marchers' protest was crushed and the protestors literally chased out of town, embittered and empty-handed.

Six months later, at the height of the Depression, Franklin D. Roosevelt was inaugurated to the American presidency. In his book *The Essential America,* Senator George McGovern describes the America that Roosevelt encountered:

> He found not only much of the nation's workforce idled, but millions of workers without organization, representation, collective bargaining rights, or unemployment insurance to protect them. He found older people haunted by the specter of insecurity and poverty in the closing years of their lives. He saw hardworking farm families losing their crops, their markets, their land, and their homes. As farmers lost their purchasing power, main-street businesses also went under. Banks were failing and closing their doors, wiping out the lifetime savings of families.[1]

Moreover, relatively few regulations shielded American workers and consumers from the depredations of big business. For almost all the nation's history, big business essentially had been free to pursue profits however they chose, no matter how many people they hurt. The motto of industrialist James "Diamond Jim" Fisk (1835–1872) expressed what seemed to be the ethos of generations of business elites: "Never give a sucker an even break."[2] Henry Flagler, the business partner of John D. Rockefeller, who was dubbed a "robber baron" for his rapacious business practices, brazenly displayed his contempt for fair dealing with both competitors and workers with a plaque prominently displayed on his desk that declared, "Do unto others what they would do unto you—and do it first."[3] It was this mix of shameless greed and lack of government oversight that led to the Great Depression.

Surveying the wreckage of the economy and the frightening levels of poverty and want, President Roosevelt vowed to Frances Perkins, his secretary of labor and close confidante, "We are going to make a country in which no one is left out."[4] He straightaway inaugurated a sea change in the nation's philosophy of federal governance—for which the corporatists and wealthy elites of America have never forgiven him. Prior to Roosevelt's presidency, the federal government had actualized little responsibility for the care of the poorest and most vulnerable Americans. Even as the pain of the Depression increased, Roosevelt's predecessor, the politically conservative Herbert Hoover, had refused to give direct government aid, which he dismissively called "handouts."

It is often overlooked that, in addition to a keen political sense, Roosevelt also brought to his presidency a deep religious sensibility: a Good Samaritan sense of responsibility for those in need. After his death, Frances Perkins explained that, for him,

> foremost was the idea that poverty is preventable, that poverty is destructive, wasteful, demoralizing, and that poverty in the midst of potential plenty is morally unacceptable in a Christian and democratic society. [He] began to see the "poor" as people, with hopes, fears, virtues, and vices, as fellow citizens who were part of the fabric of American life instead of as a depressed class who would always be with us.[5]

It was his faith and his concern for humanity that moved Roosevelt to reject America's traditional laissez faire ("let it be") approach to governance. He believed that governmental leaders had a moral responsibility to respond to the people's needs, including providing care to the poorest and most vulnerable. He said that for him this meant

> to try to increase the security and happiness of a larger number of people in all occupations of life and in all parts of the country; to give them more of the good things of life, to give them a greater distribution not only of wealth in the narrow terms, but of wealth in the wider terms; . . . to give them assurance that they are not going to starve in their old age; to give honest business a chance to go ahead and make a reasonable profit, and to give everyone a chance to earn a living.[6]

He explained his philosophy further in his 1936 nomination acceptance speech: "We seek not merely to make Government a mechanical implement, but to give it the vibrant personal character that is the very embodiment of human charity."[7]

In March 1933, just three weeks after taking the oath of office, Roosevelt created the Civilian Conservation Corps (CCC), which provided employment, meals, clothing, and lodging, plus a dollar a day, for three million young men aged fifteen to twenty-five. This was the beginning of sweeping domestic reforms that prioritized the material needs of the people and came to be known as the New Deal. It included economic stimulus policies and bank stabilization policies, financial reform and consumer protections, public works and arts and culture programs, rural and farm assistance, housing aid and mortgage reform, enhanced health and public safety protections, land and wildlife conservation policies, trade protections, and regulations that returned millions of acres of land to Native Americans. New Deal policies greatly eased the suffering of millions, laid the groundwork for the creation of the American middle class, and continue to enhance the quality of the lives of the majority of Americans to the present day. These include Social Security, unemployment assistance, and particularly critical at a time when workers had no real protections, labor law reforms.

Christian leaders widely praised the New Deal for incorporating their "social ideas and principles." No less than the head of the Federal Council of Churches (precursor to the National Council of Churches) lauded the New Deal as reflecting Jesus's recognition of the "significance of daily bread, shelter, and security," which are highlighted in the Lord's Prayer and the parable of the sheep and the goats.[8]

But despite the New Deal's focus on alleviating widespread hopelessness and misery in America, many of the nation's corporate executives and wealthy elites seethed. Not only did the captains of industry now have less influence to tilt domestic policies toward their own interests; the New Deal also substantially foreclosed certain lucrative perquisites they had come to take for granted. Explains historian Kevin Phillips, "The New Deal raised the top individual tax brackets, eliminated [Treasury Secretary Andrew W.] Mellon's fiscal favors, tightened inheritance taxes, and eliminated the personal holding companies through which some of the rich had deducted the expenses of their estates, stables, horses, and planes."[9] Wealthy elites also saw governmental oversight of markets as an insulting challenge to the positions of power and leadership they believed were the rightful possession of their class. But perhaps the New Deal's greatest sin in the eyes of the captains of industry was that it shifted the government's resources toward the masses of workers and the unemployed poor. One corporate executive complained, "You can't recover prosperity by seizing the accumulation of the thrifty and distributing it to the thriftless and unlucky."[10]

The outraged economic elites were determined to fight back. In July 1934, du Pont brothers Pierre, Irenee, and Lammot, scions of the giant plastics manufacturer that bears their family name, organized a group of wealthy businessmen to oppose the New Deal's challenge to their interests. The group called itself the American Liberty League (ALL), but in actuality they were a rich "property holders' association," as Irenee du Pont admitted in private, a group whose real concern was protecting its members' vast financial interests and their right to generate unlimited profits without the nuisance of New Deal regulatory accountability.[11] Roosevelt quipped about the ALL: "It has been said that there are two great Commandments—one is to love God and the other is to love your neighbor. The two particular tenets of this new organization say you shall love God and then forget your neighbor."[12]

Several associations of evangelical business executives were formed for the sole purpose of opposing the New Deal. For example, the Texas-based Christian American Association (CAA) was established in the 1930s by a bellicose racist, Vance Muse. Supported by Texas oilmen, the CAA "held the distinction of being one of the first organizations in the country to champion what it termed the 'God-Given-Right-to-Work Amendment,'" an obvious union busting tool meant to reduce membership and deplete dues coffers.[13] By the end of World War II, eight states had adopted versions of the CAA's anti-union proposals.[14]

In 1934 the National Association of Manufacturers, a similarly outraged group of anti–New Deal industrialists, invited a little-known Christian minister, Rev. James Fifield, to address their national convention in New York City. Fifield was a Congregationalist minister based in Los Angeles with pronounced right-wing evangelical sensibilities. In his address Fifield boldly lauded the big business opponents of the New Deal as the heroes of America, if not its saviors. The audience was so electrified by Fifield's remarks that it was jokingly said their applause could be heard in New Jersey. Conceivably, it was on that evening, in the welter of opposition to the New Deal, that the modern unholy alliance between big business and right-wing evangelicals shifted into a higher gear. For this alliance was not new. In the late nineteenth century, businessmen had enlisted evangelical organizations to help them pacify an increasingly assertive labor force. The evangelist Dwight L. Moody, founder of Moody Bible Institute in Chicago, had warned in 1886, "Either these people are to be evangelized, or the leaven of communism and infidelity will assume such enormous proportions that it will break out in a reign of terror such as this country has never known."[15] What was new, however, was the broad front of cooperation between the forces that had begun.

Riding on the crest of the business community's enthusiastic reception, in 1935 Fifield founded Spiritual Mobilization to support their interests by battling what he characterized as the New Deal's "encroachment upon our American freedoms."[16] Funded by donations from some of the nation's wealthiest businessmen, including tire magnate Harvey Firestone and J. Howard Pew Jr. of Sun Oil, Spiritual Mobilization billed itself as a Christian organization, yet there is no evidence that it ever engaged in spiritual or evangelizing activities. Its sole apparent purpose was to discredit workers' rights and increased commercial regulatory protections. Fifield propagated what he presented as biblical and theological justifications for corporations' unbridled pursuit of profits. He called New Deal policies "pagan statism," which would "destroy . . . basic freedom and spiritual ideals."[17] Claiming that the New Deal was an effort to turn the United States into a "socialist society," a tactic still employed by right-wing evangelicals against progressive policies today, he sent to more than seventy thousand ministers a tract that sought to taint Roosevelt's policies with the specter of totalitarian Soviet socialism and anti-Americanism.[18] President Harry S. Truman explained this tactic years later:

> Socialism is a scare word they have hurled at every advance the people have made in the last 20 years. Socialism is what they called public [electric] power. Socialism is what they called social security. Socialism is what they called farm price supports. Socialism is what they called bank deposit insurance. Socialism is what they called the growth of free and independent labor organizations. *Socialism is their name for almost anything that helps all the people* [my emphasis].

Faith and Freedom, Spiritual Mobilization's monthly magazine, was supposedly a Christian-based publication, but its pages regularly railed against economic concerns such as price controls, Social

Security, unemployment insurance, minimum wages, federal taxation, and even veterans' benefits. In actuality, the magazine and Fifield's public rhetoric were as much akin to libertarianism as to Christianity. That remains largely the case with right-wing evangelicals today. This is deeply problematic, because in the final analysis libertarianism and Christianity are essentially incompatible.

Libertarianism is a political philosophy that claims that a legitimate government can have only three functions: enforcing contracts, protecting private property, and keeping the peace, which includes protecting borders.[19] Missing quite conspicuously is any mechanism for caring for members of society who are in need. Indeed, the focus of libertarianism is not on the welfare of the people or the public good. Its central concern is the preservation of individual property and wealth. In fact, in its most extreme forms it considers governmental assistance to the needy as theft: an immoral use of taxpayers' dollars without their permission.[20] In this regard, libertarianism is the antithesis of biblical ethics, which, as we saw in chapter 3, repeatedly enjoins upon governing authorities the responsibility to care for the vulnerable and the needy. Libertarianism repudiates the Good Samaritan's assumption of responsibility for the welfare of his neighbor, which Jesus presented as a model for his followers to emulate ("Do likewise," he said, Luke 10:25–37).

Political philosopher Michael J. Sandel further explains, "Libertarians favor unfettered markets and oppose government regulation, not in the name of economic efficiency but in the name of human freedom."[21] But evangelicals who uphold such "freedom" as their paramount value reveal their fundamentally flawed understanding of the Bible, for the ethic that pervades the entire biblical witness is not individual freedom or liberty. The historian Kevin Kruse calls this ideological conflation of libertarianism and Christianity "Christian libertarianism," which he describes as

> an effort . . . to appropriate classic libertarian arguments, which [don't] at all have to do with religion, and put a religious veneer on them to make them palatable for Americans. . . . Christian

libertarianism is essentially an effort to appropriate a political ideology that either had nothing at all to do with religion or was antithetical to religion and instead use it toward a set of ends that had a religious gloss to it.[22]

In other words, Christianity that embraces the social irresponsibility of libertarianism is not biblical Christianity. Instead it is *ideological* Christianity, which distorts the Gospel through the prism of individualism. Ideological Christianity vilifies as Soviet-style socialism the biblical mandate to care for the poor, speaks only of individual liberty and the power to impose its will, but never of love or compassion or sacrificing for others. It is based on the nonbiblical idea that people's main responsibility is to look out for themselves, not for neighbors and communities. It answers the question posed by the murderous biblical Cain—"Am I my brother's keeper?"—with an emphatic "No!"

In fact, as was noted in chapter 3, there is no word in the Hebrew of the Old Testament for *individual*. Except for perhaps the apostle Paul's notion of individual salvation, the Bible essentially rejects individualism for a more community-centered ethos. Rather than freedom, the overarching Gospel social ethic is epitomized by the Good Samaritan's practical enactment of love for one's neighbor. The Hebrew term the Bible uses, *ha'am*—"the people"—signifies that each person is first and foremost a member of a community. As also noted in chapter 3, biblical people defined themselves and judged their actions *dyadically*, through the eyes of their communities rather than as individual actors.[23] In fact, dyadic cultural forms have characterized virtually all traditional peasant-based cultures throughout history. For instance, the Xhosa and Zulu cultures in southern Africa are based on the notion of *ubuntu*. South African peace activist Mungi Ngomane observes, "The concept of *ubuntu* is found in almost all African Bantu languages. It . . . almost always denotes the importance of community and connection."[24] Nobel Peace Prize laureate Archbishop Desmond Tutu affirms Ngomane's observation. "The lesson of *ubuntu*," he explains, "is best described in a proverb that is found in almost every African language, whose translation is, 'A person is a person through other persons.' . . . [It] is similar to the Golden Rule found in most teachings: 'Do unto others as you would have them do unto you.'"[25] Historian Thomas E. Ricks writes that even in the eighteenth-century birth of American democracy, a paramount social ethic was "virtue" or "putting the common good before one's own interests . . . was the 'lynchpin' of public life—that is, the fastener that held together the structure."[26]

The biblical ideal has always focused on the collective, the community, that we should assume life-affirming responsibility for the well-being of our neighbors so everyone might have equal access to the good things of life. The depiction of the early Christian community in Acts 4:32–37, although probably idealized, nonetheless reflects such a spirit of shared communal responsibility for the welfare of their neighbors: "The whole group of those who believed were of one heart and soul . . . everything they owned was in common." In social and political terms, that is what "love your neighbor as yourself" means: accepting responsibility for the care and welfare of the needy and the vulnerable in society and wanting the same opportunities for them as one wants for oneself. Jesus himself repeatedly condemned selfish individualism, both implicitly ("If you wish to be perfect, go, sell your possessions, and give the money to the poor," Matthew 19:21) and explicitly ("Be on your guard against all kinds of greed," Luke 12:13–37; note verse 15). The apostle Paul also specifically inveighed against being unduly self-serving ("Do nothing from selfish ambition or conceit," Philippians 2:3–4). Unfortunately, right-wing evangelicals seem to overlook these admonitions. It is because of their individualistic libertarian ethos that right-wing evangelical Christians do not in any substantive way deign to answer—nor even to ask—the Gospel question "Who is my neighbor?" Indeed, one is hard-pressed to find any instances of them publicly speaking of love or care for others; they virtually never speak of the needs of "the least of these" in the public square unless their remarks are accompanied by efforts to proselytize new followers to their ideological cause. In public they are more likely to utter derisive, hateful, conspiratorial remarks. Their unwavering support for the pathologically self-serving, self-obsessed Donald Trump is consistent with this unbiblical logic.

To be fair, not all right-wing evangelicals embrace a libertarian ethos. Some subscribe to what might be called "accountable" individualism, which is a belief that everyone has a responsibility to God to be self-sufficient as a sign of faith in God's grace. These believers contend that social safety nets not only undermine self-reliance and independence but are also morally corrupting. Perversely, despite the Gospel's teachings to the contrary, helping and being helped by others are not seen as faithfulness to the Gospel's call, but instead as a corrupting influence that disincentivizes the desperately needy from relying solely on God.

Another form of individualism is a "crucicentrist" approach, so called because it places Jesus's atoning death on the cross at the center of social policy.[27] Subscribers to this belief see their primary responsibility as saving souls. For them, poverty, emotional trauma, and physical suffering all have one purpose: to drive one to the cross to call on Jesus for relief, which they hold as the first step on the sole path to eternal life in heaven. Trauma and desperation are considered boons if they drive the sick and bereft to the cross of Jesus, where they will be "born again," meaning that their souls are saved for all eternity. Thus, letting folks suffer poverty, want, illness, and trauma is considered a great act of compassion, because that distress can bring them to the salvation of the cross.

Neither approach is consistent with the biblical witness, however. Yes, Jesus did preach reliance on God in such passages as Matthew 6:25–34 ("But if God so clothes the grass of the field, which is alive today and tomorrow is thrown into the oven, will he not much more clothe you?" 6:30). But as we have seen, even a cursory reading of the gospels reveals that by far the primary concern of Jesus's teachings is caring for those among us who are in need.

As regards right-wing evangelicals' libertarian claims, it is crucial to understand that there is no biblical basis for their desire to shrink the size of government "so small it can be drowned in a bath tub," as Grover Norquist famously put it.[28] As we saw in chapter 3, what the Bible does mandate is that governments have a responsibility to care for their people's needs, as in the description of a king's successful reign: "'He defended the cause of the poor and needy, and so all went well. Is that not what it means to know me?' declares the Lord" (Jeremiah 22:16, NIV).

In essence, what this indicates is that the optimal size of any government by biblical standards is whatever size is needed to adequately provide for its most vulnerable persons. Right-wing evangelicals' libertarian insistence on minimal government is anti-biblical because it would gut the capacity of governments to fulfill the biblical mandate. Also to be rejected is their wide-reaching opposition to consumer regulatory protections, a position they take despite having full knowledge that corporations have historically exploited workers, defrauded consumers, and recklessly degraded the natural environment when they are allowed to be accountable to no one but themselves.

In his acceptance speech at the 1936 Democratic National Convention in Philadelphia, Franklin Roosevelt offered a vision of government that was the antithesis of libertarianism. "Government in a modern civilization," Roosevelt explained, "has certain inescapable obligations to its citizens, among which are protection of the family and the home, the establishment of a democracy of opportunity, and aid to those overtaken by disaster."[29] The speech was much maligned by right-wing evangelicals, yet it was much more in line with the biblical ideal than their Christian libertarianism.

The libertarian nature of the coalition between big business and right-wing evangelicals was on grand display in 1951 when Fifield and Spiritual Mobilization hosted a series of events celebrating the libertarian notion of "Freedom under God," a phrase newly coined by Fifield himself. Private companies enthusiastically trumpeted "Freedom under God" in ads and sponsored events tailored to advance the spurious notion that Christian support of industry is both mandated by the Bible and is an integral component of the

American Way. However, the battle they were actually waging was to protect a status quo that favored the business community and the personally wealthy. In his 1957 book *The Single Path,* Fifield was careful to make that clear: "[The present] system that provides so much for the common good and happiness must flourish under the force of the Almighty."[30] His implication is clear: America's status quo is guided by God, so there is no need to institute regulations to protect rank-and-file Americans from corporate exploitation and market abuses.

The same misappropriation of the biblical witness that legitimated Depression-era businessmen's singular focus on protecting their wealth and privilege is a major component of today's right-wing Christian evangelical worldview. Its philosophical thread runs through the Moral Majority and Jerry Falwell, through Pat Robertson and the Christian Coalition, through Tony Perkins and the Family Research Council (FRC). Falwell's screed in the Moral Majority's *Journal-Champion* periodical (later the *Moral Majority Report*) could just as well have been written by any right-wing evangelical today: "The greatest threat to the average American's liberty does not come from Communistic aggression . . . but from the growing encroachments of government bureaucrats that limit the freedom of Americans through distribution of rules and regulations."[31]

This individualistic "Freedom under God" libertarian ethos can be seen in bold relief in the right-wing evangelical opposition to wearing protective masks during the height of the COVID-19 pandemic and in their pastors' resistance to limiting church gatherings to stem the flow of infections and deaths. California pastor John MacArthur, the author of *The Statement on Social Justice and the Gospel,* wrote to his congregation that he "will not acquiesce to a government-imposed moratorium on our weekly congregational worship or other regular corporate gatherings. Compliance would be disobedience to our Lord's clear commands,"[32] which for him apparently does not include the command for shepherds to protect their flocks from harm. Florida pastor Rodney

Howard-Browne not only refused to honor the quarantine and safe-distancing directives. He actually encouraged his congregants to *physically* hug. "We are not stopping for anything," he said. "The Bible School will be open because we're raising up revivalists, not pansies."[33] In March 2020, Jerry Falwell Jr., then president of Liberty University (he resigned in 2020 in the aftermath of a sex scandal), reopened the campus to students at the height of the pandemic. This prompted a faculty member to respond, "Falwell's lack of concern does nothing to mitigate these students likely becoming vectors of the pathogen roaming around Liberty's campus and the Lynchburg community, interacting with professors and staff and other townspeople." Nonetheless, Falwell refused to revisit his directive.[34] These are textbook examples of how ideological Christianity's libertarian notion of individual freedom is accorded primacy over the biblically enjoined responsibility to care for the well-being of others.

Yet for all their insistence on exercising freedom, when it comes to the interests of big business, right-wing evangelicals' libertarian sensibilities consistently fade into a fog of hypocrisy. Rarely, if ever, do they criticize government assistance to big businesses, whether in the form of outsized tax breaks, subsidies, favorable reregulation in the guise of deregulation, or even direct infusions of cash. There was little discernible outcry from right-wing evangelicals during the economic crisis of 2007–2008 when the federal government bailed out banks to the tune of billions of dollars, or when, during the COVID-19 crisis of 2020, it directed most aid not to the struggling masses but to the nation's biggest businesses.[35]

One New Deal policy found particularly galling by right-wing evangelicals and business elites like the American Liberty League and the National Association of Manufacturers was the National Labor Relations Act of 1935, which established the National Labor Relations Board (NLRB) to enforce federal labor laws governing collective bargaining and unfair labor practices. Called the Wagner Act after Robert F. Wagner, the New York senator who introduced it, the act "created the legal architecture that legitimated unions,

transforming them from organizations the employers could ignore without penalty into legally binding mechanisms that could
practice collective [rather than individual] bargaining."[36] In 1940,
the Church League of America, founded in Chicago in 1937 to
counter the New Deal policies, made the reactionary claim to its
one hundred thousand members that the Wagner Act "tied the
hands of every employer (large or small) so that any criminal . . .
could go into any plant and start organizing the employees into a
dues paying corral regardless of the merits of the case."[37] Surely
reflecting the business community's sentiments, one rich corporate executive groused, "The government and administration of
these United States has been placed by a dumb, unthinking populace in the hands of notorious incompetents."[38] Thus, a continu-
ing consequence of the unholy alliance between big business and
right-wing evangelicals is its ongoing onslaught against the only
bulwark of protection that working folk of America have against
exploitation by management: trade unions.

Nineteenth-century evangelicals differed greatly from their
twentieth- and twenty-first-century right-wing counterparts in
that they shared and honored the Bible's regard for the plight of
workers. Earlier evangelicals viewed combatting the exploitation
of workers as an important issue of biblical faith. For example, labor was an issue of major discussion at the 1873 Sixth General Conference of the Evangelical Alliance. Citing Mark 2:27 ("The sabbath
was made for man, and not man for the sabbath," KJV), Rev. Mark
Hopkins, a former president of Williams College, called for laws
to protect the Christian Sabbath because, in addition to religious
considerations, it provided workers a much-needed day of rest,
which was part of its original intent.[39] Conference attendee William H. Allen, president of Girard College in Philadelphia, called
upon the government to enact several crucial measures in support of workers, including the eight-hour workday, fair appren-
ticeship laws, allocating public lands for those who would settle
them (presumably workingmen and -women rather than specula-
tors and railroad companies), and settling labor disputes through

mandatory arbitration. Allen even called for the establishment of a bureau of labor statistics to document the status of workers and give statistical heft to their claims for parity.[40]

In all this, the early evangelicals were guided by the Bible. A number of biblical passages specifically inveigh against exploitation of the laboring poor by the rich and the powerful, as in Deuteronomy 24:14–15 ("You shall not withhold the wages of poor and needy laborers") and Leviticus 19:13 ("You shall not keep for yourself the wages of a laborer until morning"). The prophet Jeremiah proclaimed, "Woe to him who builds his house by unrighteousness, and his upper rooms by injustice; who makes his neighbors work for nothing and does not give them their wages" (Jeremiah 22:13). Jesus, himself a *tekton* ("carpenter" or "manual laborer," as he is described in Matthew 13:55 and Mark 6:3),[41] spoke specifically about the struggles of workers. In Matthew 11:28–30, he talks about lightening the load of his overwhelmingly working-poor audience ("Come to me, all you that are weary and carrying heavy burdens, and I will give you rest").[42] In Matthew 20:1–16 he shares a parable in which standing crowds of landless workers are so desperate for work that some jump at the chance to earn a denarius a day, a non-living wage that could barely feed one person, much less a family, while others jump at the employer's beckoning without even asking their wage.[43] The landowner singles out and dismisses one worker as evil simply for questioning the fairness of his compensation, which can be read as pointing to the need for worker solidarity (the original Greek for verse 15 reads, "Is your eye evil because I am good?"). The parable's foregrounding of such exploitation becomes obvious when it is stripped of the theological overlay found in many traditions that transformed the "landowner" (*oikodespotes*, literally "house master") in the parable into God. The New Testament Letter of James, believed to be written by the brother of Jesus, decries the oppression of workers in an even more pointed fashion: "Listen! The wages of the laborers who mowed your fields, which you kept back by fraud, cry out, and the cries of the harvesters have reached the ears of the Lord of hosts" (James 5:4).

Of course, not only ancient workers were sorely abused and exploited. At the outset of the Industrial Age in the mid-nineteenth century, landless workers were subjected to abuses that often were worse. To make enough money to survive, vast numbers were forced to labor sixteen hours or more per day in the dirty, dangerous conditions of factories and mines—"dark Satanic mills," as the poet John Milton famously called them. Labor historian Philip Dray observes, "The toll of workplace suffering has always been something of a hidden detail of the American work experience." However, he contends that "never more so than in the years 1880–1910, when as many as ten thousand to fifteen thousand American workers a year perished in on-site accidents, with thousands more injured and sickened."[44] But the vast majority of workers had no choice; their ability to feed and clothe themselves and their families fully depended upon the workers' complete acquiescence to the demands of profit-obsessed employers. Children as young as six years worked ten-hour days, with boys of ten and twelve years laboring as much as fourteen hours daily for the equivalent of fifty or sixty cents. In his 1906 expose, *The Bitter Cry of the Children,* the British union organizer John Spargo described the plight of children compelled to labor in coal mines:

> From the cramped position they have to assume, most of them become more or less deformed and bent-backed like old men. . . . Accidents to the hands, such as cut, broken or crushed fingers, are common among the boys. Sometimes there is a worse accident: a terrified shriek is heard, and a boy is mangled and torn in the machinery, and disappears in the chute to be picked out later smothered and dead.

Unions arose in the nineteenth century to protect workers from such egregious abuses of their safety and dignity. Unions also strived to raise wages enough for workers to afford sufficient food and shelter. Eventually they became the foremost bulwark against the exploitation by big business. Evangelicals played important roles in the early years of the American union movement. Scottish immigrant Andrew Cameron (1834–1890) was one such early union organizer. A devout, Bible-quoting evangelical who considered union organizing a virtual Gospel mandate, Cameron helped to found the National Labor Union in 1866. It was said that Cameron, a tireless crusader for an eight-hour workday, "never missed a chance to point out that Jesus had been a workingman."[45] He put his convictions in biblical terms in an 1867 edition of his nationally circulated labor paper, the *Workingman's Advocate*. "Poverty exists," he wrote, "because those who sow do not reap; because the toiler does not receive a just and equitable proportion of the wealth which he produces."[46] This truth was so clear to the church family of James W. Kline, president of the International Brotherhood of Blacksmiths, that while he was in the midst of extended strike negotiations in 1911, they sent him a telegram that read in part, "God bless you in your efforts to do that for which the Master came."[47]

But big businesses leaders in the late nineteenth and early- to mid-twentieth centuries were heedless of the Gospel message. If they appealed to biblical faith at all, they used passages like Ecclesiastes 5:18 to justify onerous, at times horrific working conditions: "It is fitting to eat and drink and find enjoyment in all the toil with which one toils under the sun the few days of the life God gives us; for this is our lot." The implication here is clear: that workers should be satisfied with what was allotted to them and not ask for more, as if their employers are the unquestioned representatives of God.

Businesses used all kinds of strategies to keep workers from organizing to defend their own interests, even stooping to brutality and, on some occasions, to outright murder. A major malefactor was John D. Rockefeller. In 1913 miners went on strike for decent wages and safer working conditions at a Rockefeller-owned mine in Ludlow, Colorado. To break the mostly peaceful strike, Rockefeller prevailed upon the governor to send in two companies of the National Guard to augment the hired goons Rockefeller had dispatched to force workers back into the mines on his terms. On April 14, 1913, without warning or provocation, the combined armed force attacked the miners and their families with flares, rifles, and Gatling guns, killing fifty-five, including many children, some of whom were burned to death in their tents.[48]

In fact, corporate executives routinely overlooked and devalued the humanity of workers. In a 1906 lecture, while explaining the philosophy behind his innovation of the assembly line, its developer, Frederick Taylor, also expressed a view of labor that was widely held by corporate managers: "We do not ask the initiative of our men. We do not want any initiative. All we want of them is to obey orders we give them, do what we say, and do it quick."[49] He is said to have repeatedly told workers, "[We] have you for your strength and mechanical ability, and we have other men for thinking."[50] Robber baron Jay Gould (1836–1892) had long ago voiced the opinion that workers were nothing but pawns to be used as employers pleased. "I can hire one half of the working class to kill the other," he said.[51] That was not braggadocio. Gould was speaking aloud a strategy that big employers continued to use successfully through much of the twentieth century as they violently pitted striking workers against the desperate, sometimes starving scabs hired to replace them. Some businesses, then as now, shut down their operations completely rather than accept unionization.[52] Major corporations like General Motors, Goodyear Tire, and Ford Motor Company hired thugs and stockpiled leftover guns and munitions from World War I to break any strikes that might occur. In 1937 a young Walter Reuther, who later became president of the United Auto Workers union, was almost beaten to death by corporate goons while participating in a strike at Ford's River Rouge plant.

The attack on unions also took other forms. In 1935, retail giant Sears, Roebuck and Company hired attorney Nathan Shefferman as its head of Human Resources, "with explicit instructions to fight unions tooth-and-nail," an order that was in direct violation of the National Labor Relations Act. According to labor historian Jane McAlevey, Shefferman "turned the human resource department into a laboratory that developed cutting edge union-avoidance strategies that remain central to the industry even now."[53] The number of antiunion specialists has increased from a hundred in the 1960s to more than two thousand today. "Union busting is a field populated by bullies and built on deceit," wrote Martin Jay Levitt in *Confessions of a Union Buster*. "A campaign against a union is an assault on individuals and a war on truth. . . . The only way to bust a union is to lie, distort, manipulate, threaten, and always, always attack."[54]

In 1947, the passing of the Labor-Management Relations Act, called Taft-Hartley after its congressional sponsors, made it permissible for businesses to directly fund antiunion campaigns, to end wildcat strikes, and to end closed shops (in which union dues were compulsory) with so-called right-to-work laws that, in reality, allowed workers to "free ride"—that is, to receive the benefit of union activities and negotiations without contributing their fair share of union dues. Taft-Hartley also banned sympathy strikes from allied unions. This effectively made it illegal to strike in solidarity with other embattled workers in their quests for better wages and working conditions, a brazen and too often successful attempt to "resocialize" workers into de facto libertarians acting in their individual self-interests rather than acting as neighbors to other workers for the collective good.[55]

In 1949, the unholy alliance between right-wing evangelicalism and the antiunion efforts of big business gained another major shot in the arm. In September of that year, Rev. Billy Graham burst upon the scene at a massive tent revival in Los Angeles. By the time the revival ended two months later, some 350,000 people had attended the services. Graham's stature in evangelical Christianity was set. Yet for all his months of preaching a gospel of love, he'd showed little love for the workers forced to band together to protect themselves against corporate exploitation. Instead, Graham scathingly likened unions and their leaders to serpents and pestilence. The Garden of Eden, he said, was a paradise with "no union dues, no labor leaders, no snakes, no disease."[56] He unreservedly denounced strikes and condemned labor leaders as godless, charging that they "would like to outlaw religion, disregard God, the church, and the Bible,"[57] suggesting that unions were composed of the unchurched. Yet he never questioned the piety of the business executives who opposed workers' fights for fairness nor the unrighteousness of managements' quests to maximize profits without concern for the workers whose labor generated them. According to an early biographer, Graham

> is equally committed to the belief that Christianity and capitalism . . . are inseparably linked and that one cannot exist without the other. When Graham speaks of "the American way of life" he has in mind [what] the National Association of Manufacturers, the United States Chamber of Commerce, and the Wall Street Journal do when they use the phrase.[58]

There is little question that without unions, the lives of most workers would be much more tenuous, especially if left solely to the mercy of a managerial class that has historically cared more about profits than the well-being of those whose labor produces those profits. Yet right-wing evangelicals, ironically including many blue-collar workers influenced by their worship leaders, typically side with management by railing against unions and calling for their destruction, as if they are spawn of the devil. Corporate malefactors have rarely been targeted by evangelicals, while union busters have been lionized. For example, Wisconsin governor Scott Walker became an evangelical hero for breaking his state's teachers' union and stripping the Wisconsin government workers' union of collective bargaining rights.[59] Unsurprisingly, Tony Perkins and the Family Research Council gave substantial financial support to Walker's union-breaking efforts, lauding Walker and loudly denouncing the unions on Perkins's popular weekly radio program.[60]

The work strike is one of the few effective tools that workers have to press for their interests in the face of the immense corporate power and wealth. Yet corporate leaders and their right-wing evangelical cohorts denounce worker strikes and protests in the most sordid terms. A classic example of this line of attack is seen in a diatribe by Herbert J. Taylor (1893–1978), a right-wing evangelical Christian and an inductee into the American National Business Hall of Fame, who portrayed worker strikes as being fueled by patently ignoble instincts. "Most strikes and lockouts," he said, "can be traced directly to selfishness, insincerity, unfair dealings, or fear and lack of friendship among the men concerned."[61] Yet one is hard-pressed to find an instance of any prominent evangelical business figure describing a corporate manager in similarly derisive terms, no matter how greedy, callous, tightfisted, or manifestly unjust their actions are proven to be.

Indeed, right-wing evangelical attacks on workers' strikes are often libertarian arguments disguised as theology. A telling example appears on a widely read right-wing evangelical website, free-bible-study-lessons.com:

> If the employee—often through unions—forces the employer to pay more in wages and/or benefits than he is willing to, then that is oppression by extortion. . . . If the union uses tactics to try and force an employer to give more than he is willing to give then we have a sinful, unBiblical, oppressive situation. No Christian should support such activity which is actually criminal extortion. . . . This means that strikes are totally wrong. No Christians should ever vote for a strike for any reason.[62]

Despite its veneer of religiosity, this position stands on a morally fallacious assumption: that employers own the moral high ground simply because they are employers, and that they will always act justly and morally responsibly toward workers. The statement offers a moral judgment that flies directly in the face of decency: that workers have no right to insist they be paid a living wage or treated with dignity.

Resonances of this attitude can be seen in the dismantling of the Professional Air Traffic Control Officers (PATCO) union in

August 1981 by the right-wing evangelical darling, President Ronald Reagan. After negotiations with the Federal Aviation Authority (FAA) failed, union members voted to mount a strike for higher wages and, citing the high-stress nature of their jobs, sought a shorter workweek and an earlier retirement date. Knowing that Reagan had once headed the Screen Actors Guild labor union and had led its first strike, that he had championed Lech Walesa's Solidarity union in Poland, and that he had earlier promised PATCO that he would help it reach their goals, the union leaders expected the president to allow them and the FAA to work toward a solution. Instead, Reagan invoked the Taft-Hartley Act to fire all thirteen thousand members of the union, many of whom were forced into bankruptcy and impoverishment after being blacklisted for life from all government employment.[63] "We had bankruptcies by the thousands. We had people commit suicide," recalled one fired PATCO member. Reagan's action signaled to grateful corporate heads that it was open season on unions. "I don't think that any other strike ever affected employers so much. Employers suddenly began to get a lot of courage from Ronald Reagan."[64] Between 1983 and 1987, corporate giants Phelps Dodge, Hormel, and International Paper were emboldened to hire striker replacement workers rather than negotiate with their unions.[65] As a result, the number of major strikes against corporations dropped from some two hundred in 1980 to seventeen in 1999 to eleven in 2011.[66] Since Reagan's 1980 action, the number of unionized workers has gone from 25 percent of all workers to perhaps 6 percent today. Not coincidentally, workers' wages (adjusted for inflation) have essentially remained flat since 1980, while during the same period CEOs have seen their salaries explode from forty times their average workers' wages to more than three hundred times. This means that the average worker would have to work three hundred years or more to earn what the average CEO makes in *one year*. Without even the diminished presence of unions, this disgraceful ratio undoubtedly would be worse. There is no biblical measure by which this state of affairs can be considered just, yet not one

major right-wing evangelical individual or organizational voice
has been raised in opposition.

One of the most striking examples of the unholy marriage between right-wing evangelicals and big business is found in a 1990
Christian Coalition leadership manual. The manual states that
"God established His pattern for work," which it explains using
four Bible passages instructing slaves to be obedient to their masters as a model for modern employer-employee relations, including this passage from 1 Peter:

> Slaves, submit yourselves to your masters with all respect, not
> only to those who are good and considerate, but also to those
> who are harsh. For it is commendable if a man bears up under the
> pain of unjust suffering because he is conscious of God. (2:18–19)

The manual explains with no sense of irony, "Of course, slavery was abolished in this country many years ago, so we must apply
these principles to the way Americans work today, to employees
and employers." Then it draws a conclusion that could have been
written in feudal times: "Christians have a responsibility to submit to the authority of their employers, since they are designated
as part of God's plan for the exercise of authority on the earth
by man."

Right-wing evangelicals are not directly responsible for the
passing of anti-labor laws and policies, but their support has
played a major role in their successful adoption. The tragic consequence is that the masses of American workers, ironically including perhaps the bulk of their evangelical followers, endure some
of the most unfair working arrangements in the industrial world:

- America is the only industrial country that does not offer
  the legal right to workers to a vacation, paid or unpaid.
- For those fortunate enough to be granted a vacation, the
  norm is two weeks, while countries with a stronger union
  tradition routinely grant four or even six weeks of paid

leave: Germany and Britain grant a full month paid vacation; France, six weeks.

- American workers average 1,780 hours of work per year. That's 70 hours (almost ten days) per year more than the Japanese, 100 hours (two and a half workweeks) more than British workers, 266 hours (two and a half workweeks) more than the French, and 424 hours (ten and a half workweeks) more than German workers.[67]
- Adjusted for inflation, the federal minimum wage of $7.25 in 2020 is 37 percent *below* its buying power in 1968. If it had merely kept pace with inflation with no increases, it would be about $10, though still not a living wage in any region of this nation.

The chasm between the rich and the poor in America is greater today than at any time since the Great Depression. According to the Federal Reserve, the top 1 percent of American households received 23.8 percent of the national income in 2016, the highest percentage since the 1920s, and controlled a record-high 38.6 percent of the country's wealth.[68] The top 10 percent now receive nearly half of the nation's income (50 percent in 2015), up from one-third in the 1970s.[69] CEO compensation has grown 940 percent since 1978, while typical worker compensation has risen only 12 percent during that time.[70] As historian Steven Greenhouse observes, "The United States now has the weakest labor movement of any advanced industrial nation, and that's a major reason why income inequality has grown worse in America than in any industrialized nation."[71]

Because of unions' contributions to economic equality and their historic fight to defend human dignity, Pope Francis has called them "prophetic institutions." "There is no good society," he has declared, "without a good union."[72] Admittedly, there have been many times that unions have not been good, when they have fallen into corruption and abuse of their members' trust. But the corruption that has occurred in unions absolutely pales in comparison to that of corporations. The accounts are legion of corporate looters purposely driving viable business enterprises into the ground to plunder their every asset, destroying the infrastructure of whole communities in their wake, knowingly poisoning the environment (including poisoning communities' drinking water), destroying workers' livelihoods and robbing retirees of the pensions they'd rightfully earned through years of toil. In fact, despite the unrelenting onslaught unions have endured at the hands of big business and their right-wing evangelical collaborators, they have played a huge part in building America's middle class, the largest and richest in the world. They had key roles in attaining for workers the eight-hour workday, paid sick days and vacations, the federal minimum wage, the time-and-a-half overtime wage premium, lunch and restroom breaks, unemployment insurance, Medicare, civil rights laws, health insurance in the workplace, and the end of child labor and sweatshops. Their efforts have led to safer working conditions in some of the most dangerous professions in the United States, including the infamously risky profession of coal mining.[73] Moreover, unions have secured better wages and working conditions for their members than those of nonunion workers.[74] Union workers earn 13.6 percent more than comparable nonunion workers after adjusting for education, age, and other factors.[75] Seventy-five percent of union workers have employer-sponsored health plans, as opposed to 49 percent of nonunion workers.[76] Quite significantly in today's economic landscape, 83 percent of unionized workers participate in employer-sponsored retirement plans, compared to 49 percent of nonunion workers.[77] Unions have not managed to fully bridge America's gender pay gap, yet female union workers' wages average 98 percent of unionized males' wages, while nonunion women average just 78 percent.[78] Unions continue to stand fast against corporations' attempts to impose neofeudal control over labor.

Right-wing evangelicals continue to play a major role in the perpetuation of the vast chasm between the rich and the poor by their identification of Christianity with libertarianism, their virtually nonexistent criticism of corporate abuse, and their never-ending attempts to unravel the social safety net that is so crucial to a semblance of decent life for so many. In large part, evangelicals' unwavering support of the Trump administration furthered the corporate onslaught against unions by scrapping numerous job safety regulations and killing a ruling that extended overtime pay to millions of workers. But worse is what the right-wing evangelicals' hero Trump has done to Franklin Roosevelt's National Labor Relations Board.

Since Roosevelt established the NLRB in 1937, wages and labor conditions in America have improved immensely. The NLRB has worked diligently to guard workers' rights against constant attempts by corporate managers to erode them. For example, until the NLRB stepped in, the Koch brothers' Georgia Pacific Corporation claimed the right to terminate workers if they shared information on social media about *their own* wages, hours, and conditions of employment.[79] In 2014, the NLRB forced the company to repeal that practice. This is just one of myriad examples of NLRB rulings in the last three-quarters of a century that have vouchsafed workers' rights and labor freedom.

But the Trump administration, undergirded by the support of influential right-wing evangelical leaders, has weaponized the NLRB to instead *dismantle* workers' hard-earned rights. Laments labor attorney Lynn Rhinehart, "In decision after decision, the [Trump] NLRB has stripped workers of their protections under the law, restricted their ability to organize at their workplace, slowed down the union election process to give employers more time to campaign against the union, repealed rules holding employers accountable for their actions, and undermined workers' bargaining rights."[80] A telling example: Trump's NLRB has ruled that a worker may be disciplined for simply *mentioning* forming a union or for merely *referencing* an organizing effort to a fellow worker during the workday. Such outrageously oppressive actions fly squarely in the face of biblical justice and decency.

Jesus declared, "The laborer deserves to be paid" for their works (Luke 10:7; Matthew 10:10, "deserve their food"), but the laborer should also be treated like a neighbor. Shouldn't there be right-wing evangelical advocacy for a minimum wage that is a living wage? Why aren't the exorbitant multiples of CEO salaries a "Christian" issue for them? Why isn't there a right-wing evangelical position on corporations exporting jobs to cheaper labor markets, destroying the livelihoods of millions of American workers simply to increase profit margins and raise their stocks' market prices or raise shareholders' dividends by a few pennies per share? Of course, there should be. But ultimately, right-wing evangelicals support an unjust status quo of vast disparities between America's rich and its poor. This is anathema to the Gospel of Jesus Christ and destructive to the fabric of our nation. This is another area of American life in which right-wing evangelicals have abdicated the moral high ground they so piously claim in order to support morally indefensible policies that are the cause of extraordinary pain to those they should be striving to serve and love as their neighbors.

A SPIRIT OF ANTICHRIST

WE HAVE SEEN HOW seriously so many of America's early evangel-icals embraced the community-affirming commandment to "love your neighbor as yourself." So seriously, in fact, that it in-spired them to actively oppose chattel slavery, to organize to offer succor to the needy, and to decry the economic exploitation of the masses. So how, then, has the love-affirming evangelicalism of the past become today's forward legion of division and exclusion, a raging Christian faction openly supporting persons and policies that are essentially antithetical to the message of Jesus Christ? I be-lieve an answer is offered by the very Bible that evangelicals profess to live by. The answer is this: that they have succumbed to what the First Epistle of John in the New Testament calls "the spirit of the antichrist" (4:3).[1]

Now, when I speak of a "spirit of antichrist" I am not talking about a monstrous supernatural being like the "beast" in the book of Revelation (which, by the way, never mentions an antichrist), or the "man of lawlessness" in 2 Thessalonians (2:3–10), or the mur-derous, manipulative figure found in popular media like Tim La-Hayes's *Left Behind* book series, or horror movies like *The Omen*. In fact, I'm not talking about a singular figure at all; 1 John uses both "antichrist" and "antichrists." What I'm talking about are ideolo-gies and public pronouncements that cynically distort the teachings of Christ—*in the name of Christ*—to serve the selfish interests of a particular individual or group. This is reflected in the identification of a spirit "not from God, . . . the spirit of the antichrist," as the motivating force of "antichrists" (see 1 John 4:2–3), by which the writer meant those who falsely portrayed the nature of Jesus and, thus, also the nature of his mission in the world. The early church father Polycarp (69–ca. 155 CE) used the term *antichrist* similarly, implying both individuals and groups.[2] First John 4:3 also indicates that the spirit of antichrist was not limited to John's time; it is an ongoing phenomenon, both "coming" and "already in the world." The great fourth-century theologian Augustine offers a clarifying summary: "For the Word of God is Christ: *whatsoever is contrary to the Word of God is in Antichrist*" (my emphasis).[3]

First John waxes tenderly about loving others and experiencing spiritual communion with God. It also offers several admonitions. Perhaps the most significant is to beware of false teachings: "I write these things to you concerning those who would deceive you" (2:26). The primary false teaching the letter is concerned with is what has come to be called the *docetic heresy*. This heresy held that Jesus was not a being of flesh and blood. Instead, its adherents asserted, Jesus was a phantasm who only seemed (*dokein,* "to seem") to have an earthly body, which was the conclusion of those who couldn't accept that the one they thought to be their victorious deliverer from worldly oppression instead died a humiliating, ignominious human death at the hands of the world.

This docetic notion of Jesus's crucifixion presented a challenge to the very foundations of the nascent Christian faith, because if it was only a phantasm of Jesus that was crucified, if it only *seemed* that Jesus himself had been crucified, then he did not die on the cross to atone for the sins of the world. Without Jesus's death on the cross there could be no resurrection, which was the confirming evidence of Jesus's divinity and the locus of Christian hope. Without the divine imprimatur of the resurrection to commend Jesus's life-affirming teachings, then if those teachings were remembered at all, they would be just another among a series of fanciful narratives, interesting parables, and pithy aphorisms circulating in the Mediterranean basin. Furthermore, if the docetic rejection of Jesus's full humanity were to prevail, there was the real danger that it would mean the demise of the budding Christian faith. Yet, John's letter reflects that his main fear was not that those outside the community of Christ believers would use the docetic heresy to attack the faith. He realized that the real danger to the faith was the misleading ideas spread by his fellow believers. As far as John was concerned, those who circulated distortions of the foundational truths of the faith—even those among his fellow Christ worshippers—were antichrists, opponents of Christ possessed by a spirit of antichrist.

I believe that like those the writer of 1 John railed against in his day, today's right-wing evangelicals are also imbued with a spirit of antichrist that has them traffic in another kind of docetic heresy, one that dismisses as illusory and phantasmic the aspects of the Gospel that do not suit their dominationist agenda. Like true docetists, they would have us believe that the social justice imperative of the Bible, its command to offer hospitality to immigrants, and the political radicality of Jesus and his commandment to "love your neighbor as yourself" are not what they seem; that they are instead figments of a mistaken biblical imagination or the product of seduction by Satan and his liberal emissaries.

It is a spirit of antichrist and the docetic heresy it has weaponized that have possessed right-wing evangelicals to support and even lead assaults on truth and decency; to cosign expressions of hate rather than striving to spread love; to spew spiteful invective against other faiths rather than accepting them as fellow children of God; and, most appallingly, to extol Donald Trump as God's chosen vessel in the highest corridors of earthly power, even as his malevolent words and deeds dishonored God by sowing chaos and deadly disunion among us. Rather than striving to build harmony, they applauded the construction of spiteful walls of division. Rather than standing on moral consistency, they offered shameless excuses for the rankest of hypocrisies. Rather than suing for peace, they embraced the death-dealing agenda of the NRA. Rather than spreading gospel affection, they demonized Muslims and "liberals" and accused those who question their machinations as being part of absurd, murderous conspiracies.

How did this come to pass? Who or what caused modern-day right-wing evangelicals to be possessed by this spirit of antichrist? Their outraged opposition to Franklin Roosevelt's New Deal protections notwithstanding, a spirit of antichrist raised its head among them in earnest in the 1970s when they made the iniquitous choice to openly defend white supremacy. But their full possession by a spirit of antichrist can be considered to have occurred when their leaders made a devil's bargain with Donald Trump to defend his avalanche of lies, hate mongering, blatant moral indecency, and outright attacks on the democratic rule of law in return for his support of their agenda to dominate American society. For this they chose to ignore all that Jesus has taught about truth, compassion, and care for community, while eschewing the love-leavened lessons of the Good Samaritan, the Beatitudes, and the Sermon on the Mount.

It is because of this spirit of antichrist that dominating American society is now more important to right-wing evangelicals than maintaining the integrity of the Christian Gospel, more important than honesty or love or care for those who look to them for truthful guidance and nurturance. In God's name they have visited upon our nation a plague of lies, a harvest of hate, the rotted fruit of unchecked corruption and moral chaos, and unleashed levels of racial antipathy and xenophobia that untold numbers of lovers of God and humanity had labored and died to keep from ever again seeing the light of day. Not only is their worldview not loving, not generous, not socially inclusive, but the notion of religious freedom they so extol extends no farther than their own ranks. They have so savaged the social justice legacy of their evangelical forebears that it is now unrecognizable.

With the rest of the world, right-wing evangelicals witnessed four years of Trump's myriad depredations—his voluminous lies,[4] his reprehensible corruption, his racism and disregard for democratic norms and rule of law. With the rest of us, they witnessed his callous betrayal of his presidential oath to protect the American people with his refusal for months to alert us to the true deadliness of the COVID-19 virus, which a Columbia University National Center for Disaster Preparedness research study concluded is responsible for at least 130,000 unnecessary American deaths.[5] As I write in December 2020, nearly a year after learning how deadly the COVID-19 virus is, when more than three thousand Americans are dying daily from it, Trump has yet to condescend to offer a comprehensive plan to address the horrendous toll in human suffering. Yet despite his unequaled agglomeration of ungodly assaults on the peace and well-being of American society, 76 percent of white evangelicals still voted to reelect him.[6] This is an abdication of moral authority of a magnitude not seen in this country since the widely entrenched Christian defense of human enslavement.

Will right-wing evangelicals ever reclaim their moral authority? That is hard to say. They do not seem to realize that they have lost their moral bearings and, therefore, are making no effort to regain them. But if one day they should seek to become fully worthy of the faith identity they claim, they would have to confront the insidious evil of their white supremacist roots and the destructive false assumptions of their Christian nationalism. They would have to admit to and repent for the political and moral carnage they have helped to wreak upon American society. They would have to strive with as much effort and conviction to repair the rends in America's social fabric as they incited to tear it apart. All this would take an inclination to humility and comity that they have yet to evince. And it must not be overlooked that many right-wing evangelicals remain unmovably mired in racism and incivility. Those persons will not change. They are comfortable with their evil. Yet, although the masses of right-wing evangelicals embrace what is terribly wrong, I believe that many among them are sincerely wrong; that is to say that they are sincere about their faith but have been woefully misled in its application. Thus, perhaps there is a measure of hope for the movement one day. Indeed, in the waning weeks of the 2020 reelection campaign of President Donald Trump, several right-wing evangelicals publicly spoke out against his efforts to remain in office, including Jerushah Duford, granddaughter of Billy Graham and niece of Franklin Graham, who courageously told the *New York Times*, "This president doesn't represent our faith." John Huffman, who once was pastor to President Richard Nixon, unreservedly disavowed Trump as "an immoral, amoral sociopathic liar who functions from a core of insecure malignant narcissism."[7]

But for the vast majority of the leaders of right-wing evangelicalism, I harbor no such hopes, for it is such as these of whom Jesus spoke:

> *Isaiah prophesied rightly about you hypocrites, as it is written,*
> *"This people honors me with their lips,*
> *but their hearts are far from me;*
> *in vain do they worship me*
> *teaching human precepts as doctrines."*
> *You abandon the commandment of God and hold to human tradition.*
>   *(Mark 7:6–8)*

I leave them to the judgment of their consciences and to the just mercy of their Lord. To the rest of us I offer the words of Paul, the apostle who served Jesus so well:

> I urge you, brothers and sisters, to keep an eye on those who cause dissensions and offenses, in opposition to the teaching that you have learned; avoid them. For such people do not serve our Lord Christ, but their own appetites, and by smooth talk and flattery they deceive the hearts of the simple-minded. (Romans 16:17–18)

ACKNOWLEDGMENTS

T HIS IS NOT the book I set out to write. It is the book I had to write in the maelstrom of madness bedeviling our nation if I was to be true to myself and the passion of my convictions. It was more than a notion to write while assailed by the daily trauma of rabid Trumpism and the day-to-day psychic drag of the pandemic quarantine, but fortunately I was gifted along the way with the support of great friends, family, and colleagues. Warm thanks to those who read early drafts or contributed helpful insights to this work, including Rodney Sadler, Joerg Rieger, Gar Alperowitz, Valerie Toney Parker, Brenda N. Johnson, Iva Carruthers, Sean Cort, and that glowing spirit and avatar of love, Bishop Yvette Flunder.

My beloved sister and brother in-law, Linda and Dennis Motley, also were gracious readers, as was my friend and brother for life Henry Rock. As always, my dear friend Stephanie Berry offered incisive remarks and critiques that helped to keep me on point. In addition, I offer a special word of thanks to my cherished friend of more than four decades, Brenda Nurah Johnson, for her loving patience with the many emails and phone calls that went unanswered during my months of writing sequestration.

For their friendship, intellectual companionship, and inspiration, I thank Michael Eric Dyson, Eddie Glaude, Marc Lamont Hill, Josef Sorett, Gary Dorrien, Raphael Warnock, and those giants of modern Christian justice-making, Reverends Jesse Jackson and J. Alfred Smith Sr. I also thank my friends and indefatigable evangelical freedom fighters Jim Wallis and Lisa Sharon Harper for their undying Gospel witness, as well as my dear brother Cornel West, whose intellectual influence and friendship are invaluable and ongoing. And I am particularly indebted to the brilliant writings of Randall Balmer and my fellow traveler Robert P. Jones for insights that greatly enriched my work.

I owe a special word of appreciation to Adrienne Ingrum, whose literary wisdom helped me envision this book. Many thanks to my wonderfully understanding and patient editor, Amy Caldwell, and all the folks at Beacon Press. And to Tanya McKinnon of the McKinnon Literary Agency: you are everything that a writer could hope for in an agent. Thank you, Michael Eric Dyson, for bringing us together.

Finally, I thank my wife, the brilliant writer and literary critic Dr. Farah Jasmine Griffin, for her ever wise counsel and spike of encouragement when I thought I could not write another word. Without her, there would be no book. But most importantly, I thank both Farah and the mercy of God for the blessing of her unflagging support and her life-sustaining love that continues to keep me from falling.

NOTES

INTRODUCTION

1. For another example of a hierarchy of gospel values, see Irene Fowler, "The Trump Brand and the Making of Christian Values," in *The Spiritual Danger of Donald Trump*, ed. Ron Sider (Eugene, OR: Cascade Books, 2020), 48.

2. Quoted in Scott Wright, *Oscar Romero and the Communion of the Saints* (Maryknoll, NY: Orbis, 2009), 68.

CHAPTER 1: WE HAVE NO KING BUT CAESAR

1. Pew Research Center, "Evangelical Approval of Trump Remains High, but Other Religious Groups Are Less Supportive'" March 18, 2019; Tom Gjelten, "2020 Faith Vote Reflects 2016 Patterns," NPR.org, November 8, 2020.

2. Hannah Butler and Kristin Du Mez, "The Reinvention of 'Evangelical' in American History: A Linguistic Analysis," *Anxious Bench*, May 31, 2018.

3. Mark S. Hamilton, "A Strange Love? Or: How White Evangelicals Learned to Stop Worrying and Love the Donald," in *Evangelicals: Who They Have Been, Are Now, and Could Be*, ed. Mark A. Noll et al. (Grand Rapids, MI: Eerdmans, 2019), 221.

4. Katherine Stewart, *The Power Worshippers: Inside the Dangerous Rise of Religious Nationalism* (New York: Bloomsbury, 2019), 4.

5. See John Fea, *Was America Founded as a Christian Nation? A Historical Introduction* (Louisville, KY: Westminster John Knox, 2011). Also see David L. Holmes, *The Faiths of the Founding Fathers* (New York: Oxford University Press, 2016).

6. Andrew L. Whitehead, Samuel L. Perry, and Joseph O. Baker, "Make America Christian Again: Christian Nationalism and Voting for Donald Trump in the 2016 Presidential Election," *Sociology of Religion* 79, no. 2 (May 19, 2018): 147–71.

7. George Barna, "National Christians: The Big Election Story in 2016," December 1, 2016. See Noll et al., *Evangelicals*, 218–19.

8. Quoted in Eliza Griswold, "Evangelicals of Color Fight Against the Religious Right," *New Yorker*, December 26, 2018. See Michael O. Emerson

and Christian Smith, *Divided by Faith: Evangelical Religion and the Problem of Race in America* (New York: Oxford University Press, 2000).

9. Robert P. Jones, *White Too Long: The Legacy of White Supremacy in American Christianity* (New York: Simon & Schuster, 2020).

10. John Fea, *Believe Me: The Evangelical Road to Donald Trump* (Grand Rapids, MI: Eerdmans, 2018), 115.

11. Jacob Jarvis, "Pastor Calls Trump 'Most Pro-Black President in My Lifetime' as New Poll Gives Biden 64-Point Lead Among Black Voters," *Newsweek,* May 22, 2020.

12. Justin Taylor, "The Supreme Court and the Convoluted Case for Trump," *The Gospel Coalition,* September 29, 2016.

13. Frederick W. Danker, ed. *A Greek-English Lexicon of the New Testament and Other Early Christian Literature,* 3rd ed. (Chicago: University of Chicago Press, 2000), 609.

14. See Jonathan Wilson-Hartgrove, *Revolution of Values: Reclaiming Public Faith for the Common Good* (Downers Grove, IL: IVP, 2019), 125.

15. Political scientist Elizabeth Oldmixon explains, "These are the folks who believe that there will be a millennium in the future, a golden age, where Christ reigns on Earth, [and] they believe that before Christ will return, there will be a tribulation where Christ defeats evil. There will be natural disasters and wars. . . . Then at the end of that period, the people of the Mosaic covenant, including the Jews, will convert. Then after their conversion, the great millennium starts." Quoted in Sean Illing, "This Is Why Evangelicals Love Trump's Israel Policy," Vox.com, May 14, 2018. Also see Chris Hedges, *American Fascists: The Christian Right and the War on America* (New York: Free Press, 2008).

16. Peter Montgomery, "Group That Runs Fundamentalist Bible Studies for Cabinet and Congress Growing 'Beyond Our Wildest Imaginings,'" *Right Wing Watch,* April 18, 2018.

17. Michael D'Antonio and Peter Eisner, *The Shadow President: The Truth About Mike Pence* (New York: Thomas Dunne, 2018), 11.

18. Stewart, *The Power Worshippers,* 40.

19. See Steven Kinzer, *Overthrow: America's Century of Regime Change from Hawaii to Iraq* (New York: Henry Holt, 2006).

20. Robert P. Jones, *The End of White Christian America* (New York: Simon & Schuster, 2017), 81.

21. See Jim Wallis, "The Religious Right Will Rise and Fall with Donald Trump," *Sojourners,* October 19, 2017.

22. Jerry Mazza, "Jerry Falwell, Jr., Calls Donald Trump the 'Dream President' for Evangelicals," *Huffpost,* April 30, 2017.

23. "Rev. Graham: Trump 'Defending Christian Faith' More Than Any Recent President," *Fox News Insider,* January 21, 2018.

24. R. Albert Mohler, "Donald Trump Has Created an Excruciating Moment for the Evangelical," *Washington Post,* October 9, 2016.

25. William J. Barber II, "Open Letter to Donald Trump's Campaign," CommonDreams.org, July 5, 2016.

26. Mark Galli, "Trump Should Be Removed from Office," *Christianity Today,* December 2019.

27. Don Nori Sr., "Is Donald Trump the President We Need?," *Charisma News,* October 2, 2015.

28. Maxwell Tani, "Trump on God: 'I Don't Have to Ask for Forgiveness,'" *Business Insider,* January 17, 2016.

29. David Brody and Scott Lamb, *The Faith of Donald J. Trump: A Spiritual Biography* (New York: Broadside Books, 2018), 152.

30. Susan Wright, "Trump Knows Easter," *Red State,* March 27, 2016.

31. Michelle Boorstein, "Trump on God: 'Hopefully I Won't Have to Be Asking for Much Forgiveness,'" *Washington Post,* June 18, 2016.

32. Matt Wilstein, "Trump to Sean Spicer: 'I've Done So Much for Religion,'" *Daily Beast,* June 3, 2020.

33. Quoted in Michael Stone, patheos.com, October 6, 2020.

34. See Tara Isabella Burton, "The Biblical Story the Christian Right Uses to Defend Trump," *Vox,* March 5, 2018.

35. This refers to Cyrus, the pagan Persian emperor called a "messiah" in Isaiah 45, because it was believed that he was anointed ("chosen by God") to bring home the descendants of the kidnapped Judahite elites from their exiled captivity in Babylon. But the comparison does not hold. This was not a simple act of compassion. It seems certain that Cyrus repatriated the Judahites to serve as bureaucrats to administer the western edge of the Persian empire that held their own people as imperial subjects.

36. Miriam Adelson and Israel Hayom, "Miriam Adelson: A Time of Miracles," *Las Vegas Review-Journal,* July 6, 2019.

37. Kyle Mantyla, "Christian Leaders and Politicians Will Be Murdered If Trump Is Not Re-Elected," *Right Wing Watch,* June 19, 2019.

38. Brian Tashman, "Mary Colbert: God Will Curse Trump's Opponents and Their Children and Grandchildren," *Right Wing Watch,* April 3, 2017.

39. Anugrah Kumar, "Prosperity Gospel Preacher Paula White Prays for Donald Trump: 'Any Tongue that Rises Against Him Will Be Condemned,'" *Christian Post,* October 3, 2015.

40. Fea, *Believe Me,* 124.

41. For Trump's pathological narcissism, see Bandy X. Lee and Robert Jay Lifton, eds., *The Dangerous Case of Donald Trump: 27 Psychiatrists and Mental Health Experts Assess a President* (New York: Thomas Dunne, 2017); and Leonardo Blair, "Robert Jeffress Thanks God for Trump's Selfless Desire to Be President," *Christian Post,* January 26, 2016.

42. Quoted in Randall Balmer, "An End to Unjust Inequality in the World," *Church History and Religious Culture* 94 (2014): 506.

43. S. H. Waldo, "The Evidence of the World's Ultimate Reform," *Oberlin Quarterly Review* 4 (July 1849): 288.

44. Charles Finney, *Lectures to Professing Christians Delivered in the City of New York in the Years 1836 and 1837* (New York: J. S. Taylor, 1837), 321. Quoted in Balmer, *Evangelicalism in America*, 57.

45. Jared Yates Sexton, *American Rule: How a Nation Conquered the World but Failed Its People* (New York: Dutton, 2020), 14–15.

46. See Carol Anderson, *We Are Not Yet Equal: Understanding Our Racial Divide* (New York: Bloomsbury, 2018), passim.

47. Jones, *White Too Long*, 81ff.

48. This verse is part of the *Haustafeln,* or "Household Code," in Ephesians 5:21–6:9 and Colossians 3:8–4:1. However, no part of the Household Code can be traced to any pronouncement of Jesus. In addition, many scholars either question or deny that Paul wrote Ephesians, citing grammatical and theological differences from Paul's letters that are universally recognized by scholars as authentic. See Victor Paul Furnish, "Epistle to the Ephesians," in *The Anchor Bible Dictionary*, vol. 2, ed. Hans Dieter Betz et al. (New York: Doubleday, 1992), 539–41. Also see n. 56 below.

49. The "curse of Ham" is an apology for slavery contrived for American enslavers. It goes like this: In the biblical narrative, Noah's son Ham laughed at Noah when finding him drunk and naked. As punishment, Ham's son Canaan was cursed by God to serve as a slave to his brothers. White supremacists claimed this as a divine declaration that all descendants of Ham, who somehow became the progenitor of all people of dark hue, should forever be slaves to Noah's other sons, who are the supposed progenitors of white people. In this way they claimed racial chattel slavery was biblically mandated and thus justified.

50. Quoted in Emerson and Smith, *Divided by Faith*, 25.

51. The following section relies heavily on Randall Balmer, *Evangelicalism in America* (Waco, TX: Baylor, 2016).

52. Balmer, *Evangelicalism in America*, 44.

53. Balmer, *Evangelicalism in America*, 511.

54. Balmer, *Evangelicalism in America*, 510.

55. "Thoughts on the Importance and Improvement of Common Schools," *Christian Spectator*, n.s. 1 (1827): 85. 5.

56. For example, see Paul T. Bristow, *What Paul Really Said About Women: The Apostle's Liberating Views on Equality in Marriage, Leadership, and Love* (San Francisco: HarperOne, 1991). Also Marcus J. Borg and John Dominic Crossan, *The First Paul: Reclaiming the Radical Visionary Behind the Church's Conservative Icon* (San Francisco: HarperOne, 2010). Of the thirteen letters in the Bible attributed to Paul, his authorship of several has long been in question because of conflicting ideas and different writing styles and terminology. There are indications, for instance, that several of the letters written in Paul's name (Ephesians, Colossians, Hebrews, 1 and 2 Timothy, and Titus) were penned by one or more of Paul's followers to address issues and circumstances in ways they believed were consistent

with Paul's teachings. This practice, called pseudepigraphy, was widely used in religious writings in late antiquity. However, this practice does not necessarily diminish their scriptural value. The letters that scholars most confidently attribute to Paul himself consistently treat women as the equals of men. In the last chapter of Paul's letter to the church at Rome, of the twenty-eight people that Paul asks to be greeted for him, ten are women, a remarkable number in the deep patriarchy of that time. In Romans 16:1, he calls Phoebe a *diakonos,* a deacon or minister, and a *prostatis,* a helper or benefactor. In verse 7, he refers to another woman, Junia, as "apostle," which is the same way he refers to himself. In 1 Corinthians 7, he painstakingly explains that women have the same social rights as men. In Philippians 4:3, he includes two women, Euodia and Syntyche, among those he calls "co-workers." Paul further attests to his belief in the equality of men and women in Galatians 3:28: "there is no longer male and female; for all of you are one in Christ."

57. Quoted in Randall Balmer, "Donald Trump and the Death of Evangelicalism," in *The Spiritual Danger of Donald Trump: 30 Evangelical Christians on Justice, Truth, and Moral Integrity,* ed. Ronald J. Sider (Eugene, OR: Cascade, 2020), 81.

CHAPTER 2: YOU WILL KNOW THEM BY THEIR FRUITS

1. See Kristen Green, *Something Must Be Done About Prince Edward County: A Family, a Virginia Town, a Civil Rights Battle* (New York: Harper, 2016). Also see William J. vanden Heuvel, *Hope and History: A Memoir of Tumultuous Times* (Ithaca, NY: Cornell University Press, 2019), 60–94.

2. See Kristen Green, "Prince Edward County's Long Shadow of Segregation," *Atlantic,* August 1, 2015.

3. Samuel Stebbins and Evan Comen, "Poverty Rates: Some of the Poorest Towns in the Country Are Found Across the Southern US," *USA Today,* June 25, 2020.

4. Mark Labberton, ed., *Still Evangelical? Insiders Reconsider Political, Social, and Theological Meaning* (Chicago: IVP, 2018), 3.

5. See David P. Gushee, *Still Christian: Following Jesus Out of American Evangelicalism* (Louisville, KY: Westminster John Knox, 2017).

6. Jeremy Weber, "Billy Graham Center Explains Survey on Evangelical Trump Voters," *Christianity Today,* October 18, 2018. Also see Julie Zauzmer, "Christians Are More Than Twice as Likely to Blame a Person's Poverty on Lack of Effort," *Washington Post,* August 3, 2017.

7. Ron Sider, "A Letter from Ron Sider," evangelicalsforsocialaction.org, July 11, 2016.

8. Randall Balmer, *Thy Kingdom Come: How the Religious Right Distorts Faith and Threatens America* (New York: Basic Books, 2007), 17.

9. Frances Fitzgerald, *The Evangelicals: The Struggle to Shape America* (New York: Simon & Schuster, 2017), 304.

10. Michael Cromartie, ed., *No Longer Exiles: The Religious New Right in American Politics* (Washington, DC: Ethics and Public Policy Center, 1993), 52.

11. "Bob Jones University Apologizes for Its Racist Past," *Journal of Blacks in Higher Education,* August 21, 2018.

12. Max Blumenthal, "Age of Intolerance," *Nation,* May 28, 2007. However, by the start of the new century, Falwell seemed to have had a change of heart. In a 2005 MSNBC television network appearance, Falwell sang a different tune: "Civil rights for all Americans, black, white, red, yellow, the rich, poor, young, old, gay, straight, et cetera, is not a liberal or conservative value. It's an American value that I would think that we pretty much all agree on." See Eartha Jane Meltzer, "Falwell Speaks in Favour of Gay Civil Rights," Soulfource.org, August 26, 2005.

13. Fitzgerald, *The Evangelicals,* 284.

14. Quoted in Fitzgerald, *The Evangelicals,* 285.

15. Robert Prear, "Falwell Denounces Tutu as a 'Phony,'" *New York Times,* August 21, 1985.

16. Fitzgerald, *The Evangelicals,* 266.

17. Quoted in Philip Gorski, *American Covenant: A History of Civil Religion from the Puritans to the Present* (Princeton, NJ: Princeton University Press, 2017), 179.

18. Fitzgerald, *The Evangelicals,* 319.

19. Max Blumenthal, "Secretive Right-Wing Group Vetted Palin," *Nation,* September 1, 2008.

20. Craig Unger, "American Rapture," *Vanity Fair,* December 2005.

21. Carol Kuruvilla, "Evangelical Pastor Claims Trump's Immigration Policies Are Biblical," *Huffington Post,* November 6, 2018.

22. "Tony Perkins," Southern Poverty Law Center, https://www.splcenter.org/fighting-hate/extremist-files/individual/tony-perkins.

23. Daniel Cox and Robert P. Jones, "Religion and the Tea Party in the 2010 Elections," PRRI, October 5, 2010, https://www.prri.org/research/religion-tea-party-2010.

24. Brian Montopoli, "Tea Party Supporters: Who They Are and What They Believe," *CBS News,* December 14, 2012.

25. Fareed Zakaria, "What Barack Obama's Memoir Leaves Out," *Washington Post,* November 19, 2020.

26. Adam Nagourney, "Campaigns Shift to Attack Mode on Eve of Debate," *New York Times,* October 6, 2008.

27. Sam Stein, "Tea Party Protests: 'Ni**er,' 'Fa**ot' Shouted at Members of Congress," *Huffington Post,* May 25, 2011.

28. Jonathan Xavier, "How Racial Threat Has Galvanized the Tea Party," *Stanford Business,* July 15, 2016.

29. See Clifton B. Parker, "Perceived Threats to Racial Status Drive White Americans' Support for the Tea Party, Stanford Scholar Says," Stanford News Service, May 9, 2016.

30. Angie Maxwell, "Tea Party Distinguished by Racial Views and Fear of the Future," Diane D. Blair Center of Southern Politics and Society, 2010.

31. Daniel Cox and Robert P. Jones, "Most Americans Believe Protests Make the Country Better; Support Decreases Dramatically Among Whites If Protesters Are Identified as Black," PRRI, June 23, 2015.

32. John Pavlovitz, "Evangelicals, This Is Why People Are Through with You," johnpavlovitz.com, January 24, 2018.

33. Michael Balsamo, "Hate Crime in the US Reach Highest Level in More Than a Decade," Associated Press, November 16, 2020.

34. Southern Poverty Law Center, "Counties in Which Trump Has Held Rallies Have Seen Hate Crimes Rise Some 226 Percent," April 15, 2018. Still, the hate crime numbers almost certainly are understated. It is estimated that half of victims of hate crimes never report the crime to police. In addition, many of the country's eighteen thousand law enforcement agencies do a poor job of collecting and categorizing hate crime data. Moreover, agencies are not required to participate in the FBI's Uniform Crime Reporting program, which gathers and compiles crime data from law enforcement to produce the data set on which the FBI hate crime report is based. In 2016, of the 15,254 agencies that participated, nearly nine out of ten reported zero hate crimes.

35. Michael Gryboski, "Paula White: Allegations of Trump Being Racist 'Come from the Pit of Hell,'" *Christian Post,* October 20, 2018.

36. Anne Gearan, Seung Min Kim, and Josh Dawsey, "Trump Condemns 'All Types of Racism' After a Week of Racially Tinged Remarks," *Washington Post,* August 11, 2018.

37. Amanda Petrusich, "A Story About Fred Trump and Woody Guthrie for the Midterm Elections," *New Yorker,* November 6, 2018.

38. Megan R. Wilson, "FBI Releases Documents Related to Trump Apartment Discrimination Case," *The Hill,* February 15, 2017.

39. Michael D'Antonio, "Is Donald Trump Racist? Here's What the Record Shows," *Fortune,* June 7, 2016.

40. Sarah Burns, "Why Trump Doubled Down on the Central Park Five," *New York Times,* October 17, 2016.

41. Donald Trump, "Donald Trump: Central Park Five Settlement Is a Disgrace," *New York Daily News,* June 21, 2014.

42. Adam Serwer, "The Nationalist's Delusion," *Atlantic,* November 20, 2017.

CHAPTER 3: WHO DO YOU SAY THAT I AM?

1. John MacArthur, *The Statement on Social Justice and the Gospel,* part 8, "The Church," September 4, 2018, https://statementonsocialjustice.com.

2. MacArthur, *The Statement on Social Justice and the Gospel,* part 12, "Race/Ethnicity."

3. MacArthur, *The Statement on Social Justice and the Gospel,* part 12, "Race/Ethnicity."

4. Bob Smientana, "Video Links Beth Moore, James Merritt to 'Trojan Horse of Social Justice,'" Religion News Service, July 23, 2019.

5. Josh Buice, "Social Justice Is an Attack on the Sufficiency of Scripture," DeliveredByGrace.com, September 13, 2018.

6. The following passages are written in Aramaic: 2 Kings 18:26; Ezra 4:7; Isaiah 36:11; and Daniel 2:4.

7. *Anchor Bible Dictionary,* vol. 3 (1992) s.v. "just, justice."

8. The egalitarian underpinning of the Bible is expressed in such passages as Proverbs 22:2: "The rich and the poor meet together; the Lord is the maker of them all" and Numbers 15:15: "For the assembly, there shall be one statute for you and for the stranger who sojourns with you, a statute forever throughout your generations. You and the sojourner shall be alike before the Lord." For his part, Jesus intoned, "He causes his sun to rise on the evil and the good, and sends rain on the righteous and the unrighteous" (Matthew 5:45). For a useful discussion of the major political philosophies of justice, including egalitarianism, see Michael J. Sandel, *Justice: What's the Right Thing to Do?* (New York: FSG, 2010).

9. That is, every male. In the unquestioned patriarchy of Israel, women were subsumed under the status of men; they had no separate status unto themselves. This is what we might call *relative* or *indirect* equality. Cultural tradition and socialization determined the degree of its acceptance. In what biblical scholars recognize as the authentic letters of Paul (those believed to have actually been written by him: Romans, 1 and 2 Corinthians, Galatians, Philippians), he repeatedly asserts the social equality of women and men. See Borg and Crossan, *The First Paul.* Yet it is not to be overlooked that the early books of the Hebrew Bible treat the social circumstance of slavery as normative.

10. See the classic discussion of justice in Abraham Joshua Heschel, *The Prophets* (Peabody, MA: Hendrickson, 2009), 200–220.

11. Simone Weil, *Waiting for God,* trans. Emma Crawford (New York: Harper & Row, 1973), 85.

12. See Bruce J. Malina, *The New Testament World: Insights from Cultural Anthropology,* 3rd ed. (Louisville, KY: Westminster John Knox, 2001).

13. David Novak, *Natural Law in Judaism* (New York: Cambridge University Press, 1998), 41. Italicized in the original.

14. Weil, *Waiting for God,* 143.

15. Exodus 22:5.

16. Exodus 23:6; Deuteronomy 1:17; Leviticus 19:15.

17. Deuteronomy 19:35–36; 25:13–15.

18. Deuteronomy 19:21.

19. Leviticus 12:8; 14:21–22.

20. Leviticus 25:10.

21. Walter Brueggemann, *Theology of the Old Testament: Testimony, Dispute, Advocacy* (Minneapolis: Fortress Press, 1997), 736–37.

22. Some commentators believe the responsibility enjoined here on kings prophesies the work of Jesus. There is no textual evidence to commend that reading.

23. Abraham Joshua Heschel, *The Prophets* (New York: Harper, 1962), 255.

24. Heschel, *The Prophets,* 268.

25. See Mark 11:11. Jesus "went into the temple" and "looked around at everything."

26. For a fuller exposition, see Obery Hendricks Jr., *The Politics of Jesus: Rediscovering the True Revolutionary Nature of Jesus' Teachings and How They Have Been Corrupted* (New York: Doubleday, 2006), 113–24.

27. Nicholas Wolterstorff, *Justice: Rights and Wrongs* (Princeton, NJ: Princeton University Press, 2008), 111.

28. See Hendricks, *The Politics of Jesus,* 61–66, and Obery M. Hendricks Jr., *The Universe Bends Toward Justice: Radical Reflections on the Bible, the Church, and the Body Politic* (Maryknoll, NY: Orbis, 2011), 126–32.

29. See *Peah* 8:7 in the Mishnah, the second-century collection and codification of Jewish laws, hereinafter signified by its conventional abbreviation "m."

30. See m. *Peah* 4:2.

31. See m. *Nedarim* 9:10.

32. See Hendricks, *The Universe Bends Toward Justice,* 113–32.

33. Hendricks, *The Universe Bends Toward Justice,* 123–27.

34. George M. Foster, "Peasant Society and the Image of Limited Good," *American Anthropologist* 67, no. 2 (1965): 293–315.

35. Bruce J. Malina, *The Social Gospel of Jesus: The Kingdom of God in Mediterranean Perspective* (Minneapolis: Fortress Press, 2001), 106–7.

36. Plato, *Laws,* vol. 1, Books 1–6, *Loeb Classical Library* no. 187, trans., R. B. Bury (Cambridge, MA: Harvard University Press, 1926), 377.

37. Eusebius, *In Hieremiam,* II, V, 2: *CCLLXXIV* 61, quoted in Bruce J. Malina, *The New Testament World: Insights from Cultural Anthropology,* 3rd ed. (Louisville, KY: Westminster John Knox, 2001), 98.

38. See Hendricks, *The Politics of Jesus,* 132–44.

39. See especially Luke 4:1–13.

40. See Hendricks, *The Politics of Jesus,* 100–112.

41. Caitlin Dewey, "GOP Lawmaker: The Bible Says 'If a Man Will Not Work, He Shall Not Eat,'" *Washington Post,* March 31, 2017.

42. For an examination of the political implications of the Lord's Prayer, see Hendricks, *The Politics of Jesus,* 101–31.

43. Adapted from Paul N. van de Water, Joel Friedman, and Sharon Parrott, "Trump 2020 Budget: A Disturbing Vision," Center on Budget and Policy Priorities, March 11, 2019.

CHAPTER 4: A NEW COMMANDMENT I GIVE YOU

1. Lorenzo Ferrigno, "Attack After Same-Sex Marriage Shines Light on Michigan Hate Crime Law," CNN.com, April 7, 2014.

2. Will Roscoe, *Changing Ones: Third and Fourth Genders in Native North America* (New York: St. Martin's, 1998), 3.

3. Quoted in Michael Bronski, *A Queer History of the United States* (Boston: Beacon Press, 2011), 4–5.

4. Scott Lively and Kevin E. Adams, *The Pink Swastika: Homosexuality in the Nazi Party* (Carbondale, IL: Veritas Aeterna, 2010).

5. Quoted in Lillian Faderman, *The Gay Revolution: The Story of the Struggle* (New York: Simon & Schuster, 2015), 350.

6. Faderman, *The Gay Revolution*, 350–51.

7. Faderman, *The Gay Revolution*, 350–51.

8. See Thomas G. Plante, "No, Homosexuality Is Not a Risk Factor for the Sexual Abuse of Children," *America: The Jesuit Review*, October 22, 2018; Alice Dreger, "Do Gay Men Have More Sexual Interest in Children Than Straight Men Do?," *Pacific Standard*, August 22, 2017.

9. Geoffrey R. Stone, *Sex and the Constitution: Sex, Religion, and Law from America's Origins to the Twenty-First Century* (New York: Liveright, 2017), 258.

10. Stone, *Sex and the Constitution*, 258.

11. Stone, *Sex and the Constitution*, 258.

12. Jennifer Agiesta, "Poll: Majorities Back Supreme Court Rulings on Marriage, Obamacare," CNN.com, June 30, 2015.

13. Michael Mooney, "How First Baptist's Robert Jeffress Ordained Himself to Lead America," *DMagazine*, January 2012.

14. Sarah K. Burris, "'God Will Finish the Job': Texas Pastor Prays for Injured Orlando Survivors to Die," *Raw Story*, June 20, 2016.

15. Derek Hawkins, "Pastor Who Called Gays 'Sinners' After Pulse Shooting Is Convicted of Child Molestation," *Washington Post*, April 12, 2017.

16. Sarah K. Burris, "These 7 Christian Leaders Showed Their Love by Celebrating the Orlando Nightclub Massacre," *Raw Story*, June 14, 2016.

17. Emily Birnbaum, "Jimmy Carter: I Think Jesus Would Approve of Gay Marriage," *The Hill*, August 9, 2018.

18. Noor Al-Sibai, "Pro-Trump Evangelist Franklin Graham Slams Jimmy Carter by Saying God Will Punish Gays with Fire and Death," *Raw Story*, July 18, 2018.

19. *Yada* is the same term used in Genesis 4:1 to connote sexual relations: "Now [Adam] knew [*yada*] his wife Eve, and she conceived."

20. Quoting *m. Avot 5.10*. See Jon D. Levenson, "Genesis," in *The Jewish Study Bible*, ed. Adele Berlin and Marc Zvi Brettler (New York: Oxford University Press, 2004), 41.

21. Jay Michaelson, *God vs. Gay? The Religious Case for Equality* (Boston: Beacon Press, 2011), 68–69.

22. See Philo, *Questions on Genesis* (Cambridge, MA: Harvard University Press, 1953). Something of a scholarly consensus recognizes multiple hands in the authorship of Genesis. Estimates of its final form center around the sixth to fifth centuries BCE.

23. Michaelson, *God vs. Gay?*, 71.

24. Michaelson, *God vs. Gay?*

25. See Richard Cavendish, *Man, Myth & Magic: An Illustrated Encyclopedia of Mythology, Religion, and the Unknown*, vol. 1 (New York: Cavendish Companies, 1995), 134.

26. Michaelson, *God vs. Gay?*, 62.

27. Michaelson, *God vs. Gay?*, 63.

28. Jacob Milgrom, *Leviticus 17–22, Anchor Yale Bible Commentaries*, vol. 3A (New York: Doubleday, 2000), 1786.

29. My acknowledgment of the practical consequences of these passages is not a comment on the divine inspiration of any portion of the Bible. Rather, it is an acknowledgment that everything touched by human agency is refracted through the prism of human inspiration.

30. Quoted in Stone, *Sex and the Constitution*, 215.

31. Michaelson, *God vs. Gay?*, 84.

32. See Andrea Ganna et al., "Large-Scale GWAS Reveals Insights into the Genetic Architecture of Same-Sex Sexual Behavior," *Science*, August 30, 2019.

33. See Institute of Medicine (US) Committee on Lesbian, Gay, Bisexual, and Transgender Health Issues and Research Gaps and Opportunities, *The Health of Lesbian, Gay, Bisexual, and Transgender People: Building a Foundation for Better Understanding* (Washington, DC: National Academies Press, 2011).

34. Michael Majchrowicz, "Conversion Therapy Leader for Two Decades, McKrae Game Disavows Movement He Helped Fuel," *Post and Courier*, September 3, 2019.

35. "Conversion Therapy," Southern Poverty Law Center, https://www.splcenter.org/issues/lgbt-rights/conversion-therapy.

36. Raphael Olmeda, "Appeals Court Strikes Down Boca Raton's Ban on Gay Conversion Therapy," *South Florida Sun-Sentinel*, November 20, 2020.

37. David Frederickson, "Natural and Unnatural Use in Romans 1:24–27: Paul and the Philosphic Critique of Eros," in *Homosexuality, Science, and the "Plain Sense" of Scripture*, ed. David L. Balch (Grand Rapids, MI: Eerdmans, 2000), 197.

38. Dale B. Martin, *Sex and the Single Savior: Gender and Sexuality in Biblical Interpretation* (Louisville: Westminster John Knox, 2006), 44.

39. Matthew Vines, *God and the Gay Christian: The Biblical Case in Support of Same-Sex Relationships* (New York: Convergent, 2014), 121.

40. Robin Scroggs, *The New Testament and Homosexuality: Contextual Background for Contemporary Debate* (Minneapolis: Fortress Press, 1984), 106.

41. Robert A. J. Gagnon, *The Bible and Homosexual Practice: Texts and Hermeneutics* (Nashville: Abingdon, 2001), 312.

42. Vines, *God and the Gay Christian*, 128.

43. Gagnon, *The Bible and Homosexual Practice*, 306.

44. Vines, *God and the Gay Christian*, 124.

45. Martin, *Sex and the Single Savior*, 42.

46. Scroggs, *The New Testament and Homosexuality*, 106–7.

47. John Boswell, *Christianity, Social Tolerance, and Homosexuality: Gay People in Western Europe from the Beginning of the Christian Era to the Fourteenth Century* (1979; Chicago: University of Chicago Press, 2015), 345.

48. John Boswell, *Same-Sex Unions in Premodern Europe* (New York: Villard, 1994), 108–61.

49. So argues Robin Darling Young, "Gay Marriage: Reimagining Church History," *First Things* 47 (November 1994): 43–48.

50. Chico Harlan and Michelle Boorstein, "Pope Francis Calls for Civil Union Laws for Same-Sex Couples," *Washington Post*, October 21, 2021.

CHAPTER 5: I HAVE OTHER SHEEP NOT IN THIS FOLD

1. In biblical Hebrew the term *ibri*, or "Hebrew," means literally "he crosses over," which reflects the Hebrews' identity and status as a class of subaltern outsiders to Egyptian society. The use of "Hebrew" as social or class description seems to be related to the early Semitic term *hapiru*, which scholars believe also connoted class status in the ancient Near East. See Norman K. Gottwald, *The Tribes of Yahweh* (Maryknoll, NY: Orbis, 1979), 401–9.

2. See James C. Scott, *The Moral Economy of the Peasant: Rebellion and Subsistence in Southeast Asia* (New Haven, CT: Yale University Press, 1977).

3. Robert P. Jones, Daniel Cox, Betsy Cooper, and Rachel Lienesch, "How Americans View Immigrants and What They Want from Immigration Reform: Findings from the 2015 American Values Atlas," PRRI, 2016, http://www.prri.org/research/poll-immigration-reform-views-on-immigrants.

4. Tara Isabella Burton, "The Bible Says to Welcome Immigrants. So Why Don't White Evangelicals?," *Vox*, October 30, 2018.

5. Hannah Hartig, "Republicans Turn More Negative Toward Refugees as Number Admitted to U.S. Plummets," Pew Research Center, May 24, 2018.

6. Michelle Boorstein and Julie Zauzmer, "Why Many White Evangelicals Are Not Protesting Family Separations on the U.S. Border," *Washington Post*, June 18, 2018.

7. Stephanie McCrummen, "Judgment Days," *Washington Post*, July 21, 2018.

8. Gordon H. Chang, *Ghosts of Gold Mountain: The Epic Story of the Chinese Who Built the Transcontinental Railroad* (New York: Houghton Mifflin, 2019), 231.

9. Ed Mazza, "Reagan Slams Border Fence, Bush Defends Undocumented 'Good People' in 1980 Debate," *Huffington Post*, May 22, 2019.

10. See discussions in Hendricks, *The Politics of Jesus*, 198–99, 202–5, 250–51, 255.

11. Daniel S. Lucks, *Reconsidering Reagan: Racism, Republicans, and the Road to Trump* (Boston: Beacon Press, 2020), 4.

12. Michael Reagan, "Who'd Take Ronald Reagan's Side on Immigration?," *Post Independent*, July 7, 2019.

13. James Dobson, "Dr. Dobson's Visit to the Border," *Dr. James Dobson Family Talk*, newsletter, July 2019.

14. Brandon Massey, "James Dobson's Anti-Immigrant Rhetoric Is Dangerous," *Sojourners*, July 3, 2019.

15. Sarah Ruiz-Grossman, "Most of America's Terrorists Are White, and Not Muslim," *Huffpost*, May 23, 2019, and Jane Guskin and David L. Wilson, *The Politics of Immigration* (New York: Monthly Review Press, 2017), 143.

16. Guskin and Wilson, *The Politics of Immigration*, 141.

17. David Gibson, "Franklin Graham Rebuts Pope on Islam: 'This Is A War of Religion,'" Religion News Service, August 1, 2016.

18. "John Hagee Warns Against Radical Islam," *Religion News Blog*, December 4, 2006.

19. Robert D. Jones et al., *Partisan Polarization Dominates Trump Era: Findings from the 2018 American Values Survey*, PRRI, November 29, 2018.

20. See Khaled A. Beydoun, *American Islamophobia: Understanding the Roots and Rise of Fear* (Oakland: University of California Press, 2018), 94ff.

21. Zak Sharf, "Riz Ahmed Missed Star Wars Celebration Because Homeland Security Stopped Him at the Airport, *IndieWire*, June 28, 2019. It is largely forgotten that Martin Luther King Jr. expressed a similar fear for African Americans: "And you know what, a nation that put as many Japanese in a concentration camp as they did in the forties . . . will put black people in a concentration camp." See Richard Lischer, *The Preacher King: Martin Luther King Jr. and the Word That Moved America* (New York: Oxford University Press, 1995), 159.

22. Ayal Feinberg, Regina Branton, and Valerie Martinez-Ebers, "Counties That Hosted a 2016 Trump Rally Saw a 226 Percent Increase in Hate Crimes," *Washington Post*, March 22, 2019, and German Lopez, "A New FBI Report Says Hate Crimes—Especially Against Muslims—Went Up in 2016," *Vox*, November 13, 2017.

23. Richard Ostling, "Do Christians and Muslims Worship the Same God?," *Religion Unplugged*, March 3, 2019.

24. Thomas D. Williams, "Franklin Graham: 'Islam and Christianity Clearly Do Not Worship the Same God,'" *Breitbart*, January 24, 2016.

25. Frederick D. Wong, "Christian Extremism as a Domestic Terror Threat," School of Advanced Military Studies, United States Army Command

and General Staff College, Homeland Security Digital Library, 2011. Also "Hate Against Americans," *Southern Poverty Law Center*, September 25, 2017.

26. To be fair, it must be noted that a number of denominational bodies and right-wing evangelical leaders have publicly questioned, and some have condemned, the separation of children from their families. These include the Southern Baptist Convention, the United Methodist denomination, even Franklin Graham, to his credit. Although it is not an evangelical denomination, it is worth noting that the United Methodist Church initiated formal expulsion proceedings against former attorney general Jefferson Beauregard Sessions for his nefarious role in the family separation travesty. But with few exceptions, evangelical churches have raised no questions about the brutality and anti-biblical offense of the zero-tolerance crackdown itself.

27. J. D. Long-Garcia, "Pope Francis Calls Trump's Family Separation Border Policy 'Cruelty of the Highest Form,'" *America: The Jesuit Review*, October 21, 2020.

28. Aric Jenkins, "Jeff Sessions: Parents and Children Illegally Crossing the Border Will Be Separated, *Time*, May 7, 2018.

29. Liz Vinson, "Family Separation Continues Two Years After Trump Administration Claims It Ended," Southern Poverty Law Center, June 18, 2020.

30. Julia Ainsley and Jacob Soboroff, "Lawyers Say They Can't Find the Parents of 545 Migrant Children Separated by Trump Administration," NBCnews.com, October 20, 2020.

31. Eddie S. Glaude Jr., *Begin Again: James Baldwin's America and Its Urgent Lessons for Our Own* (New York: Crown, 2020), xxviii.

32. The administration claimed that the family separations were not a planned part of its policy, but subsequent investigation proved that, indeed, the separations were the government's intention all along. See Lisa Riordan Seville and Hannah Rappleye, "Trump Administration Ran 'Pilot Program' for Separating Migrant Families in 2017," *NBC News*, June 29, 2018.

33. UN High Commissioner for Refugees, *Children on the Run: Unaccompanied Children Leaving Central America and Mexico and the Need for International Protection* (Washington, DC: UN High Commissioner for Refugees, Regional Office for the US and Caribbean, n.d.), accessed November 11, 2020.

34. Tara Francis Chan, "Migrant Children Say They've Been Forcibly Drugged, Handcuffed, and Abused in US Government Detention," *Business Insider*, June 21, 2018.

35. Flores et al. v. Sessions et al. May 2018.

36. Caitlin Dickson, "Border Patrol Is Confiscating Migrant Kids' Medicine, U.S. Doctors Say," *Yahoo News*, June 4, 2019.

37. Kristine Phillips, "'America Is Better Than This': What a Doctor Saw in a Texas Shelter for Migrant Children," *Washington Post*, June 18, 2018.

38. Serena Marshall and Lana Zak, "Doctor Compares Conditions at Immigrant Holding Centers to 'Torture Facilities,'" *ABC News Digital*, July 23, 2019.

39. Matthew Kahn, "Document: Federal Judge Orders Government to Reunite Families," *Lawfare*, June 26, 2018.

40. Kahn, "Document: Federal Judge Orders Government to Reunite Families."

41. Editorial Board, "Migrant Children Are Still Confined and Vulnerable. It's a Gratuitous Act of Cruelty," *Washington Post*, May 25, 2020.

42. "COVID-19 Escalating in ICE Detention Centers as States Hit Highest Daily Records—and ICE Deportation Flights into Northern Triangle Continue," International Rescue Committee, August 3, 2020.

43. Ralph Drollinger, *What the Bible Says About Our Illegal Immigration Problem*, Capital Ministries Members Bible Study, February 18, 2019. Quoted in Stewart, *The Power Worshippers*, 50–51.

44. Carol Kuruvilla, "Evangelical Pastor Claims Trump's Immigration Policies Are Biblical," *HuffPost*, November 6, 2018.

45. Meagan Flynn, "Detained Migrant Children Got No Toothbrush, No Soap, No Sleep. It's No Problem, Government Argues," *Washington Post*, June 21, 2019.

46. Neil Vigdor, "Pence Defends Conditions at Migrant Detention Centers in Texas," *Washington Post*, July 13, 2019.

47. American Civil Liberties Union, *Warehoused and Forgotten: Immigrants Trapped in Our Shadow Private Prison System* (New York: ACLU, June 2014).

48. Spencer Ackerman and Adam Rawnsley, "$800 Million in Taxpayer Money Went to Private Prisons Where Migrants Work for Pennies," *Newsweek*, December 27, 2018.

49. Nick Miroff, "Migrants Say U.S. Border Patrol Detention Centers Are 'Iceboxes,'" *Chicago Tribune*, August 7, 2018.

50. Nicole Goodkind, "ICE Used Taxpayer Money to Pay Private Prisons $800 Million to Detain Migrants in 2018," *Newsweek*, December 27, 2018. Also see Monsy Alvarado et al., "'These People Are Profitable': Under Trump, Private Prisons Are Cashing In on ICE Detainees," *USA Today*, December 20, 2019.

51. Margaret Talbot, "The Challenge at the Border Shows No Signs of Abating," *New Yorker*, May 26, 2019.

52. Nicholas Kristof, "Food Doesn't Grow Here Anymore. That's Why I Would Send My Son North," *New York Times*, June 4, 2019.

53. Toni Morrison, *The Source of Self-Regard: Selected Essays, Speeches, and Meditations* (New York: Knopf, 2019), 5.

54. Katherine Witsman, *U.S. Lawful Permanent Residents: 2017* (Washington, DC: US Department of Homeland Security Flow Report, August 2018).

55. These measures include "free trade," the ironically named forced removal of tariffs. It was crafted to protect local farmers and manufacturers

from being overwhelmed by foreign firms that are able to offer lower prices because their own governments subsidize them. The imposed austerity measures include forced privatization of key governmental functions that can leave tens of thousands of public employees without a source of income. In the case of demonized Mexico, one of the stipulations of the North American Free Trade Agreement (NAFTA) was to reduce or eliminate entirely protective tariffs. This severely cut agricultural profits, which resulted in the severe loss of agricultural jobs. More than 1.5 million Mexican farmers lost their sources of income, forcing them to sell or abandon their farms. In the final analysis, NAFTA caused the loss of more than two million agricultural jobs in Mexico. To add insult to injury, the Trump administration has ordered the Department of State to cut $450 million in aid to Central America, much of which was earmarked to fund economic development and reduction of crime in El Salvador, Guatemala, and Honduras—measures that would greatly improve the plight of those seeking asylum from poverty and crime.

56. An apparent exception appears in Mark 7:25–30. But although Jesus appears to turn away a Syro-Phoenician woman who sought healing for her seriously ill daughter, declaring, "I have only come to the lost sheep of Israel," nonetheless he did not refuse her request.

57. However, in recent years evidence has been presented that Gandhi ignored the suffering of black Africans during his years in South Africa and used racially derogatory terms to refer to them. As problematic as that may be, that cannot detract from his later leadership, sacrifices, and example of the viability of nonviolent resistance under certain circumstances. See Ashwin Desai and Goolem Vahed, *The South African Gandhi: The Stretcher-Bearer of Empire* (Stanford, CA: Stanford University Press, 2015).

58. Martin Luther King Jr., "Palm Sunday Sermon on Mohandas K. Gandhi," *The Papers of Martin Luther King, Jr.*, vol. 5 (Berkeley: University of California Press, 2005), 148.

59. Mary Jo Dudley, "These U.S. Industries Can't Work Without Illegal Immigrants," CBSNews.com, January 10, 2019.

60. Kathleen Boyle et al., "Migration and the Economy," *Citi GPS*, September 2018.

61. Morrison, *The Source of Self-Regard*, 15. This is a slightly truncated version.

62. Jim Meisner Jr., "The U.S. Migrant Crisis Is a Test for Christians," *Patheos*, June 30, 2019.

CHAPTER 6: YOU SHALL NOT ADD TO THE WORD WHICH I COMMAND YOU

1. Thomas Kidd, "Were Evangelicals Really Silent about Roe v. Wade?," The Gospel Coalition, September 25, 2018.

2. Vicki O. Wittenstein, *Reproductive Rights: Who Decides?* (Minneapolis: Twenty-First Century Books, 2016), 44.

3. See Kira Schlesinger, *Pro-Choice and Christian: Reconciling Faith, Politics, and Justice* (Louisville, KY: Westminster John Knox, 2017), 30.

4. Schlesinger, *Pro-Choice and Christian*, 32.

5. Schlesinger, *Pro-Choice and Christian*, 31.

6. John Fea, "A Brief History of Modern Evangelical Social Engagement in America," in *Catholics and Evangelicals*, ed. Ronald J. Sider and John Borelli (Eugene, OR: Cascade, 2018), 3.

7. Fea, "A Brief History of Modern Evangelical Social Engagement in America," 5.

8. Randall Balmer, "The Real Origins of the Religious Right," *Politico Magazine*, May 27, 2014.

9. David Roach, "How Southern Baptists Became Pro-Life," *Baptist Press*, January 16, 2015. Quoted in Jemar Tisby, *The Color of Compromise: The Truth About the American Church's Complicity in Racism* (Grand Rapids, MI: Zondervan, 2019), 169.

10. Balmer, "The Real Origins of the Religious Right."

11. Steven P. Miller, *Billy Graham and the Rise of the Republican South* (Philadelphia: University of Pennsylvania Press, 2009), 54.

12. Sanjana Karanth, "Trump Pushes Dangerous Abortion Lies at Green Bay Rally," *HuffPost*, April 28, 2019.

13. Leonardo Blair, "SBC Leaders Albert Mohler, Russell Moore Criticized for Honoring John Lewis Due to Liberal Record," *Christian Post*, July 12, 2020.

14. Schlesinger, *Pro-Choice and Christian*, 57.

15. Richard B. Hays, *The Moral Vision of the New Testament: Community, Cross, New Creation* (San Francisco: HarperSanFrancisco, 1996), 448.

16. R. C. Sproul, *Abortion: A Rational Look at an Emotional Issue* (Sanford, FL: Reformation Trust, 2010), 88.

17. The New International Version, New King James Version, and New American Standard translations, along with biblical commentators like theologian John Piper, argue that the Hebrew term *weyatse'u* in 5:22 should more properly be translated as "born prematurely" rather than "miscarriage." Thus, Piper argues, "There is no miscarriage in this text. The child is born prematurely and is protected with the same sanctions as the mother. . . . Therefore, this text cannot be used by the pro-choice advocates to show that the Bible regards the unborn as less human or less worthy of protection than those who are born." See John Piper, "The Misuse of Exodus 21:22–25 by Pro-Choice Advocates," desiringGod.org, February 8, 1989. However, Hebrew Bible scholar Jeffrey Tigay, in his discussion of the book of Exodus, agrees with the NRSV translation quoted in this chapter, noting that halakhic exegesis (interpretation of the body of Jewish laws derived from the Written and Oral Torah) also does not consider an unborn fetus a living person. See "Exodus," Berlin and Brettler, *The Jewish Study Bible*, 154. Jewish Talmudic ethics expert Fred Rosner, author of *Biomedical Ethics and Jewish*

Law (New York: Ktav, 2001), agrees. Moreover, the Mesopotamian Code of Hammurabi (196–214), which predates the earliest biblical writings by several centuries and is recognized as influencing the Exodus prescriptions, similarly places a lesser value on the unborn fetus. See Yung Suk Kim, "*Lex Talionis* in Exodus 21:22–25," *Journal of Hebrew Scriptures* 6, art. 3, 2006.

18. Dionysius of Halicarnassus, *Roman Antiquities*, 2.15.1–2.

19. Susan Page, "Barbara Bush's Long-Hidden 'Thoughts on Abortion,'" *Atlantic*, March 29, 2019.

20. Thomas Aquinas, *Summa Theologica*, 1, q. 118, part 2.

21. Leslie J. Reagan, *When Abortion Was a Crime: Women, Medicine, and Law in the United States, 1867–1973* (Berkeley: University of California, 1998), 250.

22. Reproductive health expert Mary Ann Castle observes that "the Christian Right raises billions of dollars to support ultraconservative state-level candidates and legislators to promulgate their religious views. These philanthropists have developed interconnected funding priorities and strategies to advance their public policy agenda. For example, they provide fellowships and offer professional supports to public officials. Networks of regional and state policy right-wing think tanks and advocacy organizations have been created to provide testimony to legislators and directly influence them. Money from corporate businesses, wealthy individuals, conservative family foundations and owners of media strengthen and expand their ability to influence public policy." Mary Ann Castle, "Abortion in the United States' Bible Belt: Organizing for Power and Empowerment," *Reproductive Health*, January 5, 2011.

23. Page, "Barbara Bush's Long-Hidden 'Thoughts on Abortion.'"

24. See "Shout Your Abortion" (shoutyourabortion.com), a website that bills itself as "a decentralized network of individuals talking about abortion on our own terms."

25. Rob Schenck, "My Reversal on Abortion Rights," *New York Times*, May 31, 2019.

CHAPTER 7: THOU SHALL NOT MURDER

1. Kristine Phillips, "With Crowns on Their Heads and AR-15s in Their Arms, Couples Exchange Vows in Pro-Gun Church," *Washington Post*, March 1, 2018.

2. Kate Shellnutt, "Packing the Pews: The Connection Between God and Guns," *Christianity Today*, November 8, 2017.

3. Shellnutt, "Packing the Pews."

4. "A Brief History of the NRA," nra.org.

5. John Houston Craige, *The Practical Book of American Guns* (New York: Bramhall House, 1950), 84–93.

6. Michael Waldman, "How the NRA Rewrote the Second Amendment," Brennan Center, May 20, 2014.

7. This was primarily in response to the Brady Handgun Violence Prevention Act of 1993 and two Supreme Court rulings. *Burton v. Sills* (1969) upheld New Jersey's strict gun control law. *Lewis v. United States* (1980) supported the federal ban on possession of firearms by convicted felons.

8. Adam Winkler, *Gun Fight: The Battle over the Right to Bear Arms in America* (New York: W. W. Norton, 2013), 25.

9. Quoted in Jessica Dawson, "Shall Not Be Infringed: How the NRA Used Religious Language to Transform the Meaning of the Second Amendment," Palgrave Communications, July 2, 2019.

10. Bobby Ross Jr., "Jesus Loves Me and My Guns: Faith and Firearms Touted at the NRA's Prayer Breakfast," *Washington Post*, May 7, 2018.

11. David A. Graham, "Wayne Pierre's Cynical Exploitation of Outrage," *Atlantic*, February 22, 2018.

12. David Barash, "Guns, God, and Trump: New NRA President Says It's Her Job to 'Save' America," *New Civil Rights Movement*, May 6, 2019.

13. Chelsea Bailey, "More Americans Killed by Guns Since 1968 Than in All U.S. Wars—Combined," NBC.com, October 4, 2017.

14. Charles Marsh, "The NRA's Assault on Christian Faith and Practice," *Religion and Politics*, January 3, 2018.

15. Neil J. Young, "Why Do Evangelicals Oppose Gun Control?" *The Week*, August 11, 2019.

16. Young, "Why Do Evangelicals Oppose Gun Control?"

17. Young, "Why Do Evangelicals Oppose Gun Control?"

18. "Report on Gun Suicide—Confronting the Inevitability Myth," Giffords Law Center to Prevent Gun Violence, September 13, 2018.

19. Quoted in David Harsanyi, *First Freedom: A Ride Through America's Enduring History with the Gun* (New York: Simon & Schuster, 2018), 231.

20. Michael Powell, "The NRA's Call to Arms," *Washington Post*, August 6, 2000.

21. James B. Trefethen, *Americans and Their Guns: The National Rifle Association Story Through Nearly a Century of Service to the Nation* (Mechanicsburg, PA: Stackpole, 1967), and Violence Policy Center, *Blood Money: How the Gun Industry Bankrolls the NRA* (Washington, DC: VPC, April 2013).

22. "How America's Gun Industry Is Tied to the NRA," NPR.com, March 13, 2018.

23. Michael Posner, "In the Wake of Mass Shootings, It's Time to Focus on Gun Manufacturers," *Forbes*, August 5, 2019.

24. "Wayne LaPierre Fights for the Second Amendment Before the United Nations," Institute for Legislative Action, July 12, 2012.

25. Ben Smith, "Obama Most Anti-Gun Candidate Ever, Will Ban Guns," *Politico*, August 6, 2008.

26. "Firearms Ammunition Economic Impact Report," NSSF, April 10, 2018.

27. Kiera Lerner, "After Falsely Claiming Obama Would Take Away Guns, NRA Now Makes Same Claim About Clinton," *ThinkProgress*, May 21, 2016.

28. Elspeth Reeve, "Two Decades of Paranoid Pronouncements by the NRA's Wayne LaPierre," *Atlantic*, January 30, 2013.

29. Sexton, *American Rule*, 244.

30. Wayne LaPierre, "Stand and Fight," NRA Institute for Legislative Action, February 1, 1983.

31. Matt Gertz, "NRA's Wayne LaPierre: Buy a Gun or You Will Die," MediaMatters, February 13, 2013.

32. Kayla Hicks, "The NRA Shows How It Feels About African-Americans," Coalition to Stop Gun Violence, November, 2015.

33. Melissa Hickman Barlow, "Race and the Problem of Crime in 'Time' and 'Newsweek' Cover Stories, 1946 to 1995," *Social Justice* 25, no. 2 (72) (Summer 1998): 149–83.

CHAPTER 8: THE WORKMAN IS WORTHY OF HIS KEEP

1. George McGovern, *The Essential America: Our Founders and the Liberal Tradition* (New York: Simon & Schuster, 2004), 95.

2. Alan Greenspan and Adrian Wooldridge, *Capitalism in America: A History* (New York: Penguin, 2018), 124.

3. Hal Bridges, "The Robber Baron Concept in American History," *Business History Review* 32, no. 1 (1958): 1–13; 1. Historian Bridges explains that the term reflects the notion that "business leaders in the United States from about 1865 to 1900 were, on the whole, a set of avaricious rascals who habitually cheated and robbed investors and consumers, corrupted government, fought ruthlessly among themselves, and in general carried on predatory activities comparable to those of the robber barons of medieval Europe."

4. John F. Woolverton and James D. Bratt, *A Christian and a Democrat: A Religious Biography of Franklin D. Roosevelt* (Grand Rapids, MI: Eerdmans, 2019), 116.

5. Woolverton and Bratt, *A Christian and a Democrat*, 127.

6. Quoted in Woolverton and Bratt, *A Christian and a Democrat*, 126.

7. Quoted in Woolverton and Bratt, *A Christian and a Democrat*, 114.

8. Both quoted in Kevin Kruse, *One Nation Under God: How Corporate America Invented Christian America* (New York: Basic Books, 2015), 5–6.

9. Kevin Phillips, *Wealth and Democracy: The Politics of the American Rich* (New York: Broadway Books, 2002), 220.

10. Kim Phillips-Fein, *Invisible Hands: The Making of the Conservative Movement from the New Deal to Reagan* (New York: W. W. Norton, 2009), 12.

11. See Hendricks, *The Universe Bends Toward Justice*, 106–7.

12. Quoted in Kruse, *One Nation Under God*, 4.

13. Darren E. Grem, *The Blessings of Business: How Corporations Shaped Conservative Christianity* (New York: Oxford University Press, 2016), 28.

14. Grem, *The Blessings of Business*, 28.

15. Grem, *The Blessings of Business*, 20.

16. Kruse, *One Nation Under God*, 6.

17. Kruse, *One Nation Under God*, 12.

18. Kruse, *One Nation Under God*, 13.

19. See Robert Nozick, *Anarchy, State, and Utopia* (1971; New York: Basic Books, 2013), xix.

20. See Nozick, *Anarchy, State, and Utopia*, 170–74.

21. Michael J. Sandel, *Justice: What's the Right Thing to Do?* (New York: FSG, 2009), 59.

22. Quoted in Emma Green, "Why Donald Trump Appeals to Evangelicals," *Atlantic*, August 8, 2016.

23. See Malina, *The New Testament World*.

24. Mungi Ngomane, *Everyday Ubuntu: Living Better Together, the African Way* (New York: HarperCollins, 2020), 14.

25. Ngomane, *Everyday Ubuntu*, 8.

26. Thomas E. Ricks, *First Principles: What America's Founders Learned from the Greeks and Romans and How That Shaped Our Country* (New York: Harper, 2020), 5. Ricks cites Joyce Appleby, *Liberalism and Republicanism in the Historical Imagination* (Cambridge, MA: Harvard University Press, 1992), 21.

27. Myriam Renaud, "Three Reasons White Evangelicals Hate Obamacare," *Sightings*, University of Chicago, April 12, 2018.

28. Quoted in Robert Dreyfuss, "Grover Norquist: 'Field Marshall' of the Bush Plan," *Nation*, May 2001.

29. Woolverton and Bratt, *A Christian and a Democrat*, 113.

30. Quoted in Phillips-Fein, *Invisible Hands*, 73.

31. Quoted in Phillips-Fein, *Invisible Hands*, 229.

32. Morgan Lee, "When John MacArthur Reopens His Church Despite COVID-19 Orders," *Christianity Today*, July 29, 2020.

33. Lee Brown, "Evangelical Pastor Mocks 'Pansies,' Won't Close Church for Coronavirus," *New York Post*, March 17, 2020.

34. Marybeth Davis Baggett, "Dear Liberty University Board: Please Stop Jerry Falwell Jr. Before It's Too Late," Religion News Service, March 22, 2020.

35. Alana Abramson, "'No Lessons Have Been Learned': Why the Trillion-Dollar Coronavirus Bailout Benefited the Rich," *Time*, July 18, 2020.

36. Jane McAlevey, *A Collective Bargain: Unions, Organizing, and the Fight for Democracy* (New York: Ecco, 2020), 47–48.

37. Woolverton and Bratt, *A Christian and a Democrat*, 29.

38. Quoted in Phillips-Fein, *Invisible Hands*, 20.

39. John Fea, "When a Christian America Meant Something," *Pantheos*, March 23, 2011.

40. William H. Allen, "The Labor Question," in *History, Essays, Orations, and Other Documents of the Sixth General Conference of the Evangelical Alliance: Held in New York, October 2–12, 1873*, 670–74.

41. Some scholars contend that the term has a weightier meaning than that of a craftsman. Jewish scholar Geza Vermes suggests that *tekton* is the

biblical Greek rendering of *nagger*, a colloquialism for a "learned man" in Jesus's everyday Aramaic tongue. However, this is not a widely held scholarly opinion. See Geza Vermes, *Jesus the Jew* (London: William Collins, 1973), 21.

42. Many biblical commentators interpret this passage in theological terms. But workers in first-century Israel were literally burdened and work weary. Archaeologists have found skeletal remains of workers who had become physically deformed from carrying heavy loads and were also malnourished, surviving on an estimated average daily caloric intake as low as 1,400 calories. See Hendricks, *The Universe Bends Toward Justice*, 131; and David A. Fiensy, *The Social History of Palestine in the Herodian Period* (Lewiston, NY: Mellen, 1991), 89.

43. See Hendricks, *The Universe Bends Toward Justice*, 131. Also see David Mealand, *Poverty and Expectation in the Gospels* (London: SPCK, 1980), 6.

44. Philip Dray, *There Is Power in a Union: The Epic Story of Labor in America* (New York: Doubleday, 2010), 276.

45. Heath W. Carter, "The Church of Organized Labor," *New Republic*, July 12, 2015. Also see Eric Arnesen, *Encyclopedia of U.S. History and Working-Class History*, vol. 1 (New York: Routledge, 2006), 205.

46. Carter, "The Church of Organized Labor."

47. Carter, "The Church of Organized Labor."

48. See Julia May Courtney, "Remember Ludlow!," in *Voices of a People's History of the United States*, ed. Howard Zinn and Anthony Arnove (New York: Seven Stories, 2004), 281. Originally printed in *Mother Earth* 9, no. 3 (May 1914).

49. Robert Kanigel, *The One Best Way: Frederick Winslow Taylor and the Enigma of Efficiency* (New York: Viking, 1997), 169.

50. Kanigel, *The One Best Way*, 226–27.

51. Greenspan and Wooldridge, *Capitalism in America*, 124.

52. Steven Greenhouse, *Beaten Down, Worked Up: The Past, Present, and Future of American Labor* (New York: Knopf, 2019), 14.

53. McAlevey, *A Collective Bargain*, 62.

54. Martin Jay Levitt with Terry Conrow, *Confessions of a Union Buster* (New York: Crown, 1993), 1.

55. Levitt, *Confessions of a Union Buster*, 59.

56. Kruse, *One Nation Under God*.

57. Kruse, *One Nation Under God*, 39.

58. Grem, *The Blessings of Business*, 57.

59. Caitlin Emma and Daniel Strauss, "Scott Walker Broke the Unions. Now He Says He's the 'Education Governor,'" *Politico*, July 21, 2018; and Karen Tumulty, "Wisconsin Governor Wins His Battle with Unions on Collective Bargaining," *Washington Post*, March 10, 2011.

60. Josh Harkinson, "The Religious Right's Anti-Union Crusade," *Mother Jones*, April 4, 2011.

61. Quoted in Harkinson, "The Religious Right's Anti-Union Crusade," 35.

62. Glenn Davis, "Are Unions Biblical?," free-bible-study-lessons.com, n.d.

63. Greenhouse, *Beaten Down, Worked Up*, 136.

64. Greenhouse, *Beaten Down, Worked Up*, 136.

65. Joseph A. McCartin, "The Strike That Busted Unions," *New York Times*, August 2, 2011.

66. Eugene V. Resnick, *AP United States History*, 2nd ed. (Hauppauge, NY: Barron's, 2014), 36.

67. Greenhouse, *Beaten Down, Worked Up*, 12.

68. Jesse Bricker et al., "Changes in U.S. Family Finances from 2013 to 2016: Evidence from the Survey of Consumer Finances," *Federal Reserve Bulletin* 103, no. 3 (September 2017).

69. Greenhouse, *Beaten Down, Worked Up*, 12.

70. Lawrence Mishel and Julia Wolfe, *CEO Compensation Has Grown 940% Since 1978: Typical Worker Compensation Has Risen Only 12% During That Time* (Washington, DC: Economic Policy Institute, August 2019).

71. Mishel and Wolfe, *CEO Compensation Has Grown 940% Since 1978*, xii.

72. Michael Sean Winters, "Labor Unions Are Prophetic, Innovative, Pope Says," *National Catholic Reporter*, July 6, 2017.

73. Alison D. Morantz, "Coal Mine Safety: Do Unions Make a Difference?," *Industrial and Labor Relations Review* 66, no. 1 (2013): 88. Morantz reports, "My best estimates imply that overall, unionization predicts a 13–31% drop in traumatic injuries and 27–83% drop in fatalities."

74. Greenhouse, *Beaten Down, Worked Up*, 9–10.

75. "The Benefits of Collective Bargaining: An Antidote to Wage Decline and Inequality," fact sheet, Economic Policy Institute, April 14, 2015.

76. US Department of Labor and US Bureau of Labor Statistics, *National Compensation Survey: Employment Benefits in the United States, March 2018* (Washington, DC: BLS, September 2018).

77. US Bureau of Labor Statistics, Employment Benefits Survey, Retirement Benefits, Bureau of Labor Statistics, March 2017.

78. Elise Gould and Celine McNicholas, "Unions Help Narrow the Wage Gap," Economic Policy Institute, April 3, 2017.

79. Jonathan D. Frieden, "National Labor Relations Board (NLRB) Settles Claims Based on Employer Social Media Policy," *National Law Review*, January 25, 2014.

80. Lynn Rhinehart, "Under Trump the NLRB Has Gone Completely Rogue," *Nation*, April 7, 2020.

EPILOGUE

1. The term *antichrist* occurs in the Bible only four times. All the references are found in the First and Second Letters of John: 1 John 2:18; 2:22; 4:3; and 2 John 1:7.

2. Polycarp's Letter to the Philippians, par. 7.

3. Cited in Richard K. Emmerson, *Antichrist in the Middle Ages: A Study of Medieval Apocalypticism, Art, and Literature* (Seattle: University of Washington Press, 1981), 64.

4. As of September 2020, the *Washington Post* had documented that Trump had lied to or substantially misled the American people almost twenty-three thousand times. See The Fact Checker, "In 1,323 Days, President Trump Has Made 23,510 False or Misleading Claims," *Washington Post*, September 3, 2020. Also see Glenn Kessler et al., "Trump Is Averaging More Than 50 False or Misleading Claims a Day," *Washington Post*, October 22, 2020.

5. Irwin Redlener et al., "130,000–210,000 Avoidable Covid-19 Deaths—and Counting—in the U.S.," National Center for Disaster Preparedness, October 21, 2020.

6. Robert P. Jones, "Trump's Election Support from Evangelicals Shows We're the Biggest Obstacle to Racial Justice," NBC.com, November 16, 2020.

7. Both quoted in Nicholas Kristof, "She Is Evangelical, 'Pro-Life' and Voting for Biden," *New York Times*, October 22, 2020.

INDEX